A THEORY OF LAW

A
THEORY
OF
LAW

Philip Soper

HARVARD UNIVERSITY PRESS
Cambridge, Massachusetts
and London, England
1984

Copyright © 1984 by the President and Fellows
of Harvard College
All rights reserved
Printed in the United States of America
10 9 8 7 6 5 4 3 2 1

Publication of this book has been aided by a grant
from the Andrew W. Mellon Foundation

This book is printed on acid-free paper, and its binding
materials have been chosen for strength and durability.

LIBRARY OF CONGRESS CATALOGING IN PUBLICATION DATA

Soper, Philip.
A theory of law.

Includes index.
1. Law—Philosophy.   2. Political science.   I. Title.
K355.S65   1984   340'.1   84–711
ISBN 0-674-88025-0 (alk. paper)

To my parents

PREFACE

T HIS BOOK owes its existence to the conviction that the nature of law debate, as currently conducted, is largely meaningless. It owes its structure to the belief that the debate can be made meaningful by connecting it to issues in moral and political philosophy.

The dual heritage has left its imprint on the content and style of what follows. First, though I have called it a "theory of law," it is a theory that requires developing an account of the obligation to obey law as well as of the concept of law. Thus this book is intended as a contribution to political theory and the problem of political obligation as much as to legal theory. Second, my determination to relate legal theory to practical concerns has led me throughout to use language and arguments that do not require extensive familiarity with the specialized literature in the field. In consequence, I have had to summarize entire works and schools of thought in ways that may seem unfairly short, though not, I trust, inaccurate, to those who do know this literature. Such readers I urge to consult the notes for further clues to the place of the argument in the contemporary debate.

Acknowledgments of aid and assistance in a work of this sort are inevitably owed to more people than one can reasonably list in a preface. I am particularly grateful to three of my colleagues: Donald Regan and Thomas Green, who read an early version of the manuscript and made many valuable suggestions, and Joseph Vining, who provided inspiration and encouragement in numerous discussions.

A fellowship from the American Council of Learned Societies, with funds provided by the National Endowment for the Humanities, enabled me to devote a sabbatical leave in 1980 to this project, as did generous assistance from the W. W. Cook Endowment at the University of Michigan Law School.

CONTENTS

I INTRODUCTION 1

*The Problem of Motivation 1   Legal and Political
Theory 7   Etiology and Prognosis 12*

II LEGAL THEORY 16

*Classical Positivism: Taking Austin Seriously 17   Modern
Positivism: The Search for Normativity 26   A Fresh Start:
Taking Obligation Seriously 38   Natural Law and Other
Nontheories 51   A Theory of Law 55*

III POLITICAL THEORY 57

*Preliminaries 58   Failure of the Standard
Paradigms 65   Autonomy and Authority 75   A Theory
of Political Obligation 80   Legal and Political Theory
Revisited 87*

IV CONNECTIONS 91

*Political Theory and the Concept of Law 91   Legal Theory
and the Concept of Obligation 95*

V APPLICATIONS 101

*Law, Morality, and Certainty 101   Courts and
Legislatures 109   The Claim of Acceptability 117   The
Concept of Rights 125   The Right to
Discourse 134   Death and Transfiguration 143*

VI IMPLICATIONS 148

*Nihilism and Other Maladies 148   The Problem of
Commitment 154   Choosing a View 157*

NOTES 163   INDEX 187

INTRODUCTION

I

T O SAY PRECISELY when legal theory reached its current dead end would be more difficult and less to the point than describing the nature of the impasse and its causes.

By "legal theory" I mean that body of speculative thought about the nature of law that has dominated analytical jurisprudence since John Austin's lectures on the subject a century and a half ago.[1] By "dead" I mean what the term implies in ordinary speech: lifeless, drained of connections to any of the purposes that give meaning to human life. "Dead end," I suggest, rather than "dead" *simpliciter* because, unlike others who mock the sterility of these disputes,[2] I do not believe that the basic enterprise is misconceived so much as misdirected. Legal theory has taken a turn that can end only in an increasing divergence between the phenomena it analyzes and the actual experience of ordinary citizens.

THE PROBLEM OF MOTIVATION

Those inclined to doubt these claims or to suspect that they are exaggerated should consider this: what could possibly motivate an intelligent person to explore the "maze of metaphysical literature"[3] on the question, What is law? The uninitiated can be forgiven for assuming that the answer to this question is the obvious one: surely the persons most likely to profit from such a study are professionals or citizens forced by career or circumstance to investigate legal relationships—to find out, in short, just what the law is. In fact these people—judges, lawyers, law teachers, potential litigants, all "insiders" of the legal system,

· 1 ·

as I shall call them—are the least likely beneficiaries of legal theory. Countless judicial opinions line the shelves of countless professional libraries mutely attesting to the irrelevance of legal theory by their utter disregard for this body of scholarship. To maintain in the face of such evidence that academic speculation about the nature of law has anything at all to do with the practical problem of finding out what the law is can be done comfortably only by those so used to the smell of the lamp that they no longer notice it.

But this charge of insider irrelevance rests on more than the evidence of empirical observation. Legal theorists virtually ensure the irrelevance of their results for this class of people by making insider opinions about what law is determinative of the truth of their theoretical claims. In this respect the legal theorist is like the scientist whose theories, say about animal behavior, cannot themselves be a part of animal experience. If bees and apes fail to conform to theory, it is theory that must change to keep pace. The possibility of animals consulting theory for its behavioral implications is ruled out, not just empirically, on grounds of inadequate consciousness, but logically, on grounds of absurdity. So too, when the legal theorist tests claims about the nature of law by considering whether they mirror the opinions of litigants, judges, or professionals, insider irrelevance must result. The old saw "Law is what the judges say it is" has been replaced by a new one, "Law is whatever insiders say it is."[4] In neither case is the definition of any use to the insider.

Who else then asks, What is law? and what else might such a person be seeking if not information about existing legal relationships? Given the fact of insider irrelevance, it is natural to assume that the person to whom legal theory is addressed must be an outsider of some sort. Indeed, much of the speculative writing about law, where it displays awareness of the motivation problem at all, seems to be based on the assumption that the critical viewpoint for conducting and evaluating the analysis is that of the external observer; but what kind of observer, and what does he or she want to know?

To answer that question one must, as it were, become an observer of legal theory itself, from which perspective a rather bizarre prospect appears. The aim of the legal theorist, it is usually said, is to describe those features that are most important in distinguishing legal from other forms of social control—from moral or coercive bonds, for example; or the goal is to distinguish legal systems from other systems of social organization, such as the more primitive forms of a tribal society or the less cohesive forms of international cooperation. With this as his aim, the theorist reestablishes the relevance of the analysis to the stated goal, but only at the cost of raising an equally puzzling problem: who cares? What is the point of marking off the distinguishing features of legal systems?

It would be one thing if, say, anthropologists turned to legal theory for help in deciding whether or not to classify a social structure as legal. By and large, though, they do not, and for good reason. Once the major features of various societies have been described and compared, it is difficult to see what further information is conveyed by adding the label "legal" to some and not to others. The label, like all classifications, lumps together common characteristics; but the question why just these characteristics should be selected for special attention is not an anthropological one.[5]

The same conclusion holds for other outside observers who might be suggested as the intended beneficiaries of legal theory. Social psychologists describe and compare legal, moral, and coercive influences on behavior without recourse to legal theory to check the accuracy of their labels. Sociologists record and predict behavioral responses to variations in the law without first consulting legal theory to ascertain what law is.[6] Policy scientists identify the legal impediments to needed change, distinguishing these from the cruder barriers of desire and will, without prior recourse to definitions of law and power. Outsiders in short resemble insiders in at least this respect: both make distinctions between law, morality, and force commonly and daily, but at levels and for purposes that have nothing to do with the apparent purposes and level of abstraction of legal theory.

This observation suggests that the problem of explaining the point of legal theory is but one aspect of the broader problem of explaining what underlies and motivates classification and definition in general. For most people, it will seem obvious that the way in which we divide the world and categorize its contents depends on our purposes in doing so. We distinguish chairs from couches because the functions of each in human life are sufficiently different in ways that are sufficiently often demonstrated to justify two categories rather than one. Most people have one concept of snow, but skiers know corn snow and powder, and Eskimos have distinct concepts for even more forms of solid precipitation. Indeed, languages are natural in part just because they permit this kind of modification: new experiences justify breaking an existing concept into several new concepts, each distinguished from the other by differences previously neglected but now worth taking into account.

All of this is familiar enough if not entirely uncontroversial. But recounting the familiar allows one to explain from a different angle the problem of trying to discover who might be interested in what legal theorists have to say. The problem is not that social scientists, judges, lawyers, and citizens have no need for the distinctions between law, morality, and coercion that lie at the heart of legal theory. The problem, rather, is that they seem to have no need for the fine tuning that legal theorists add to the grosser discriminations that are more than satisfactory for ordinary people and for other disciplines. The citizen's main concern is to know the probable consequences of past or contemplated action. For that it is enough to know that law is, roughly, a set of directives issued or accepted by officials who enforce the directives with organized sanctions. Morality, in contrast, substitutes for the official source and the organized sanction an appeal to conscience to consider the impact of action on others. In contrast to both of these, an order backed only by a threat is neither part of an organized system of sanctions nor the subject of a claim of legitimacy but depends for its efficacy entirely on the perceived likelihood and severity of the threat. These rough definitions are enough for most people in the same way that a broad, undifferentiated concept of snow is enough for the farmer whose only concern is the possibility of a late frost.

One may, of course, pick at the rough definitions in a variety of ways. One may try to show, for example, by emphasizing the similarities in the motivating sanction of each that what is at first taken to be three distinct phenomena can be reduced to one.[7] Conversely, one could explain to the farmer why the skier finds useful a more finely tuned definition of snow. But who is the analogue to the skier in legal theory? Whose purposes are served by the more careful distinctions drawn by the analytic philosopher between law, morality, and force and the notions of authority and legitimacy?

If we continue to press for an answer to this question by observing what legal theorists themselves profess as their goal, two final possibilities emerge. The first denies the above assumption that citizens and other insiders can operate adequately within their own areas of concern armed only with the rough definition of law. But this denial takes us back to where we started—to the fact that theories of law are simply not among the tools insiders use to predict the consequences of action. At some point, to insist that philosophical analysis yields sounder conclusions about what the law is when such conclusions are reached without reference to such analysis is to impose the philosopher's goals on those he purports to aid, thus redefining the problem. Recognition of this fact may explain why recent theorists are more cautious in their claims, suggesting that only certain insiders—judges and officials—are in need of the theorist's tools. Unreflective definitions of law, it may be thought, particularly with their heavy emphasis on the predictive interests of insiders, may serve well enough for the layman and the lawyer, but they are of little use to the judge. Judges, after all, must distinguish between legal and nonlegal sources of authority, and, at least in difficult cases, unreflective definitions are far too crude to be of much help.

Whatever the explanation for this central position of the judicial institution within legal theory, one thing is clear: it does not solve the motivational puzzle. When one compares the conclusions of current legal theorists with the actual function of the judge, it is clear that judges are no better equipped to determine the law in difficult cases with the theorists' definitions than they are with the unreflective definition. Master test, rule of recognition, basic norm, and law of nature—all these are concepts far too abstract to be used in actually deciding cases. Indeed, candid theorists usually confess that the picture of law they paint is not meant to be representational even in the judge's chambers.[8]

Nor will it do to suggest that the value of the picture is symbolic, reminding judges of the limits placed by role on the power to decide cases by reference to personal morality or other subjective views. Such a reminder is of little use when the theory does not itself undertake to show where these limits are reached. Left to struggle with that question alone, judges will not perceive a difference between, on the one hand, filling gaps in open-textured language by the exercise of one's best judgment and, on the other hand, extrapolating from clear cases to the institutionally required solution in the difficult case. From the viewpoint of the judge there is little to choose between predictive theories of law that are viciously circular and their current alternatives, which are vacuously abstract.[9]

There remains a final possibility. The effort to mark off the distinguishing features of legal systems may be thought to be a task worth pursuing for its own sake, without regard to the practical implications for other human endeavors. "Knowledge for its own sake" has a reassuring ring, particularly to academic ears, and boasts a renowned lineage in both humanistic and scientific fields. Indeed, much of the analysis that has dominated moral philosophy for the better part of this century seems predicated less on the assumption that it will actually aid in the making of practical moral judgments than on the assumption that philosophical clarity is desirable for its own sake. To be sure, a connection between conceptual clarity and less confused judgments is often invoked; but the connection is difficult to demonstrate, and, in any event, it seems clear that the analysis would proceed and be thought worthwhile regardless of its practical value.

As a solution to the motivational problem, this justification for legal theory is remarkably uninspiring. For one thing, it wrongly analogizes social phenomena to the phenomena of the natural sciences. The idea of pure research directed at discovering, for example, the nature of the atom makes sense regardless of one's views about whether such knowledge will ever have practical consequences. By "makes sense" I mean both that such investigations are possible and that the impulse behind them is psychologically plausible. Objects can be described and differences and similarities noted without ever stopping to consider what purposes might justify marking off these distinctions. The motivation for such disinterested analysis—exploration of one's environment for its own sake—is, moreover, from crib to lab a familiar part of human experience. In contrast, it is difficult to defend both the possibility and the plausibility of maintaining a disinterested attitude toward the investigation of social phenomena. The possibility is problematic because social phenomena and correlated concepts may themselves be affected by the theorist's analysis. If law is unmasked as force, attitudes toward law may change, and previously perceived distinctions between tax collectors and muggers may blur. The theorist who ignores these possibilities does so at the risk of discovering that yesterday's theory no longer explains today's data.[10]

As for the plausibility of the enterprise, even assuming one could control for the interaction between theory and data, it is hard to explain why such a disinterested dissection is undertaken in the first place. Unlike the physical universe, social reality consists of the internal attitudes of people as well as their observable behavior. The motivation for studying just the behavior while deliberately ignoring the underlying attitudes—the hopes, fears, dreams, and desires that determine behavior—is comparable to the impulse that leads one to do crossword puzzles and brain teasers. These activities *are* pursued simply for the inherent enjoyment of discovering or manipulating logical or preconstructed relationships. They are psychologically plausible largely because they make no pretense of being relevant or meaningful beyond the context of the game itself. If the motivation for legal theory is analysis for its own sake in this sense, it should come as no surprise that the endeavor lacks relevance for ordinary purposes and appears to many to be a professional philosopher's pastime.

Instead of trying to infer the purpose of legal theory from the existing literature on the subject, it may be more profitable to ask directly what purpose legal theory ought or could be made to serve. What reasons beyond the interest in conceptual analysis for its own sake could motivate serious inquiry into the nature of law? Providing an answer to that question is as simple as attempting to infer it from the existing literature is difficult. Legal theory is a branch of philosophy, and the central questions of philosophy, from Plato to Kant, have never changed. What can I know? What ought I to do? and What may I hope? remain the cognitive core of every serious attempt to confront the human condition. If legal theory is viewed as an attempt to answer the second of these questions—What is law that I should obey it?—the motivational problem is solved: the inquiry into the nature of law is connected to a persistent human concern. Moreover, by viewing legal theory as a branch of moral philosophy, one can explain the nature of the wrong turn that has been taken in this field of jurisprudence. The problem is not, as some would have it, that legal theorists are guilty of essentialism—that is, of assuming that law is somehow "out there" with a unique essence awaiting discovery.[11] Modern theorists are all too eager to deny that charge, insisting that their goal is simply to describe important features of legal systems, with "importance" being measured by the purpose that the feature serves. The problem is that even this more modest descriptive task is assumed by current theorists to require one to measure importance and thus to test competing models of law with an epistemological goal in mind rather than a moral one. It is not the question of what to do but of what one can know that has come to dominate analytical jurisprudence, even though the answers legal theory provides to this epistemological question are poorly designed to aid those who might be thought to be most interested in it—anthropologists, say, or lawyers, judges, and litigants. The problem is analogous to delivering at a watchmaker's convention a discourse on the question, What is time? when all that could conceivably interest those in attendance is the problem of how to measure time more accurately. Fortunately, one has more than metaphor to illustrate and defend this claim.

LEGAL AND POLITICAL THEORY

Nothing better reveals the curious state of affairs in this field of philosophy than the gulf that presently separates political and legal theory. The central question of political theory is that of legitimacy: Why should I, or anyone, obey the state?[12] Political theorists thus confront directly what I have identified as the moral question that ought to guide legal theorists as well. Indeed, classical philosophy did not distinguish these as separate disciplines. Thrasymachus' challenge to distinguish might from right is as much a preface to every serious contemporary investigation into the nature of law as it is to Plato's *Republic*, although in Plato's case the preface is to a far more exciting and elaborate story than the tale typically told by modern legal theorists. The latter turn the challenge into a request to dispel linguistic confusion; Plato accepts the challenge as requiring an investigation into the nature and basis of the just state, which necessitates in turn a wide-ranging inquiry into the substantive issues of moral and political philosophy.

This difference in approach reflects more than a difference in story-telling tastes; it reflects as well a difference of view about the connection between political and legal theory. That such a connection exists should hardly surprise. The political theorist's goal of characterizing the just state seems to require the cooperation of the legal theorist in two ways. First, in order to know what constitutes a good legal system one must know what a legal system is. Thus legal and political theory are related in the sense that an adequate legal theory is a logical prerequisite for an adequate political theory. Second, if one views legal theory as a first step toward an adequate political theory, the analysis of the concept of law itself is guided by the problem of political obligation that motivates it: the central question for the legal theorist, for example, becomes whether or not 'legal system' might just mean those organized social systems that have some legitimate moral claim on us.

Contrast now the relationship between political and legal theory as actually practiced today. Two events in the last two decades have led to a resurgence of interest in both fields. In legal theory H. L. A. Hart's *Concept of Law* revived debates about the nature of law and furnished the foil then, as it continues to now, for those who challenge the positivist view that Hart endorsed. In political theory a nonliterary event, the experience in the United States of an unpopular war, revived philosophical interest in the question of political obligation, spawning innumerable discussions of the nature and basis of the obligation to obey the law. Despite the classical and apparently logical connection between these two fields, however, the briefest glance shows that each is oblivious of the other. Consider first the problem of political obligation. One could select at random any of a number of recent efforts to explain why and whether there is an obligation to obey the law and discover a similar pattern. First, the author poses the question and by way of introduction nods in the direction of its historical importance and contemporary relevance. Second, a brief explanation of the concept of obligation is given, along with a reminder of the distinction between prima facie and absolute senses of the term. Third, potential grounds for political obligation are examined. Recently these efforts have culminated in the conclusion that there is not even a prima facie obligation to obey the law,[13] a remarkably counterintuitive claim to which I shall return.

The point is that the entire analysis of political obligation in even the most respectable of these pieces proceeds without the slightest hint that one first needs to know what law is in order to decide whether there is an obligation to obey it. In contrast, a good deal of legal theory has its origins in, and continues to be preoccupied with, the problem of explaining whether and how law differs from force. Hart begins his book with a uniquely important explanation of why Austin's analysis of law as command is inadequate: commands or orders backed by threats only oblige; they do not obligate. In the end, Hart's account also fails to connect law and obligation,[14] but the point remains that a strong tradition associates law with force and clearly separates the concepts of validity and obligation. Explaining what is wrong with this view is not an easy task, but these recent accounts of political obligation ignore the problem altogether. If the tradition is right, then the literature on the obligation to obey confronts a straw man from the start. If law is only force, one does not need pages of discussion about the nature and extent of the obligation to comply: there is none. The analysis could end as quickly as Hart dismisses Austin's model of law as the "gunman situation writ large."[15] The political theorist, in short, who concludes that there is no prima facie obligation to obey the law without first examining what is meant by 'law' risks the charge that his political theory is both incomplete and trivial: incomplete because it depends critically on a preconceived idea of law that is not defended; trivial because that idea about what law is already entails the conclusion about the obligation to obey.

The situation with respect to legal theory is no better; indeed, it is the mirror image of the problem in political theory. Where political theory ignores the need to define law in a way that does not trivialize further investigation into the grounds for obligation, legal theory ignores the phenomenon of political obligation in the account it provides of a legal system. The best way to illustrate this claim is to consider developments in legal theory since the appearance of *The Concept of Law*, which at first glance appears to be a counterexample to the claim. Hart begins his investigation, as noted, with the problem of accounting for obligation as the key to his criticism of Austin. From that beginning the investigation shifts increasingly toward what I have called the epistemological inquiry: the focus is on the kind of entities (rules) that make up law and the ways in which varieties of these rules combine to yield a legal system. In the end it is this quest for a descriptive model of legal systems and a theoretical test for legal validity that dominates the analysis rather than an inquiry into how rules accepted and enforced by officials can be said to be rules of obligation.

Developments since Hart's book have led even more clearly to an eclipse of the insider's moral concerns by the outsider's epistemological one. Two examples will illustrate. Joseph Raz, who follows in Hart's positivist steps, has produced an account of legal systems that carefully refines the analysis of the kind of entity law is and the relationships that characterize the combining of laws into a legal system. Raz also seems to insist even more strongly than Hart that a model of law must reflect the insider's perception that legal rules obligate.[16] After developing this model of law, Raz turns to the apparently separate question of whether this perception of obligation is in fact correct. Raz's current conclusion is that law does not entail even a prima facie obligation to obey.[17] Not only does the epistemological interest dominate the legal theory, but, when Raz does take up political theory, it turns out that one might as well have stopped with Austin as far as the moral question is concerned: neither commands nor rules that are merely perceived to obligate necessarily obligate in fact.[18]

My objection at this point is not to the specific conclusion but to the method. It may well be that law does not obligate. Indeed, the choice between a view that equates law with force, thus dispensing with obligation, and the alternative view developed in this study is not one that analysis can dictate. The problem with the method is twofold. First, by analyzing the concept of law at the outset and then deriving implications for obligation, one prejudges the question of whether the obligation to obey is part of the data to be accounted for in the theoretical construct. The virtue of the moral approach to legal theory is that it accepts the persistent association of obligation and law as elements of a legal system that must be explained; to ignore this feature is to prejudice in advance one's conclusions concerning the nature of law and its relevance to moral duty.

The second problem is again the motivational one. The inquiry into the nature of law has practical interest only to the extent that one can use the resulting analysis to aid the moral inquiry: what ought I to do? An analysis that concludes that there is no prima facie obligation to obey the law certainly has negative implications for that question, at least in that one no longer has to worry that disobeying a law is wrong per se. The problem is that the theorist who attempts to defend this claim will ultimately be forced to confront his own implicit definition of law. If that definition, in the epistemological interest of embracing as wide a species as possible, qualifies any effective regime as a legal system but only by excising obligation as a necessary concomitant, then it is still for all practical purposes a useless definition. The only response to the moral inquiry is, whether or not you have an obligation depends on the kind of legal system you are in. With that as an answer, our inquirer can only turn back to political theory, convinced that the legal theorist has nothing to tell him:

"What must law be if it *is* to obligate?" asks our inquirer.

"I don't know that," responds the theorist, "but I do know this: it doesn't obligate if it is characterized only by features X, Y, and Z. And, by the way, features X, Y, and Z, you understand, constitute the minimally sufficient conditions for qualifying as a legal system."

It is the "by the way" in this exchange that no one with a practical interest cares about. What people do care about is what the legal theorist can only admit he does not know.

For a second example of the current epistemological emphasis in legal theory consider Ronald Dworkin's views, which are, at least in spirit, antagonistic rather than sympathetic to positivism.[19] Dworkin's theory, with its initial concern over the distinction between rules and principles and the question of how to reach correct legal decisions, seems a perfect example of the preoccupation of legal theory with the problem of determining what kind of entity law is. This epistemological goal, however, soon gives way in Dworkin's subsequent writings to an agenda more closely related to a moral issue: what is the obligation of a judge in a legal system? That this moral question, phrased in terms of judicial discretion, should turn out to be the centerpiece of Dworkin's theory, eclipsing entirely the earlier wrangle over rules and principles, is further evidence of the centrality of the issue in any adequate legal theory. But the moral issue, even in Dworkin, remains obscure for reasons related to the theory's epistemological false start. First, by phrasing the question of judicial obligation in terms of legal validity, Dworkin's theory appears only to add an even further refinement to the positivist's already impractically theoretical test for law. The effort required to find the law under this theory requires abilities so far beyond those of ordinary mortals that even professional philosophers, let alone judges, have now mostly despaired of discovering any practical way to distinguish the difference in discretion that Dworkin posits.[20]

Second, and perhaps more fundamentally, there is no clear answer in Dworkin's theory, any more than in Hart's, to the question of why a judge has an obligation to apply the law in the first place. Confining a judge's discretion may make judicial decisions more legitimate within liberal democratic theory, as Dworkin suggests, but this claim of legitimacy remains hypothetical so long as no justification of democratic theory itself is forthcoming. Political theory, in short, again confronts legal theory as an indispensable ingredient of the latter—a point that Dworkin continually asserts but can never explain so long as political theory remains, as it seems to for him, primarily an incorporated part of his own, more generalized test for legal validity. It is the thesis of this study that Dworkin's approach reverses cart and horse. The question of judicial obligation, like the more general question of political obligation, should be confronted directly by asking what law must be if judges are to have an obligation to apply it. Having answered this question, one can then consider the implications of the resulting concept of law for the question of legal validity and judicial discretion.

ETIOLOGY AND PROGNOSIS

It is worth pausing at this point to speculate about the causes of the current condition of legal theory. What explains the preoccupation with epistemological questions? What caused the classically conceived unitary inquiry to dissolve into separate inquiries, each apparently blind to the other? Part of the answer no doubt lies in the nature of analytic philosophy itself, which increasingly in this century has taken its task to be the presumably value-free one of dissecting language to reveal meaning and to correct mistaken ways of thinking and talking. One need not disparage this enterprise to note the risk it entails of producing puzzles that are puzzles only for philosophers, not for ordinary people. One can push at the boundaries on the map created by language at almost any point and discover how easily the lines blur. But most people do not push. When they do it is in response to specific problems, sufficiently unique to make old categories become suddenly less useful.

In science these concept frontiers are crossed continually, but by an ever-smaller group of experts. In ethics the opposite is the case: everybody is an expert (which means nobody is), and at the same time the moral categories and concepts used in making practical judgments differ little from those in use two thousand years ago in Greece. There is simply no analogue in moral philosophy to the proliferation of concepts in, say, particle physics. The consequence is a powerful incentive to try to accommodate philosophy to the scientific model, to turn what should be moral inquiries, where progress is difficult, into scientific inquiries, where progress, at least in the form of new classifications and distinctions, is possible. Unfortunately, to stake claims to moral progress on this analogy to science comes at the cost of any conceivable relevance for human affairs.

These speculations help explain one further feature of current legal theory that this study, in contrast, does not share—namely, a preoccupation with linguistic distinctions and difficult cases. Whether law is properly characterized as a rule, a principle, a norm, or a command and how to find the law in a hard case are two examples of the kinds of questions that remain outside the focus of this study. My focus instead is on what I have called the rough definition of law—the easy case, the simple directives of an organized society that citizens confront every time they stop to think about the speed limit sign they are passing. What must be true about such directives—law in the simple sense—if they are to yield obligation?

Two final matters deserve attention. One concerns terminology, the other the problem of definition. Philosophers have devoted enormous resources in this century to an analysis of moral language and ethical concepts, dwarfing in volume all the literature that legal theorists are ever likely to produce. Accordingly, to suggest that legal theory must proceed by keeping in mind the problem of grounding political obligation may seem to set a hopeless task, requiring one first to settle intractable disputes in moral philosophy before considering the questions that legal theory poses. How does 'obligation' relate to 'ought'? How do moral reasons differ from prudential, aesthetic, or other reasons for action? What is a reason for action, and what is the process by which conflicting reasons are reconciled into a single sufficient reason for acting? These are examples of questions that touch a considerable literature and are necessarily implicated in a discussion of political obligation. For the most part, I shall simply indicate where necessary the sense in which moral terms are used here, and I shall also try to employ terms likely to be familiar to people who are not philosophers. I have two excuses for the resulting appearance of professional naiveté. First, those who find the moral language inadequate may always substitute a more adequate terminology without detracting from the basic framework of this study. My claim is that law can best be understood by connecting legal and political theory. If the connection I make in this essay proves the claim plausible, then those who prefer a different connection may be encouraged to continue this effort at redirecting legal theory.

My second excuse is less an excuse than a belief, which I shall not pause to defend, that the closer one sticks to plain talk in analyzing ethical concepts, the less prone one is to that peculiar kind of philosophical error whose technical name is "nonsense." Take, for example, the structure of this inquiry. Since the question that guides it is hypothetical—what must law be if it is to obligate?—and since I believe that the phenomenon of prima facie obligation is universally associated with the institution of law, I might have described the study in language that in some circles would have lent it an air of instant profundity. I might have said, "I am embarking on a transcendental deduction of the conceptual framework that makes law (*überhaupt*) possible." But what would be the point except to obscure?

The hypothetical nature of the question does, however, force one to confront again the problem of definition. What does one accomplish even if one manages to show what law must be in order to obligate? If one shows that man in order to fly would have to have wings and a different bone structure, one proves only that the creature described is not what we mean by man. So too, after completing an analysis of law that preserves a place for fidelity, how does one respond to the outright dismissal of the analysis on the ground that that is just not what we mean by law? In part I have already answered this question. We have seen that others, Hart for example, also take as a starting point the claim that an adequate concept of law must at least connote obligation. I simply go one step further: what better way, after all, to show that law connotes obligation than to show that it obligates in fact? In that sense, by insisting that actual obligation is one of the phenomena of legal systems for which theory must account, one is no less arbitrary in the selection of data than are those who focus only on that other entity, the legal directive. But the matter is not entirely an arbitrary choice of which aspects of social systems to emphasize. The burden of this study will be to show that the account of law given here not only entails obligation but also explains a variety of other phenomena, including standard jurisprudential puzzles, in ways that make it plausible to view the theory as an explication of the concept of law rather than as a purely stipulative definition.

In the end, however, no final answer to this question is possible. Law is a concept that balances precariously between the view that it is nothing but, and the view that it is something more than, force. My choice of metaphor for the definitional task ahead is not that of the blind men and the elephant but that of the drawings that can be seen as either a duck or a rabbit, a young girl or an old crone, stairs rising or stairs descending—the symbol capable of totally different interpretations that cannot be reconciled by so simple an act as walking around the beast. Yet these alternative interpretations, though in one sense irreconcilable, are not completely arbitrary; they are obviously bounded by the objective reality of the phenomenon. The duck-rabbit cannot plausibly be seen as a female nude except on the psychiatrist's couch. Something like a creative, self-fulfilling choice must determine which of the objectively plausible views one takes. This study can only suggest what is at stake in that choice and how the most familiar aspects of a legal system can be seen coherently from either direction. As things currently stand, the only vision to be found in contemporary legal theory is one that cannot, except by fiat, distinguish law from force. How it is possible to see law as more than this without also simply declaring by fiat that law and morality coincide is what I aim to show.

These then are the goals of this study: to reconnect political and legal theory and to construct in the process *a* theory of law (with the emphasis, but not too much, on the indefinite article). The pretentiousness of this goal I am happy to balance with the precaution contained in the observation that "most philosophical ideas are simple enough ... The difficulty ... comes when the philosophers attempt to prove they are right."[21] The theory advanced here is indeed simple enough and may be found in slogan form at the end of the next chapter. In that chapter I examine the failure of current legal theory to connect the ideas of law and obligation and from this examination I extract the additional feature that must be included if the connection is ever to be established. In this sense I show that the feature is a necessary condition of any theory that hopes to distinguish law from force. In Chapter III, I examine political theory with the aim of showing that the same feature that is necessary for an adequate legal theory is also sufficient (in conjunction with a second feature) to ground political obligation. In Chapter IV, I defend the connection between this conclusion of moral philosophy and the inquiry into the nature of law. In the remaining chapters I examine the implications of this view of law for a selection of jurisprudential puzzles, both old and new. I conclude by returning to the problem of definition and the choice between alternative, equally plausible visions of the world, relating these problems in the context of this brief study to the broader themes they touch of hope and despair in the search for objective value.

LEGAL THEORY

II

B EGGARMAN, mugger, tax man, thief. All but the first take my
money whether I will or no. The thief's stealth spares me the direct
confrontation with his insult to my autonomy, but that is too small a sol-
ace to spare him in turn the same outrage with which I instinctively
greet the mugger. Even if in calmer moments, or as a result of city-
dulled sensibilities, I do not react exactly with outrage, I, like others,
will find absurd the suggestion that the interchange with mugger or
thief deserves my respect in any sense.

Contrast now the typical response to the tax collector. He too confronts me with a demand he is prepared to back with force. He, like the
mugger, cares only that I am in his jurisdiction, subject in an equally de
facto sense to his power. Questions of consent, considerations of reci-
procity (what did the tax collector or his regime ever do for me?), esti-
mates of whether the tax will do more good in the public coffers than in
my pocket are as irrelevant to the law's insistence that I comply as they
would be to the mugger. Yet the common response is not outrage but
respectful attention. How might one explain the difference? More important, is it a difference that can be justified on reflection, or must one
be content to make a few commonplace observations about the effect of
habit and conditioning on attitudes and behavior?

To look for answers to these questions in current accounts of the nature of law is to expect too much of legal theory. Legal theorists, as
noted, insist that their task has nothing to do with the justification, as
opposed to the characterization and identification, of specifically legal
attitudes. As far as the legal theorist is concerned the question should be

· 16 ·

not whether the more favorable response toward law is justified but whether that response is in fact one that essentially characterizes legal systems. I shall leave the question of justification for the next chapter. But even if the investigation is reformulated as an inquiry into the characteristics of insider attitudes toward law, it is not easy to find a satisfactory answer in current legal theory.

CLASSICAL POSITIVISM: TAKING AUSTIN SERIOUSLY

If one were to begin the inquiry into how law differs from force by looking to common opinion on the matter rather than to legal theory, one would undoubtedly discover sentiment for the view that there is no difference. The plausibility of that view lies in the above descriptions of the mugger and the tax collector: both confront one with demands backed by threats that ignore entirely the wishes of the person addressed. What is this but a description of force? The only apparent difference is that many people seem to respond differently to the demands of each.

This difference in response or attitude toward the law's demands has become so important in modern legal theory that it is helpful to review some common ways of describing the difference. The response to the gunman, I suggested, is moral outrage or indignation. That is a natural way to describe the intuitive reaction to directives that rely solely or primarily on the fear of threatened sanctions to induce compliance. Systems that employ such directives I shall call coercive. The response to the tax collector, in contrast, I described as respect, which suggests that compliance is sought for reasons that are not necessarily connected to the threatened sanction. These reasons presumably appeal to the values, desires, or interests of the person addressed in ways intended to make compliance largely voluntary.

Some theorists use the term 'norm' to include both kinds of directives—those that coerce as well as those that seek voluntary compliance.[1] The gunman, after all, is also prescribing a course of conduct and appealing to one's prudential interest in avoiding the threatened sanction. Thus, even his order might be called a norm if that term simply designated prescriptions for behavior which one has some reason to follow. In this study, however, I shall limit the term 'norm' and the idea of a normative system to include only directives and systems that seek compliance primarily for reasons other than the fear of threatened sanctions. With this clarification, the puzzle with which this chapter begins and that provides its focus can be put in the form of a deceptively simple question: are legal systems coercive or normative systems?

Coercion as the Essence of Law

Modern positivism owes Austin an immense debt. By characterizing law as a command he did two things. First, he answered the above question by providing a simple and elegant model of law that is essentially coercive and thus reflects and elaborates on much common opinion. Second, by using the language of 'command', he provided later analysts, who took their task to be that of describing the kind of entity that law is, with a beautiful target. 'Command', it turns out, is the wrong linguistic category for law. A better one is that of a rule or a social standard or a norm of a certain sort.

These objections concerning the kind of linguistic entity law is I shall call analytical objections. Analytical objections aim at getting the linguistic category right. One corrects Austin just as one might correct the child who has tried to put the square piece in the round hole. Such objections succeed mainly by pointing to observable differences between the assigned and the correct slot. One may also object to Austin's claim that law is essentially coercive. Objections of this sort, because they raise the question of whether the idea of a legal system connotes more than simply force, I shall call connotational objections. Connotational objections focus on meaning and significance, as one might in explaining to a child what is meant by 'round' and 'square'. The criteria for success here are more difficult to articulate and quickly lead to discussions about the nature of definition which I shall temporarily postpone.

The analytical objections to Austin's command theory are well known. No one has summarized them better than Hart. Whereas I have focused on the ways in which the tax collector and the mugger are alike, Hart reminds us of ways in which many laws differ from this simple model of an order backed by a threat. Two differences strike one at once. First, many laws do not appear to order one to do anything at all but simply make it possible to do things like make contracts or wills. Second, even when laws do order one to do or to refrain from doing something, they typically apply to the lawgiver as well as to the person addressed. Thus, unlike the mugger, the tax collector or legislator must also respond to the requirement to hand over his tax dollar. These differences lead Hart to suggest that laws are better seen as officially accepted rules rather than as simple coercive orders.[2] In addition to making this analytical correction to Austin's account, Hart also sets out to remedy the even more serious connotational defect he sees there. The command theory implies that legal systems are essentially coercive; but modern positivists from Hans Kelsen through Hart insist that they are normative. Hart proposes to correct this connotational defect with the same revision that he uses to correct the analytical mistake: by replacing the idea of a sovereign's command with that of an officially accepted rule.

Before I examine modern positivism's attempts to explain and defend the normativity of law, it is important to see why these objections to Austin's account might be thought to miss the point of legal theory—at least as understood by classical theorists such as Austin. The point of the classical enterprise was definitional: to explain the meaning of law in a way that reveals something about the concept as well as the phenomenon the concept reflects. I shall say more about the nature and plausibility of this enterprise in the next section but for now wish only to suggest two reasons why this definitional perspective lessens the force of Hart's objections.

First, whether law is a command or a rule has no practical implications for anyone bent on finding out what the law is (the epistemological inquiry). No lawyer, judge, or scholar thinks that a conclusion about the consequences of attempting to create a will or a contract or a tax shelter is affected by whether the law in question is best described as a command or a rule. Insiders, in short, do not share the philosopher's concern for putting legal directives in their proper linguistic category. This conclusion leaves as the only possible practical interest in the analytical enterprise the connection between that enterprise and the connotational one. Is the difference between commands and rules one that has moral implications?

But now the analytical objections prove pointless for a second reason: whether law is best described as a command or a rule has no bearing on whether legal systems are seen as essentially coercive. This lack of connection between the connotational and the analytical objections is shown by the fact that substituting 'rules' for 'commands' in the description of mugger and tax collector is not likely to affect one's intuitive judgment about the coercive character of the situation. Gunmen or terrorists who issue only orders consistent with rules accepted by the gang or its leaders are no less coercive. It is true that this image of gangsters following rules implies an uncoerced attitude among the members of the gang; they at least follow the rules willingly, not just because of a threat directed at them. But this feature does not take one beyond the coercive character of the command model of law. Austin's sovereign too, presumably, has at least this same minimal "normative" attitude toward his position of power: nobody threatens him, he just accepts his position (or the rules he says define it) for reasons that may range from simple self-interest to the disinterested desire to serve others.

One reaches the same conclusion by starting with the tax collector. Just as gangsters who happen to follow rules do not seem any the less gangsters, so too the normative attitude that modern positivists believe typifies law does not depend on viewing legal directives as rules. Tax collectors could operate in regimes that issue commands traceable to the will of a personal, Austinian sovereign. The Austinian account of sovereignty, that is to say, is usually thought to be defective not because it involves a logical contradiction but only because it fails to account for all cases. Particular examples of legal systems can be produced or imagined that do not seem to have a single identifiable sovereign. But whether any particular society has such a sovereign is an empirical question.[3] If we now imagine such a society—one in which the account of law as command *does* fit, as perhaps in some modern examples of military regimes or historical examples of monarchies—the normative attitude that modern positivists find in law still exists, at least among the rulers or commanders of the society. The sovereign and his underlings accept their position for reasons not essentially connected to the fear of a sanction. If this attitude of acceptance toward one's status as sovereign-commander is enough to constitute the normative attitude that is essential to law, then nothing has been added that is not already implicit in the Austinian account.[4]

Definition as the Essence of Legal Theory

The force of Austin's account derives from viewing his theory as an attempt at definition—at discovering what is meant by a legal system.[5] Definition invites one to move beyond the mere description of an object to selecting and defending certain features as more important than others in explaining how a term is used. Definition invites the question, What would we say if . . . (would it still be a chair if it didn't rock, it didn't have cushions, and so on?). A complete explanation of what definition is all about, as noted in Chapter I, can quickly lead beyond both legal and moral theory into a morass of metaphysics. Undaunted, let us pursue a simple example to illustrate the most commonly recognized elements of the problem.

The preanalytic phenomenon. If you and I are debating whether to call a love seat a chair (rather than, say, a couch), we must first agree on what we are trying to define. If you do not know what a love seat is, I can point to one, or I can describe it in language you and I already share (a piece of furniture just large enough to accommodate two adults sitting side by side). But what is the preanalytic phenomenon in the case of law? Obviously we cannot point to the thing or bring it into the room to analyze or describe as we might in the case of the love seat. And almost all legal theorists agree that one cannot simply take as the preanalytic phenomenon everything that is referred to in ordinary language as law, for that would include laws of nature and other obviously unintended referents. We face the danger at the outset, then, that subsequent disputes may not really be disputes at all because we may be talking about different things—as in the case of the blind men and the elephant.

A rough approximation of the preanalytic phenomenon in the case of a legal system is that of organized social systems. One would need to add a few qualifiers, stressing that the system is effective and purports to be comprehensive and supreme in a way that excludes social clubs and similar lesser-included social systems; but even with these qualifiers, it is still not clear that this is the phenomenon whose definition or description is at issue among legal theorists. Some theorists, for example, want to exclude certain kinds of social organizations—like the despotic rule of a tribal chieftan—even though these organizations are just as comprehensive and supreme as more mature societies; others specifically include these more primitive systems among the data to be analyzed.[6] Given this kind of disagreement about the very thing we are trying to describe, how do we guard against the possibility that subsequent disputes are simply the consequence of different starting points?

Description versus definition. One way to avoid the problem is to start at the other end, with the concept of chair rather than with the troublesome borderline case. Thus we should select an example that everyone agrees is a legal system, see what we can say about it, and then see whether the reasons we are sure it is a legal system help us decide what we should say about a particular borderline case such as the despotic tribal society. Finally, we must recognize that there will always be borderlines and that the point of the theoretical enterprise is not to provide necessary and sufficient conditions for the use of a term but to understand the features that typify the standard case.[7]

But after we have described a standard social system and the tribal chieftain's society, there arises the problem alluded to in Chapter I: what is there left to do that is of any intellectual interest? Why not be content with descriptions that show the extent to which the two societies resemble and differ from one another? To say that one system is legal and the other is not adds no new information, although we may for convenience's sake decide to use the shorter label "legal system" as a synonym for a selected set of descriptive features.

The legitimacy of definition. At this point, one possibility remains for the theorist bent on selecting some of the descriptive features of a society as the essence of law. Definitions are tested by reference to human purposes and the impact on those purposes of two things: the phenomenon in question and the prior classification scheme that language provides. Why do we have separate concepts for chair and couch in the first place rather than a single concept of furniture that can be variously described in terms of length, shape, size, and so on? One possibility is that we encounter the need for an object on which to recline as well as sit often enough to justify a separate concept for things that serve the purpose, saving us the need to repeat the more cumbersome description each time. If this is the most plausible explanation of the "latent principle which guides our use of [the words],"[8] then we are well on our way to deciding some borderline cases, such as whether a love seat is a chair or a couch. If it is not long enough to accommodate the average recumbent body, it is probably better classified as a large chair rather than a couch. If we begin to distinguish purposes uniquely served by the two-seater large chair that are important for us (or for a large subset of us, such as lovers), we may decide that we do need a new concept: hence, 'love seat'—"neither chair nor couch, though like and unlike in the following ways."[9]

From the perspective of definition it is easy to see how a classical positivist like Austin might respond to the objection that the command model of law does not account for the normative attitude of many people. The response would be that such an attitude is no more essential to law than cushions or rockers are essential to chairs. That many people have such an attitude is simply a contingent fact about their personalities or about the coincidental convergence of their interests with the demands of a particular legal system; the attitude is not a necessary feature of law. After all, some people might respond positively toward gunmen too, sympathizing with a particular mugger's plight or with the justice of a terrorist's cause. Yet that possibility would not lead one to revise the judgment that in general the confrontation with gunmen is coercive. Moreover, gunmen too, as we have seen, presumably have a minimal normative attitude toward their own position of power if all one means by 'normative' is "uncoerced." Thus, even the universal existence of such an attitude among the officials of society would not by itself count against the claim that legal systems are essentially coercive.

The analytical objections to Austin's account, already lacking practical import, also seem to lose what descriptive force they have when viewed from this perspective. If Austin's goal is to defend the threatened sanction as the essence of law, he has a simple reply to the claim that the coercive model does not do justice to the variety and range of application of laws. From Austin's viewpoint power-conferring laws are of interest only to the extent that one's desires or wishes in enforcing exchanges or transferring property will be frustrated unless one makes the contract or will as commanded. In such cases, the potential sanction of nullity is just as real as any other sanction, so that even these laws can be fit into the model of orders backed by threats.[10] Similarly, the objection that law binds the sovereign as well as those commanded loses some of its force if one has merely replaced "the sovereign" with "the officials." For to the extent that officials too can ignore the existing rules, accepting and imposing new rules at will in an enterprise where "all that succeeds is success,"[11] Austin's claim must be conceded: the constraints on those in charge will lie in what can be gotten away with, not in the law.

The definition of a legal system. Austin too must defend his claim about the important thing in classifying a system as legal. By comparison the chair example seems relatively simple. Internal attitudes about other important aspects of chairs all seem unrelated to the definitional problem, because it is easy to see that chairs are mainly for sitting, however much one may recognize other interests in such things as color or comfort. But what are legal systems mainly for? The preanalytic phenomenon suggests that it is social control that interests us. That is the genus or general category. And just as our distinct interests in sitting and reclining may explain why we divide the genus furniture into chairs and couches, so one looks now for purposes or interests that might explain why we should further differentiate the general category of organized social system. One possibility is that we are interested in the different means of exercising social control—in distinguishing social groups according to the nature of the bond that makes the society both effective and a system instead of a coincidental convergence of behavior.

The appeal of the classical positivist's position is now easy to explain. Force or coercion is the bond claimed to characterize the legal order, and the widespread prudential interest in avoiding organized sanctions is the interest that is invoked in defense of that claim. We use the term 'legal' to mark off those social systems that back directives with effective threats of force from those that do not—just as we developed 'couch' to designate furniture on which one can recline. Like moral philosophers who define "primary goods" as things everyone desires, whatever else might be desired (thus avoiding the problem of specifying the full range of things people might or ought to want), so Austin and Bentham and Hobbes might defend the coercive view of law, or the bad man's viewpoint: whatever else one is interested in, everyone at least wants to know the prudential consequences of disobedience. If one is also interested in the moral relevance of the fact that something is law or in the social expectations that go with something's being law, let him go to the priest or the moral philosopher or the sociologist, not to the legal theorist or the lawyer.

If a modern positivist is to respond to the claim of the classical positivist, he must explain why it might be important to reflect in a classification scheme the idea of voluntary allegiance, at least among officials, along with the idea of coercion in calling a social order legal. What general human purpose or interest would explain including respect for accepted social standards without regard to their coercive aspect? The only answer Hart offers to this question is the suggestion that the puzzled or ignorant person might want to conform to society's expectations, regardless of accompanying sanctions.[12] But to make the interests of the would-be conformist so important seems out of line with common experience. Everyone has an interest in avoiding organized sanctions, but few people actually pass themselves off as conformists simply for the sake of conforming. The concern not to commit a social faux pas ranks so far below the concern not to be punished that, forced to choose between Austin and Hart, Austin's seems the preferable point of view— with respect to the classification question.[13] At best the puzzled man is like the person whose main interest in chairs is comfort: he does not define 'chair' by reference to that interest, even though he may make it the main, perhaps exclusive, consideration in selecting chairs. So too, the would-be conformist may be interested in law primarily as a clue to official expectations, but that is no reason to think that he would deny that the main interest in deciding what law *is* is the one identified by Austin.

To see just how difficult a task one faces in defending the claim that a normative attitude is essential to the idea of law, consider how one might respond to the "what if" question in this case: what if a particular organized social system did not exhibit the normative attitude that modern positivists believe typifies legal systems? What if nobody used language of obligation in connection with legal claims but only talked about what one was obliged to do? Would one still call such a society a legal system?

The point of this question does not lie in the assumption that every object must fit into the existing language scheme. One uses borderline cases not in the belief that there are necessary and sufficient conditions for the application of every term but as a way of testing the claim that a particular feature is an important part of the standard or paradigm case. We might not know, for example, what to say if asked whether a piece of furniture with only three legs is still a chair (rather than, say, a stool) because our language may not map quite so precisely. But we would know what to say if asked whether the object must have rockers or cushions in order to be a chair. So too, if one confronted Austin with the question of what to say of a society that attached no sanctions to its directives, it is easy to understand the appeal of his hypothetical response that the system just is not a legal one. If nothing can happen to me if I ignore a prescription, it is indistinguishable from moral or other social standards of society. So a first start at improving upon Austin justifies a similar question: what would one say if the normative attitude that modern positivists believe typical of law did not exist in a particular society? Four possible answers occur:

1. One might claim that it is logically impossible for such a society to exist. The very idea of exercising power implies at least some person or persons whose allegiance to the system is uncoerced, and this voluntary acceptance of one's position is all that is meant by the existence of a normative attitude. But if this is what is meant by the normative attitude within a legal system, we have already seen that, far from being inconsistent with the coercive model, it is implied by it.

2. One might deny the empirical possibility of purely coercive regimes, claiming that only regimes with a sufficient degree of voluntary acceptance will survive. But legal theorists do not conduct surveys to test the truth of their claims about the normative attitude that typifies law. Moreover, the claim seems empirically false. Coercive regimes can and do exist with no voluntary allegiance, beyond what is implied in the idea that those in charge voluntarily accept their role.[14] Finally, the empirical claim, even if it were true, would not answer the definitional inquiry any more than the fact that all swans appear to be white proves that whiteness is an essential aspect of the meaning of 'swan'.

3. One might concede that organized coercive systems could exist and might still be legal systems, content with the modest claim that the normative attitudes described are important additional features found in most standard legal systems. Unfortunately this response is so modest as to be no response at all. It evades the claim that law is essentially coercive by substituting description for definition as the goal of legal theory. But if one is only describing various important features of standard legal systems rather than insisting that some are essential to the idea of law, one has not produced a counterexample to Austin's theoretical claim. Moreover, one could just as plausibly claim that since most standard legal systems tend to reflect certain minimum moral standards, the connection between law and morality is as firmly established as the connection between law and normativity. Yet modern positivists usually hasten to dismiss as merely contingent the fact that most legal systems reflect moral standards.[15] If the normative attitude toward law is also

just one among many features that happen to be found in most mature legal systems, it too can be dismissed as merely contingent.

4. The final possibility is to admit that a purely coercive system could exist but to deny that it would be a legal system. This claim directly confronts the classical view of law as essentially coercive. But the claim must now be defended; one must show what it is about the concept of law that makes it plausible to think that the term extends only to non-coercive regimes.

In sum: (1) Austin's model of law is an effort at definition. It claims that the essence of law is coercion and that other features are not essential. (2) This claim that law is coercive is compatible with the existence of a normative attitude among some people; indeed, even the idea of an order backed by a threat entails at least one normative (uncoerced) attitude on the part of the person or persons doing the ordering. (3) To advance beyond the coercive model two requirements must be met: first, one must describe the normative attitude that is essential to law in a way that distinguishes it from what is implicit in any exercise of de facto power; and second, one must defend as a matter of definition the claim that this particular attitude is an essential part of what is meant by a legal system.

MODERN POSITIVISM: THE SEARCH FOR NORMATIVITY

The best example of the dilemma that confronts modern positivism in meeting Austin's challenge may be found by comparing the theories of Kelsen and Hart. Both theorists develop noncoercive models of law that attempt to capture the alleged normative element in law. Both theories fail in different ways to meet the two requirements for an adequate theory just described. Kelsen meets the first requirement by suggesting, somewhat cryptically to be sure, that the normative attitude distinctive of law is not just any uncoerced attitude of the sort one might find even among gangsters but a strong endorsement of the rules comparable to the moral endorsement that characterizes an individual's attitude toward his most basic system of values. But Kelsen makes no attempt to meet the second requirement of explaining just why this attitude of strong moral endorsement must exist if one is to speak of legal systems. Hart, overly sensitive to the problem of definition which the second requirement entails, appears to abandon the definitional enterprise altogether by substituting description as the goal of legal theory. The result is a description of the normative attitude toward law that fails to distinguish law from force and that seems to contradict Hart's own claims about the importance of preserving the idea of obligation in a model of law.

The Price of Purity

Kelsen's "pure theory of law," as he called it, is aptly named. The difference between the gangster and the tax official, as he explains it, is that behind the official there is a law and behind the law a constitution; if we presuppose that we should respect the constitution, then that explains why we respect the tax official as well.

Children play games of this sort that begin, "If your mother had wheels . . ." The unabashedly hypothetical nature of Kelsen's account leaves untouched (hence the theory's "purity") not only the question of justification but every other conceivable problem concerning the difference between law and force that might be of intellectual or practical interest. Instead of attempting to explain or characterize, much less justify, the difference in normative response by reference to objective differences between the gangster and the legal order, Kelsen tells us only that if one presupposes the normative validity of the underlying legal system, consistency will spread that normative response to embrace the logically linked parts of the system as well. In fact, one gets exactly the same analysis of the problem of characterizing the response to any externally imposed demand or occasion for action. Does the beggar's request provide one with a moral reason to give alms? "Only if a general norm—established, for instance, by the founder of a religion—is valid that commands 'Love your neighbor.' And this latter norm is objectively valid only if it is presupposed that one ought to behave as the religious founder has commanded."[16] Does my plant's need for water trigger a respectful response in me? If it does, then it does. Does the bull or the cow deserve veneration? If you think so, then you think so. Does the moon demand to be worshiped? If it is part of your normative structure to so regard it, then you will so regard it. Just how tautological and useless these responses are as answers to any meaningful inquiry should be evident.

The closest Kelsen comes to indicating what gives rise to the critical normative attitude in the case of law is his terse discussion of the difference between the legal community and a gang of robbers. The latter does not constitute a legal order "because no basic norm is presupposed according to which one ought to behave in conformity with the order. But why is no such basic norm presupposed? Because this order does not have the lasting effectiveness without which no basic norm is presupposed . . . The coercive order regarded as the legal order is more effective than the coercive order constituting the gang." Let the gang, continues Kelsen, establish its effective control over a certain territory and "the coercive order may indeed be regarded as a legal order and the community constituted by it may be regarded as a 'state.' "[17]

Here at least is consistency. If one cannot explain the difference in normative response, then one must be prepared to concede that gunmen too can come to be regarded with the proper normative attitude. All it takes is a little conditioning. Mugging, perhaps, is too infrequent and random. But let muggers organize, or better yet convert their enterprise into a protection racket, visiting neighborhood merchants as regularly as the tax collector, and one may expect to see the appropriate change in response from moral outrage to moral respect.

Sterility. That Kelsen here seems to be offering "social science stabs at the psychology of the law abiding citizen" which seems "outside the scope and interests of the pure theory of law"[18] is only the least of the problems with this approach. The more serious problem is that it dooms legal theory to sterility from the start for reasons suggested in the preceding chapter. Insiders who want to know whether there are good reasons for the difference in response, who are prepared to challenge their conditioning, will find nothing of use to them in Kelsen. Even the empirical suggestion that links the normative response to the effectiveness of the coercive order is falsified by a good deal of human experience. Protection rackets are still rackets, however effective; and entire regimes can be regarded by their subjects as outlaw states with no more right to rule than gangsters despite years of effective control.

It is not only insiders who will find their concerns so curiously ignored. Outsiders too will find nothing of interest in this treatment of the difference between law and force. The distinction between a legal and a purely coercive system becomes a distinction that serves simply as a label to designate those authority relationships that do and those that do not rest unexplainably on the asserted normative basis. Confronted with any actual regime, one must look to see whether the appropriate normative attitude exists; the label and the analytical exercise add nothing to what one discovers from this empirical survey of people's attitudes.

The preceding discussion of the challenge that Austin presents makes it easy to see what is lacking in Kelsen's account. Kelsen meets the first condition for going beyond the coercive model of law: that is, he distinguishes the type of normative attitude toward law—a moral one—from the minimal attitude of voluntary acceptance that one finds even in the case of gangsters. But Kelsen mounts no defense of his apparent semantic claim that the concept of legal system necessarily implies the existence of such an attitude. At the risk of some repetition it is worth emphasizing just how large this gap in Kelsen's account is. Let us assume *arguendo* that Kelsen is correct in claiming that gangsters who succeed will, by the very fact of success, generate a new and distinctive normative attitude toward their imposed rule, either among the gang members themselves or the citizens they control. That claim seems to be true at best only as an empirical or psychological generalization; it does not seem to be a semantic truth, such as the claim that bachelors are unmarried men, or even a universally true empirical proposition, such as that all swans are white. Thus one can imagine without contradiction an effective regime that is purely coercive, with nobody, including the rulers, endorsing or presupposing the rules in Kelsen's sense; one could probably even find existing or historical examples of such regimes.[19] If Kelsen intends his claim about normativity to be semantic—a claim about the meaning of 'law'—he must defend that claim by explaining why as a matter of definition we should not count these purely coercive regimes as legal.

The attempt to fill in this gap for Kelsen by arguing that purely coercive systems do not count as legal presents the positivist with a dilemma. One cannot defend this claim without abandoning the exactly opposite position of the positivist when it comes to proposals to limit 'law' to exclude morally iniquitous systems. In the latter case the positivist advances both theoretical and practical reasons for preferring the wider to the narrower concept. As a theoretical matter, the positivist insists, nothing but confusion can result from leaving the study of iniquitous laws "to another discipline, and certainly no history or other form of legal study has found it profitable to do this."[20] But the same can be said of leaving to the study of another discipline those regimes that rely entirely on coercion for the enforcement of their directives, without the normative endorsement of any particular group, including officials. The organized sanction, after all, is the most salient feature of the specific method of social control under study. In some societies this form of control may be supplemented by official normative attitudes toward the basic rules of the regime that may or may not be correct according to critical morality. In other societies, as we have seen, there may be no official normative attitude at all but only effective enforcement accompanied at best by passive acquiescence in the imposed rule. In both cases it is the effectiveness of the social regime that creates a functioning society and thus an apparent entity for study. There is nothing in the positivist's account to explain why it is artificial to exclude from such studies those entities that are immoral but not artificial to exclude those that work by force, fear, and inertia alone.[21]

The positivist's practical objection to excluding iniquitous laws from the concept of law follows from the claim that the question of moral obligation is independent of the determination of legal obligation. Immoral systems can thus safely be counted as legal without affecting the ultimate question of what to do; indeed, this view of the matter, it is claimed, sharpens and clarifies the moral inquiry. But this argument applies even more clearly to the individual who finds himself within a coercive regime: he too must separate the moral question of what to do from the 'legal' requirements he confronts. What then is the practical advantage of excluding purely coercive systems from the definition of law? If anything, it is the attempt to do so that confuses moral inquiry because of the implication that there are different consequences for moral obligation in normative as compared to coercive systems. But that is a proposition that the positivist never asserts, indeed cannot assert, given his self-imposed constraint on engaging in substantive moral inquiry.

The dilemma here can be briefly summarized. The positivist's insistence on maintaining his theory's purity forces him to say nothing about either the grounds for or the nature of normative judgments. Yet at the same time the positivist insists that law is a normative system. Insistence on the first position results in a theory that provides neither insider nor outsider with criteria to explain or justify the normative attitude that the second position posits as a characteristic of any legal system. As a result, the second position itself—the insistence that law is normative—begins to appear arbitrary.

Inconsistency. Escape from this as from any dilemma lies in either of two directions. One can discard the claim that law is essentially normative, thus conceding that tax officials and gunmen differ only in the extent and degree of their effectiveness and organization. Or one can supply criteria to characterize the distinctive legal attitude in a way that aids in identifying and explaining the distinction between law and force.

The latter course is Hart's, whose variations on the theme sounded by Kelsen consist almost entirely of a more detailed description of the normative attitude that characterizes rules of obligation and of the legal order. The features described, it should be noted, are still of one kind only: the kind that can be used by the outsider, the external observer, to identify the appropriate normative attitude. Furnishing criteria for the insider to ground or justify the normative attitude continues to be eschewed as a matter for political or moral philosophy. The purity of the positivist's program is thus preserved while at the same time the legal theory's differentiating power is presumably increased. The result is a study in inconsistency.

The inconsistency in Hart's account can be quickly described.[22] Hart begins as does Kelsen: orders backed by threats oblige; law by contrast obligates. He ends with an account designed to preserve this feature of obligation in a legal system. That account, as noted, replaces the idea of orders backed by threats with the idea of rules accepted by officials. Yet Hart's descriptions of a society's rules of obligation on the one hand and of the official acceptance of legal rules on the other differ markedly. Rules of obligation are characterized by serious social pressure to act in ways that are thought essential to a prized feature of social life and that typically conflict with self-interest.[23] In contrast, official acceptance of rules "may be based on many different considerations: calculations of long-term interest; disinterested interest in others; an unreflecting inherited or traditional attitude; or the mere wish to do as others do."[24] The first description of obligation is of a strong normative attitude much like the moral sense which Kelsen too seems to posit as the basic attitude underlying a legal system. The second description of rule acceptance is the weakest possible sense of normativity: it is no different from the attitude implicit even in the coercive model; indeed, it is little more than an explication of voluntary allegiance. If rule acceptance can be nothing more than allegiance to a system for reasons of self-interest, it is clear that the strong sense of obligation and the features that Hart says identify it are not necessary features of a legal system—even among the officials who accept it. The normative terminology that appears in statements about the law need reflect no more than the force of a prudential "ought." "You ought to obey the tax man" becomes the normative equivalent of the mugger's, "You ought to hand over your money."[25]

This conclusion, that statements of legal obligation are equivalent in meaning to assertions that there is some chance of being punished if one fails to comply, is, of course, Austin's conclusion. If Hart's model yields an idea of obligation that is no stronger than this, it means either that Hart's connotational objection to Austin is unwarranted, or that one must add other features to the model to give a different sense of legal obligation. I shall explore the second possibility in the next section of this chapter. But the first possibility deserves consideration here. Why are modern positivists so convinced that Austin was wrong and that claims of legal obligation mean more than assertions about what one is *obliged* to do?

A standard answer to this question relies on examples in which, it is claimed, one would still say there is a legal obligation even though it is not likely that a sanction will be imposed—because, for example, one has bribed the court or left the country.[26] But these examples are the wrong examples. All that Austin's account requires is that there be some chance, however slight, of a sanction's being incurred, which is not the same as saying that it is *likely* that a sanction will be imposed. Thus, the examples of bribing courts or leaving the country or getting off without a sentence after conviction (because the law in question provides only a maximum penalty but no minimum) do not carry the intended force. In each of these cases there is some empirical chance that the sanction will be (or might have been) imposed. The bribe might be discovered; the exile might be brought back or might come back accidentally or voluntarily; the judge might have imposed a sentence within the authorized maximum. Each of these possibilities is consistent with the claim that to say there is (or was) a legal obligation means no more than to say there is (or was) a chance of harm.

What must be imagined if one is to test Austin's claim is a case in which there is absolutely no chance of punishment. But the only such cases that come to mind are those in which death (or even law itself, as in the case of the statute of limitations) has intervened, and in these cases we probably would *not* say that legal obligation still exists. In short, if one keeps the right examples in mind, it is plausible to conclude that a contradiction *is* involved in saying one has a legal obligation even though there is no chance of punishment. Austin's view is too pervasive to be disproved by appealing to linguistic practices that are likely to reflect the same uncertainty that divides legal theorists.

A similar conclusion applies to the argument that Austin's view makes it impossible to distinguish a tax from a fine.[27] This argument also begs the question whether we do, in fact, make a *legal* distinction between taxes and fines where that distinction is not reflected in the possibility of an additional sanction in the latter case. If one decides to view the parking ticket as a "tax" and park in the zone reserved for the handicapped in order to avoid being late for an important meeting, what does it add to explain that such conduct is disapproved of as well as "taxed"? Such information means no more to the "bad man" than to be told that the city council has passed a resolution expressing the sense of the city that one should not park in handicapped zones but has added no sanction for doing so. Austin's claim that such sanctionless laws are indistinguishable from positive morality and hence are not law cannot be disproved by noting that fines attach to conduct that is censured, whereas taxes do not. The question is whether this is *legal* censure and hence results in a *legal* obligation. Indeed, where society does want to make clear the distinction between a tax and a fine, it ensures that the deliberate decision to treat the fine as a "tax" will incur some risk of an additional penalty. Thus, punitive damages in torts deter the deliberate decision to pay a "tax" for the harm caused in return for the pleasure of hitting someone, and scofflaw provisions may similarly increase the penalty for those who willfully violate parking regulations. These facts underscore the Austinian-Holmesian view. Unwilling to rely merely on the expression of societal disapproval to distinguish fines from taxes, we reflect that disapproval where it matters (legally) in the possibility of an additional sanction for the willful attempt to convert a fine into a tax.

A third argument against Austin's account is that predictions of harm, even if they explain what 'legal obligation' means to many people, cannot explain what judges mean by these words. Judges refer to law as a reason for imposing the sanction, not as a means of predicting the incidence of sanctions.[28] The problem with this objection is that it does not provide any alternative account of what obligation *does* mean for the judge, other than the suggestion that such language is just another way of talking about legal validity: to say that one has an obligation to register for the draft, under this view, is simply to report that there is a rule to that effect among the rules judges accept. But this is a use of 'obligation' that is not normative at all. If this is what obligation amounts to in Hart's model, it helps explain the contradiction in his account. Hart suggests that legal rules are to be classified among a society's basic rules of obligation. That claim seems inconsistent with a model of law that makes a rule legal just in case it is valid—that is, accepted by officials for any reason whatsoever and not necessarily for reasons that reflect important social purposes as in the case of other rules of obligation. It is a mistake to think that one can infer anything about obligation (in any sense other than validity) from such a model.[29]

In sum, if claims of legal duty are simply reports about what rules have been accepted (comparable to a *description* of the rules of chess), they are not normative claims at all. If such claims are predictions of a chance of harm, they are indistinguishable in meaning from orders backed by threats. Only two possibilities remain. The first is to show that claims of legal obligations have the same basic meaning as claims of moral obligation. The second possibility is that 'legal obligation' refers to something altogether different: not moral obligation, but not simply a sanction theory of duty either.

This second possibility in contrast to the first one seems odd. It suggests that instead of one root idea of obligation, which philosophers argue about in connection with moral obligation, there are at least two such ideas, related but distinct. Yet when one talks, say, of promissory obligation or of family obligation, no one would think that one is talking about new forms of obligation but only about the moral obligation to keep promises or to provide for family needs. So too, the nonmisleading way to talk about legal obligation, as a concept distinct from legal validity, is to talk about the moral obligation to obey the law. This study defends this common-sense view. Even if this defense fails, however, the alternative does not seem to be that one must imagine a different (but inexplicable) sense of obligation; the alternative seems to be that Austin was right. Of course, explaining what moral obligation itself means is no easy task, and many philosophers conclude that moral language too can be reduced to a sanction-based theory of duty.[30] But precisely because it is so difficult to say just what moral duty means, it seems odd to suggest that there is room for yet another even more esoteric concept of obligation. If claims of legal obligation do not share the same root meaning as claims of moral obligation, then they probably are only reports of legal validity or predictions of a chance of harm.[31]

The Demise of Definition

A final round in the modern attempt to explain the normative element in law may be found in the dispute between Hart and Joseph Raz. Raz, who studied under Hart and originally developed a theory much like his, has since modified his views in ways that resemble what we have seen in Kelsen. Raz suggests that the normative attitude toward law, at least among the judges or officials who accept and enforce the system, is of the strong, moral variety.[32] A judge's decision that something is my legal duty entails a claim about my moral duty, at least in the sense that in pronouncing my legal duty, the judge implies that he believes the duty is consistent with, or even required by, morality. This connection between law and the claim or belief that law is just is precisely the connection that I propose to defend as an essential feature of law. In this respect both Raz and Kelsen, in suggesting that wherever one finds legal systems one finds an official belief in the justice of that system, provide strong empirical support for the theoretical claim advanced here. The problem once again is to show that this connection between law and the belief in justice is more than an empirically contingent phenomenon.

To see the difference between the claim that must be defended and the only claim found in Raz or Kelsen, consider an analogy. Suppose one is investigating the essence of social organizations that occur on a smaller level than the state—social clubs, for example. Clubs also have rules that members must follow on pain of expulsion or other penalty; and those who promulgate the rules presumably have at least the weak attitude of acceptance implicit in any voluntary organization. Suppose now that an observer bent on providing an analysis of the idea of a social club announces a discovery: he has observed that those who promulgate the rules also believe that the rules are just. Thus, he concludes, a belief in the justice of the rules is characteristic of the idea of a social club.

The problem with this discovery is that it can be true in a trivial sense that has no bearing on the question of what is meant by a social club or organization. It is true in a trivial sense that people probably do not take any nonfrivolous action—that is, action that has consequences for others—if they do not think the action is consistent with morality. But that fact of human psychology does not tell one anything peculiar about social clubs and certainly does not entitle one to conclude that the very idea of such a club entails a belief by its members in the justice of the club's rules. The club, after all, may have nothing to do with morality or justice; it may exist, for example, just to allow lovers of Dickens to pursue their interest or chess enthusiasts to pursue their hobby. No one thinks such pursuits are unjust, and in that sense one may be entitled to infer that the club members believe their rules are consistent with morality; but at the same time no one thinks there is any need to defend the rules of these social clubs beyond simply pointing to what has been accepted. No one, that is, has to defend Dickens as a better object for a literary club than some other author or chess as a better game than go. It is enough that Dickens or chess is the chosen basis for the organization. Moreover, the motives for forming or joining the club may range as variously as those described by Hart from self-interest or unthinking tradition to a view of Dickens as the greatest author the world has ever produced. A social club, in short, fits nicely into a model whose only necessary normative element is the weak attitude of acceptance. That model remains adequate even though it may also be trivially true that, should the issue arise, members of the club would hasten to acknowledge that there was never any thought of their engaging in anything immoral.

This response to the claim that law connotes a belief in justice is in essence the response that Hart gives Raz. And it is consistent, as we have seen, with Hart's own model of law: judges may accept the rules for all kinds of reasons having nothing necessarily to do with morality. Furthermore, though I have suggested that as an empirical matter it is probably true that social organizations do not believe that what they do is immoral, that is not a necessary or universal truth. One can imagine club members admitting that their rules for membership or their pursuits in the club are immoral yet continuing in the enterprise because self-interest is too strong or because members simply have no concern for morality. Hart is willing to say that the same is true of law: it is possible that judges might even admit that the rules they accept are immoral yet continue to enforce them.[33] If this is so, all that remains of the claimed connection between law and the belief in justice is an empirical generalization about the link between action and psychology: people normally persuade themselves that what they do is not immoral. Even if it is a generalization that holds true in most cases, there is no reason to think that it must be true in order for us to speak of a legal system.

What is important to note about this dispute is how futile it is to try to decide who is correct without first knowing, once again, whether it is a definition or a description that is at stake. The empirical facts that Hart points to as counterexamples to an alleged connection between law and the belief in justice can hardly be denied. Organized social systems can be created and maintained by rulers with motives as diverse as those that Hart decribes and can even be openly admitted by those in charge to be evil. Even Raz concedes this empirical possibility, suggesting that judges who do not believe in the morality of the rules they accept will be forced to pretense.[34] But if these empirical possibilities must be conceded, there is only one level on which dispute can continue: the level of definition. One must explain why systems that do not include the official belief in justice do not count as legal systems. Rather than deny the empirical possibility of various judicial attitudes, one must defend the conceptual claim about the connection between law and the belief in justice.

To see how such a conceptual argument escapes the force of the empirical arguments so far considered, compare another analogy: the institution of promise keeping. It is usually agreed that part of the very meaning of promise is the idea that one commits oneself to act in the future in a way in which one would not otherwise be obligated to act. If that is what a promise means, it yields an example of the kind of meaning that must be constructed for law as well, for now all of the empirical propositions considered before can be admitted without affecting the claim about meaning. Thus, one can imagine people who do not in fact intend to commit themselves nevertheless making promises. Those people, one would say, are forced to pretense. Indeed, the whole point of the pretense lies in taking advantage of what the pretender knows is understood within society whenever the language of promise is used. It is also true that the motives for making promises may be as various as those described by Hart, ranging from self-interest to a view that oath taking is a dignifying act in itself. But even if the motive is only self-interest, the step into promise making is a serious one: one takes the step knowing (or pretending) that a moral obligation has been assumed. Finally, even one who has decided that there is no moral obligation to keep promises, not even in the prima facie sense, may still recognize that the meaning of promise entails the belief by others that such a moral obligation ensues.

Here then is a conceptual connection between a concept (promise) and the belief in a moral claim (an obligation to keep the promise).

Moreover, the conceptual meaning remains intact even though (1) one thinks that the moral belief is false—that is, that promises do not really obligate; (2) one has no intention of keeping the promise; (3) one makes the promise for reasons that are purely self-interested. What one cannot do is make a promise and simultaneously deny any intention of keeping the promise or any belief in an obligation to keep promises. In that case, the promisee understands that no promise has been made, but at most only a statement of future intent.

Applying the same analogy to the alleged connection between law and the belief in justice results in a similar conclusion. One may concede the empirical possibility that judges may not believe the laws are just yet note that the system in which they operate assumes such a belief. Such judges will be forced to pretense. What they cannot do is openly confess their cynicism, for then, as in the case of the promise, they would reveal that this is no longer a legal system but only its alternative—a coercive system. It should also be clear now that what was missing in Kelsen's account is also missing in Raz's: a defense in terms of meaning and definition of the claim that coercive systems do not count as legal systems any more than stating an intent to act while denying any commitment to do so counts as a promise.

Why is there no such defense in legal theory of this conceptual claim for a normative model of law? One reason has already been suggested. If the goal of legal theory is description, then Hart is right: there is no reason to insist on one particular kind of normative attitude as the only one to be found in organized social systems. But it is also clear that if description is the goal, there is no reason not to include in the account another commonly encountered empirical fact: the general tendency of such systems to reflect minimal moral requirements. The descriptive goal, in short, is incompatible with positivism's central tenet about the lack of connection between law and morality. Yet if the dispute between Hart and Raz is definitional, Raz's claim remains as undefended as Kelsen's, and Hart's has not advanced beyond Austin's.

There is, I believe, another explanation for the positivist's reluctance to enter the definitional arena and engage in the argument that is necessary to establish the connection between law and any particular normative attitude. Consider again the difference between the idea of a promise and that of a social club. Why is it plausible to assume in the first case that the connection between the concept and the moral belief is essential, whereas in the second it is at best contingent? Presumably it is because one could if pressed justify these assumptions by saying something about promise keeping and its importance to people as well as something about the nature of moral obligation. That suggests that to defend the conceptual claim about law and the belief in justice, one must similarly be able to explain why it might matter to people that this particular attitude toward law should exist. In doing so, one may find it impossible to avoid engaging in evaluation and substantive moral argument, departing from the purity of the positivist's program to account for the importance of the attitude toward law in the only way that makes sense—from the viewpoint of the insider himself.

A FRESH START: TAKING OBLIGATION SERIOUSLY

This brief review of positivism's struggle to defend a normative model of law has produced two competing descriptions of the attitude that is distinctive of law. The weak attitude is simply the attitude of uncoerced acceptance of the power structure—an attitude that typifies any voluntary organization. The strong attitude parallels that of moral obligation: officials accept the power structure because they think it is just. If consistency alone were the goal, Hart's account could simply be altered to delete one or the other of these different ideas as an explication of the necessary normative attitude. Hart's repeated insistence on the weak attitude of acceptance as all that is necessary suggests, as noted, that it is the idea of obligation that should be dispensed with in a model of law, though that requires withdrawing the connotational objections to Austin. The structure of the present inquiry requires the second option. Before one concedes that officials are only variously motivated henchmen in an essentially coercive system, it is worth pursuing the implications of a view that insists on preserving the stronger features of obligation that Hart originally identified: (1) serious social pressure to conform to rules that (2) are thought to advance prized aspects of social life and (3) that often conflict with self-interest. What would this characterization of the official normative attitude toward law imply for the insider who wants to know why law deserves his respect?

The View from Inside

To answer this question one must be more precise about insiders—who they are, how they come to inquire into legitimacy, the nature of the response such an inquiry requires. These questions lead in turn to a more fundamental problem for legal theory than that of explaining the normativity of law. It is a problem that extends beyond legal theory to embrace almost all modern examples of empirical sciences that purport to describe and systematically treat the realm of value in human life solely from the outside, without attending to the subjective features of that realm as they appear to those who struggle honestly to create and live within it.

Nonsubjecting subjects. Hart's analysis shares with other legal theories the tendency to divide insiders into two groups: those who rule and those who do not. Only the former, according to all the positivists thus far considered, need exhibit the normative attitude that characterizes a legal system. The normative allegiance of the latter group, though desirable, is not necessary for the system to be legal. Moreover, Hart even suggests that subjects who do not accept the system can only conclude that law obliges but has no tendency to obligate, thus ending once and for all, at least for them, the effort to distinguish law from force.[35]

This picture of a legal system, which contemplates complete normative estrangement between ruler and ruled, puts an end to more than the dissenting citizen's inquiry into why he should respect the law. It also puts an end to two thousand years of political philosophy that addresses just that question. The whole point in asking whether there is an obligation to obey the law is to find out what there is about law qua law to justify moral respect, apart from one's independently established normative attitudes toward the goals the law seeks to promote. If one already believes, for example, that murder is morally wrong, there is no need for an independent obligation to obey the law against murder. The quest for grounding political obligation begins, in short, where this picture of law ends: with citizens who do not share the official normative attitude toward the rules imposed on them but who nonetheless can be said to have a rational basis for obligation. Whether such a basis for obligation exists is another matter, to be considered in the next chapter. The point is that a theory of law whose implications for dissenting citizens ignores a possibility that political theory seriously explores must have gone astray somewhere.

Where it went astray is not hard to see. We began with the assumed separation of rulers and subjects as respects each group's normative attitudes toward the social structure that unites them. To this substantive disagreement on the merits of a society's basic rules was then added a further and much more divisive wedge, describing the normative attitude of rulers in a way that dispensed with even the claim that allegiance is due from dissenting subjects. If legal systems may be based solely on rulers' self-interest, even to the point of their openly admitting that "morally, they ought not to accept" the system but "for a variety of reasons continue to do so,"[36] there is no possibility for further dialogue between rulers and dissenting subjects; the only remaining argument for compliance is that of the gun.

This account explains how one moves from existing legal theory to a conclusion that seems to dismiss the concerns of political theory. But one may benefit from speculating as to why the move occurred. The phenomenon of social structures that operate to the disadvantage of large, identifiable groups is all too familiar in history, with slave societies constituting only the most blatant example. The legal theorist's determination not to let judgments of substantive morality determine how the term 'law'should be applied leads to a definition that embraces these as well as more enlightened regimes. But the definition is too loose: it does more than qualify slave societies as legal, with the consequence of eliminating any idea of obligation among the slave group; it has the same consequence for any citizen who happens to disagree with the rulers' judgment about the merits of the legal system.

How does the situation change if one requires that the normative attitude of rulers reflect the stronger features of obligation? A complete answer to that question must await the examination of the basis for political obligation in the following chapter. At this point it is enough to note that this stronger view of obligation, which requires group reference to prized features of social life, gives a very different picture of the relationship between rulers and ruled by suggesting that officials hold out the system they administer as one that deserves the allegiance of dissenters and supporters alike. Such a claim is not a universal concomitant of social orders. Societies may establish dominant and purely coercive relationships vis à vis other groups—most obviously in the case of slaves or subjects of conquered territories. Indeed, what makes these groups different from dissenting citizens is the attitude of the rulers in the case of the slave group that nothing but force or power matters. The allegiance of the subordinate group is not sought, for there is no interest in making the reciprocal gesture that the demand for allegiance requires: a claim that there are mutual benefits to be realized from the organized rule that is imposed.

These considerations suggest that an adequate legal theory must leave room for the possibility of a moral attitude toward law even among subjects who reject the basic value structure of society. Where rulers make no pretense that the system serves any interests but their own, further attempts to ground obligation among dissenting citizens are probably useless; but in other cases, one deals with the very essence of political theory by trying to explain how respect for the attempt to rule justly is warranted even though one believes that attempt to be a failure. The positivist at this point might respond by admitting to undue haste in suggesting that obligation cannot exist without coincidence of normative outlook. But grounding obligation is not his aim. The variety of reasons for official acceptance may correlate with a variety of morally appropriate attitudes on the part of subjects, depending on one's political theory. The essence of the positivist's claim is simply that the only necessary condition for the existence of a legal system is that officials display the appropriate normative attitude toward the basic structure. To test the implications of this claim, one must consider how it is that questions of obligation and duty arise among officials and what kind of response such questions require if one is to find obligation even within this group.

Unruly rulers. The fundamental problem for the official is not why he should obey the law but why he should enforce it. He may confront the former question in his role as citizen, but in his official role he confronts the need to justify, at least to himself, the imposition on others of the organized sanctions he administers. This justification may take the same form as the justification for obedience to law, but it need not. Thus a judge may believe that although civil disobedience is appropriate, he is nevertheless obligated to enforce the law until it is changed.

This possibility suggests that the source of official obligation is not the same as the source of political obligation in general. Indeed, the more one reflects on legal theory's struggle to give an account of the normative attitude among officials that makes a system legal, the more difficult it becomes to understand the necessity for the struggle. In contrast to political theory's task of explaining why the dissenting citizen has a prima facie obligation to obey the law, it is child's play to explain why a judge ought to apply the law. One need not point to a mystical juristic hypothesis or to a complex social practice that is simply accepted. One need only recognize that officials who voluntarily assume positions with attendant duties thereby agree, expressly or implicitly, to perform a certain role, to play by the rules, in short to apply the law.

Judges may of course decide that the rules are too iniquitous to enforce and thus face the same conflict between duties that characterizes the problem of civil disobedience. But while the question of obligation to obey the law has been widely discussed, there is virtually no literature on the question of the judge's obligation to apply the law, although there is a huge body of literature on the question of *how* a judge determines the law and thus fulfills this obligation. What distinguishes officials from subjects is precisely what makes the problem of political obligation so difficult. Subjects do not necessarily consent or agree in any ordinary sense to the system in which they find themselves. But officials do. If political theorists could point to the same voluntary acts in the case of citizens that one finds in the case of voluntary assumption of office, all the elaborate (and ultimately unsuccessful) attempts to construct tacit consent from, say, the decision to vote or to remain in the country would be unnecessary. Why then does legal theory take such a circuitous route in accounting for the basis of official obligation and its characteristics?

Note that one consequence of this consent-based view of obligation is that legal systems become essentially like the games or social clubs discussed earlier, in which members or players participate voluntarily and thus agree to abide by the rules. This agreement provides the prima facie obligation that prevents a judge from determining his duty through an independent evaluation of the rules. This view of law as game[37] may even serve to reconcile the textual discrepancies in Hart's account. The various reasons for acceptance, in the weak sense, are like the various motivations for agreeing to play a game. Having once agreed, one finds that one has incurred group obligations, in the strong sense, as evidenced by critical reactions to deviation designed to remind one of the agreement. But if this is what the normative base of law amounts to, it could have been said more simply. Moreover, this explanation contrasts markedly with the apparent assumption of both Hart and Kelsen that the critical normative attitude obtains toward the rules themselves rather than toward an agreement to play by such rules.

There is one very good explanation for the unwillingness of legal theorists to rest the observed normative element in law on a direct analogy to the normative basis of a game, although it is an explanation that jeopardizes the entire enterprise. Unlike game players and club members, an official in a legal system must play by rules that apply to nonmembers and nonplayers. Those who have not consented or joined may nonetheless be punished, fined, deprived of goods, life, and liberty—all because the rules the judge agreed to play by require these results. Since the judge knows that these are the consequences of his decision to become a judge, it would be an abuse of the notion of promise to suggest that he could create a countervailing duty to existing moral duties—for example the duty not to inflict wrongful injury—by promising to inflict such injury. Contracts or promises known to require illegal or immoral acts do not yield obligation, prima facie or otherwise. Thus for the judge the normative attitude must be toward the rules he is about to agree to enforce. That is why it is the basic rules that must be hypothesized or accepted.

Note the consequences of this explanation. First, one passes over a perfectly adequate external account of official obligation, in terms of implicit agreement, in favor of an account that focuses on the insider's reasons for deciding to enter the agreement. Second, the explanation seems to require weightier reasons for acceptance than self-interest or the mere wish to do as others do, for otherwise the game analogy would be entirely appropriate. Third, by ignoring the implicit agreement in the account one gives of official obligation, one theoretically invites every judge to question anew why he should enforce the basic rules of the legal system. That question can no longer be answered by referring to the conditions of the trust that was accepted. It must instead be answered by directly showing in what respect the basic rules are to be acknowledged as rules of obligation. And that brings us back to where we started: the attempt to find and characterize obligation among the officials of a legal system.

We haved already seen that obligation cannot result from the mere fact that others accept rules solely because they serve their own self-interest. In such a regime officials and subjects alike have only prudential reasons for compliance: punishment for the subject, loss of preferential status for the official. How does the matter change if one requires that the official attitude toward the rules of the system be of the stronger variety, characterized by the more serious reaction to deviation that is a mark of rules of obligation? Such a test suggests that an official could foresee two principal kinds of reaction to his failure to conform: serious pressure from his peers, and reminders that the rules serve prized features of social life. Of these reactions it is tempting to dismiss the first as simply another form of threat, like the gun, that by itself cannot provide any but prudential reasons for compliance. Indeed, if there were nothing to this account of obligation but a reference to social pressure to conform, the matter would not differ essentially from the gunman situation.

But there is more. Compared to the gun, social pressure is far less immediately threatening, however subtly effective in the long run. Social pressure still appeals to the voluntary acquiescence of the individual; the pressure is merely an attention-getting device. The critical feature in explaining obligation is the group belief that the rules serve prized features of social life, a belief that precedes and gives rise to the pressure. While Hart appears content to give equal weight to the pressure and the claim of value that accompanies the pressure, the view from inside emphasizes the latter, with the former at most an incidental by-product.[38]

The outsider's description of obligation suggests a stark image: a vise of social conformity in which individuals are slowly squeezed to the accompaniment of sweet talk about the independent value of the rules. From the inside the view is quite different. There is no vise apart from that of the individual's own conscience. One twists and squirms in response to two features of the group reaction: first, a recognition of the possible merits of the claim of value, which is likely to conflict with self-interest, creating tension between self- and other-regarding impulses; second, even if one is persuaded that the group's judgment is in error, the need and desire to belong and the recognition of one's own ability to err make painful the decision to deviate. That both of these pressures are internally generated in a way that the pressure of a vise or a gun is not is evidenced by the ability of the individual to release the pressure himself through nothing more than the strength of his own faith and courage. The dissenter, confident of the correctness of his convictions and unconcerned over the prospect of estrangement from the group, feels no pressure though he may still hear the claims of value.

From whatever direction one approaches the attempt to characterize obligation—whether from the point of view of the judge who wants to know why he should enforce the law or the citizen who wants to know why he should obey—one ends with the same conclusion. Both perspectives require a response that at least claims value for the rules in question, and both seem to discount as largely irrelevant the fact that force or pressure accompanies the claim. Can one say more than this without totally abandoning legal theory for moral philosophy? Can one characterize the nature of the claim of value that confronts deviating officials or citizens? In particular, is it sufficient for the group simply to iterate that these are their values, or must they be prepared at least in theory to demonstrate that these are values that dissenters ought also to embrace?

Recent investigations of this problem suggest that these alternatives spring from competing theories of obligation: a practice theory, which traces the justification of rules to a social practice or convention about which nothing more can be said; and what might be called a purpose theory, which requires the statement that a group believes a rule to be obligatory to entail the statement that the group is prepared to show that the rule serves some purpose in terms of defensible group interests.[39] The difference in terms of the response to an insider's "Why should I do it?" is the difference between, "Because that is what we all do," on the one hand and, on the other, "Because it serves certain important functions, which is why we all do it and why you should too."

From the discussion thus far it should be clear that the only adequate account of obligation from the viewpoint of the insider corresponds to the purpose theory. "Because we all do it" is a reply that can create a variety of motives to conform—from the mere wish to do as others do to the more compelling need to belong. But serious inquiry into what one ought to do begins by confronting impulses and instincts with a view to finding a rational basis to govern their influence on action. The occasions on which the brute fact of social convention alone seems to supply such a rational ground for conforming are likely to be instances in which the convention is only an elliptical reference to some other reason for conforming, apart from the convention itself. Coordination problems that require group harmony (for example, which side of the road to drive on) are familiar examples. Games too foreclose reevaluation of the conventional rules in the midst of play not because "that's just the way we play," but because of the implicit prior agreement. Even rituals and ceremonies, whose value in celebrating and strengthening community may be thought to depend on participating just because others do, are but further instances of a kind of coordination problem. Not all instances of conforming action serve ritualistic values; determining which ones do requires independent judgment and thus, once again, reference to something beyond the mere fact of convention.

I do not mean to suggest that those who insist on separating legal and political theory are logically committed to an erroneous view—the practice view—of obligation. To the contrary, one may agree that the purpose theory is the better account of obligation while still remaining disengaged from the question of what purposes matter. In this manner one maintains the perspective of the outsider, leaving to moral philosophy the problem of guiding the internal dialogue that binds dissenters to the group. But whatever the logic of the matter, there is an undeniable empirical tendency for legal theorists to prefer what appears to be the practice theory of obligation. The explanation for that tendency may lie in the attempt to accommodate within the concept of legal system two extreme examples of functioning societies: the very primitive society and the highly integrated one. Tribal societies that engage in practices and rites that strike us as odd or nonsensical may simply be demonstrating the purpose theory at work in a group whose values and world view we do not share. It is also possible, however, that such societies are in a stage of moral development that is as primitive as the "science" that underlies their taboos. Jean Piaget's studies suggest that the child's development of moral reasoning follows a course from the unthinking devotion to convention for its own sake to the dawning recognition and acceptance of one's power to evaluate and change convention.[40] So too is it possible that social organizations may never progress to the point where challenge and evaluation of existing taboos is even conceivable. In such cases outsiders will see only a practice unaccompanied by attempts to justify beyond merely pointing to the rule that the deviant has disregarded. At the opposite extreme is the thoroughly conformist society in which the justification for the basic structure is so well known and so completely internalized that the problem of justification never arises. All of us find ourselves in this state on some occasions, for we could hardly function if each step had to be preceded by a reexamination of basic normative premises. A society that finds itself in this position for any length of time—whose members have no occasion to dissent, question, or challenge—also provides nothing to observe but the practice. But these are unusual cases. The characteristics of the paradigm case of obligation in modern societies cannot be extracted from societies that have not yet awakened or that have gone back to sleep.

If it is paradox that one seeks rather than mere tendency, one must look beyond the choice between practice and purpose accounts of obligation to the more fundamental commitment of legal theory to the view of the outsider. It is that commitment, alluded to earlier, that generates the consistency problems I have been discussing, and it is to that problem that I now turn.

The View from Outside

So far we have seen that any attempt to find a distinction between law and force in current legal theory confronts the following problems:

1. The insistence that law is normative and thus differs from force is an assertion of a difference, not an explanation or a defense of it.

2. The positivist's objection to making the concept of a legal system depend on the correctness of the normative attitude toward law applies equally to making the concept depend on the existence of such a normative attitude.

3. The claim that an adequate model of law must connote the idea of obligation tends to be followed either by no description of obligation at all, as in Kelsen, or by a description of the normative attitude toward legal rules that conflicts with the description of the attitude toward rules of obligation, as in Hart.

4. The suggestion that obligation will be acknowledged among subjects only if they accept the same normative outlook as rulers ignores a long tradition whose whole point is to ground obligation in the face of normative disagreement.

5. The criteria used to determine when a group has a rule of obligation focus on the pressure to conform in a way that obscures and distorts the central role of justification in the formation and maintenance of such rules.

To claim that each of these is an instance of conflict, contradiction, or inconsistency is to use a logical vocabulary poorly suited to the moral dimensions of this inquiry. It is usually thought, for example, that purely logical inconsistency can be avoided so long as one takes care to distinguish statements about the existence of normative attitudes made by outsiders who do not share that attitude from similar statements made by insiders.[41] But it is this distinction between outside and inside views that gives rise to the moral analogue of the logical vocabulary: frustration, sterility, and confusion await those who look to legal theory for answers to questions that have meaning in human affairs. The more one compares the features that enable the outsider to say that a group has a rule of obligation with the features that members of the group themselves use to identify and support claims of obligation, the more difficult it is to demonstrate that outsiders and insiders are still talking about the same phenomenon. The common discourse that unites both points of view ensures that the external observer can remain pure only by removing himself so far from the scene of discourse that he can no longer observe and becomes himself imperceptible.[42]

Belief and action. One can illustrate and defend these claims by contrasting two kinds of human characteristics: those that mediate at least in part through mind and those that do not. Normative attitudes and value judgments, which can be formed, modified, abandoned, and re-formed through reflection, thought, and dialogue, are examples of the former. Colds and fevers are not. The latter may be controlled by discovering and altering the conditions that cause them, but they cannot, except in their psychosomatic forms, be reasoned out of existence.

Both kinds of phenomena may be observed as well as experienced. "You can tell a person has a fever when he becomes flushed, shows a temperature, and so on" is the observational analogue to "You can tell a group believes action is obligatory when they react to deviation by criticizing, pressuring, and so on." The most obvious point of such purely descriptive statements is the dictionary one of explaining how a particular language is used. The foreigner may now identify and appropriately label fevers and normative attitudes whether or not he himself has ever known what it is to be ill or strongly committed. Indeed, the virtue of this purely descriptive approach is thought to lie precisely in rendering unnecessary any reference to subjective states, to the nature of the internal experience that accompanies the observed behavior.

Here the strain of trying to maintain the analogy begins to be felt. Armed with the theorist's lexicon, I can determine not only when others have fevers but when I do as well, for the diagnostic criteria are the same. The only variable is the mouth into which I put the thermometer. Not so in the case of obligation or other judgments of value. I may use the lexicon to make a good guess about whether those around me believe something to be obligatory, but I cannot similarly use it to find out whether I entertain the same beliefs. I cannot check external signs of my behavior in order to find out what I believe as I might to determine if I have a fever. Even psychological models that probe for hidden motives

· 47 ·

to explain observable conduct assume that once such hidden structures are brought into consciousness, the automatic nature of the link with behavior is severed. Indeed it is only by assuming that all value formation is unconscious, induced like hypnosis through processes totally uncontrolled by mind, that the analogy with physiological phenomena can be maintained at all; but that assumption, with its roots in determinism and the modern taste for behaviorism, is hardly compatible with an observer's attempt to remain uncommitted in describing the commitments of others.

What is true of the individual—the behavior-free nature of his process of value formation—is true of the group. Each may identify the apparent belief of those around him by observing their behavior, but one's recognition of the distinction between belief and action prevents such identification from ever being more than tentative. It is this distinction between belief and action that ultimately prevents making the latter, which is all that the observer can see, an automatic test for the former. Strong moral beliefs do not guarantee action, any more than highly coercive forms of group retaliation prove the existence of underlying, strongly held moral beliefs.[43] Thus, the tendency toward contradiction. Legal systems are the most visible forms of social retaliation for deviant behavior and by that test alone appear to the outsider to be normative systems. But the outsider's very use of the language of normativity means that he knows how sharply the insider's use of that terminology distinguishes between fiat and reason, force and persuasion, action and belief. The attempt to shuttle back and forth between inside and outside perspectives as if one were simply switching hats leaves behind unmistakable traces of contradiction: descriptions from the outside that are infected by unexplainable (because unobservable) references to value; descriptions from the inside of the motives for accepting a legal system that no longer provide a basis for the insider to distinguish between law and force.

Belief and reality. The dilemma for the outsider runs deeper than this tendency toward contradiction through the conflation of belief and action. Nothing prevents the legal theorist from acknowledging the point, and indeed Hart makes it a central feature of his own theory, that there is a great difference between the purely external, predictive view of social rules and the internal view that sees in deviation a reason for retaliation. The problem is that once this difference is recognized, it has serious implications for a theory of law that purports to leave untouched the substantive question of what is a good reason for forming beliefs. The source of legal theory's sterility is in conceding that the insider's perspective is critical to the understanding and existence of normative systems while refusing to consider how such perspectives are developed and maintained in the face of challenge. This makes legal theory's claim that law is normative either arbitrary or empty—arbitrary if one simply has to take the assertion on faith, empty if one looks to the theory for help in deciding whether his own system includes the appropriate normative attitude and hence qualifies as legal. The most that current legal theory can say in response to the latter inquiry is that the system is legal if, for example, the official group believes that it is just. But what the insider asks, and what each member of the official group potentially and continually asks, is whether it is just. It is the distinction between belief and reality now, rather than between belief and action, that the outsider's perspective distorts.

In one sense, of course, we always operate on belief, even in the world of fact. Yet we know what it means to believe one has a fever but to be in fact mistaken. Similarly, the insider knows the difference between stating that the group to which he belongs believes that something is valuable and stating that it is in fact valuable. Indeed, it is the interchange between believers and nonbelievers as to what in fact has value that characterizes the formation and defense of claims of obligation. The legal theorist's determination to remain neutral in this particular interchange while still insisting that law differs from force leads to a view of law that equates belief with reality: all that is necessary for a system to be normative in the appropriate legal sense is for officials to display the appropriate normative belief, however false or even insincere.

The impetus for this conflation of the belief in value and the reality of value is not hard to find. The variety of possible beliefs is as unlimited as the capacity of mind to imagine objects or states of affairs which passion can then embrace. Witches and demons and spirits that live in the trees, oracles in caves and kings appointed by God, majority votes and tablets miraculously carved in stone all are capable of serving as foundations for beliefs and commitment on which elaborate normative structures can be built and to which the organized sanctions distinctive of law can be attached. Were one dealing with the realm of fact, one would proceed to distinguish between superstitious and rational beliefs; but the realm of value is another matter. However strong the tradition that places value judgments within the reach of rational appraisal, an equally strong tradition emphasizes the essential arbitrariness of such judgments. The legal theorist's willingness to make belief, however apparently irrational, the key to the identification of legal systems seems to stem from an attitude that reflects and builds on the view that value judgments are essentially arbitrary. Just as the pure outsider is most comfortable with the philosophy of determinism when constructing his criteria for identifying normative systems, so the legal theorist who admits the importance of the internal view that characterizes normative judgments but refuses to provide rational criteria to guide that internal view is most comfortable with the ethics of relativism.

One must be careful, however, not to overdraw the indictment. I am not suggesting that legal theory is logically committed to relativism, nor even that the moral relativist is the only person with good reason to refuse to be drawn into the substantive debates that characterize the development of internal normative attitudes in a legal system. The logical relationship between moral relativism and one's choice of a legal theory holds in only one direction. If one is a relativist, as Kelsen is thought to have been, one is likely to conclude that there is no point in proceeding beyond a belief-based theory, for the essence of relativism just is the denial of the reality of a realm of value with which to test and evaluate belief. Yet one may be prepared to evaluate moral judgments in other contexts, as both Hart and Bentham are, while still urging disengagement from the moral issue in identifying legal systems. After all, it is precisely the variety of ideologies encountered in a survey of past and present societies that strengthens the theorist's determination to retain his purity. Why disqualify any of these from being legal, however silly or wrong their basic normative judgments, particularly when evaluation of the normative judgment can proceed separately from the identification of the system as legal?

What the theorist treats as separate questions, however, the insider treats as one; for unless he is also a relativist, the insider's beliefs, and with them his allegiance and acceptance, are always potentially subject to challenge and rational defense. The theorist who remains aloof from the defense of value is from the insider's perspective indistinguishable from the relativist. And when the legal theorist switches hats and becomes the moral philosopher, criticizing the insider's normative structure, he attacks not just the latter's beliefs but with it, according to the theorist's own definition, the identification of the system as legal.

One need not deny the merits of the positivist's program in trying to make the concept of law wide enough to embrace the variety of ideological structures that underlie functioning societies. The mistake lies in thinking that the only way to achieve this program is to make belief in value critical, with the reality of value eliminated altogether as a test for law. There is another way that promises to achieve the theorist's program without disparaging the insider's insistence on the distinction between what is accepted as valuable and what is in fact valuable. What is needed is a confrontation with the substantive issues of political theory with the aim of showing the insider how the beliefs of others, however wrong, can nevertheless yield real obligation for him. The choices are not restricted to a view that sees law as based on normative attitudes whatever they may be and a view that restricts law only to morally correct systems. There is another view that defends the normative base of law by showing how even the erroneous beliefs of others can entail obligation, thus answering the insider's fundamental moral question, albeit only by abandoning the purity of the outsider's position.

Chapter III deals with this basic problem of political theory. First, however, I shall describe more carefully the alternative view I have suggested and trace its connections to a strand of legal theory about which I have as yet said very little.

NATURAL LAW AND OTHER NONTHEORIES

It will have occurred to readers familiar with the literature that I have been using one particular view of law—that of the positivist—as the basis for the preceding discussion as well as the source of the specific examples used to illustrate the problems of legal theory. Though I have said enough to indicate that I do not expect the critique, even if construed primarily as a critique of positivism, to lead to natural law as the alternative, I have not yet said much about how the tradition of natural law fits into the picture I have been painting. There is a good reason for this omission, and that is that natural law theories are hardly theories at all. What goes by the name of natural law, at least where legal theory is concerned, is at best a sustained emphasis on one particular feature of legal systems, rather than an attempt to construct a theory uniting various features, and at worst a slogan invented by positivists in the first place which distorts the natural law insight.

I begin with the slogan: to say that unjust law is not law is to start and stop a theory in a single sentence. As far as the concept of law is concerned, the slogan initiates an inquiry exclusively into moral and political philosophy, leaving questions about the identification and structure of legal systems mere by-products of the moral inquiry. The slogan thus presents the mirror image of positivism's struggle against sterility: while positivism purports to identify law but fails to explain how it differs from force, the natural law slogan preserves the distinction between force and obligation but fails to identify law apart from the substantive moral inquiry into justice. The question, What is law that I should obey it? remains unanswered in both cases, by the positivist because he has no answer and by the proponent of natural law because his only answer is in the form of a tautology.

There is a similar mirror image of the problem of inconsistency. Where positivism struggles to retain the purity of the outsider's perspective at the cost of distorting the internal view of normativity, the natural law slogan is faithful to the insider's view but at the cost of ignoring what any outsider can plainly see: social orders can and do impose officially sanctioned consequences on the insider that do not depend on the substantive merits of the system. Indeed, the slogan flaunts its own contradiction: to say that unjust law is not law requires formal tests for legal validity of the positivist's sort in order to apply substantive tests.

The very obviousness of this contradiction should have been enough to alert the early positivists, who took such delight in attacking the slogan, to see it as an attempt to express a different idea from that of providing criteria to identify law. The classical natural law writers were never bothered by the modern positivist's concern for precision in modeling validity. For them, as for the ordinary citizen, rough definitions sufficed. The theoretical problem from the beginning was the moral one, and the slogan accordingly represented an attempt not to define or analyze law but to explain the moral consequences that follow from law.[44] As the problem is treated in Aquinas it has a dual aspect. First, he shows how law, though manmade, can nevertheless add to obligations whose roots are otherwise found exclusively in moral and religious law. The merely *mala prohibita* become *mala in se* by virtue of the lawmaker's decision. But there must be a limit to this power of man to make his own will the source of obligation, and that limit is reached when man's will conflicts with God's—that is, with what is already *malum in se* by reference to moral or religious law. Hence, manmade law that is unjust is not God's law; it does not obligate.[45] That is all the slogan says, and in that form it is a statement that even the positivist can embrace without violating his strictures against confusing the legal and the moral.

In the literature of this century the slogan is rarely found, except as an object of attack in the literature of positivism itself. What one does find is a sustained concern that the positivist has overlooked a vital aspect of the meaning of law. Yet the positivist's response has generally been to see in this expression of concern nothing more than another attempt, however indirect, to repeat the discredited slogan.

Lon Fuller's writings provide the best example of both the nature of the discontent as well as the tendency of positivism to dismiss the concern. Fuller's scholarly life was dominated by a fascination and love for the role of reason, purpose, justification in the development and maintenance of legal rules. The fascination took several forms. In its descriptive form it emphasized the role of purposive reasoning in the actual development of Anglo-American law, particularly the common law. It is here, in Fuller's descriptions of the process of legal reasoning and his illustrations from the common law that one finds some of his most elegant and influential work.[46]

The role of reason in the legal process also had for Fuller a normative aspect reflected in his belief that "when men are compelled to explain and justify their decisions, the effect will generally be to pull those decisions toward goodness."[47] Finally, it is probably true that Fuller also meant his views to be in some sense conceptual, a claim about the meaning of law itself.[48] It is on the conceptual claim that positivism pounced. "All his life . . . in love with . . . purpose," but surely one must know that purposes may be evil as well as good.[49] So much for the attempt to deduce a connection between law and morality from the bare fact that law is purposive. Moreover, the normative aspect of Fuller's views, interpreted as an empirical claim about the relationship between reason and goodness, has also become a target for modern skeptics: some of the most evil regimes, we must remember, have tried to mask the noise of their atrocities behind the sweet voice of reason. For that matter, one does not have to look to evil regimes for counterexamples but only to human nature itself and the inability of reason in the face of passion and will to serve any but a rationalizing role for aims that run the gamut of moral acceptability.[50] Even Fuller's descriptive claims are now facing a new generation of skeptics eager to debunk purpose as a thin disguise for various narrow interests—economic, social, class.[51] So much, one might conclude, for Fuller's sustained concern.

There is another view, however, of the phenomenon that Fuller was trying to describe, a view that avoids the thrust of these attacks and at the same time connects his concern to the problems of legal theory that I have been discussing. Both the conceptual attack on Fuller and the normative disagreement about the value of reason are aimed at a view that tries to connect legal systems either conceptually or empirically with substantive goodness. They are, in short, attacks based on the assumption that the emphasis on reason and purpose and their relationship to goodness are simply variations of the old natural law slogan. But one does not need to make the slogan's conceptual claim to see in the emphasis on purpose and reason the ingredient that seems to be missing in current models of law. It is not the actual correctness or justice of the purposes invoked that is crucial to law but the fact that purposes are invoked at all—that reason and justification rather than fiat and will dominate the manner in which rules are formulated, defended, modified, and reformulated. The conceptual claim need only be that there is a link between law and a particular process of rule justification rather than between law and any particular substantive outcome that may result from the process.

As for the attack on Fuller's description of this process, even those most eager to find ulterior interests behind the avowed goals that fuel judicial development and transformation of legal doctrine hesitate to ascribe to the legal mind awareness of the alleged discrepancy between real and apparent ends.[52] At most it is the accusation of self-deception and illusion that awaits those who participate in the process, believing it to be guided by reason. That accusation, with its roots in legal realism (ironically at its heyday just when Fuller was also at his most influential), leaves intact the reality of what I have identified as a neglected aspect of legal theory: the claim of value, reflected in the readiness to back demands for allegiance with arguments designed to show that the system serves the interests of all.

A second example of current discontent with positivism, which also takes neither the form of the classical natural law slogan nor that of a full-blown alternative conceptual theory, is provided by Ronald Dworkin.[53] This is not the place to recount the debate that Dworkin's view of the legal process has inspired, particularly since I have already suggested that much of the debate seems to lead to an epistemological dead end. What is worth recounting are the respects in which Dworkin's views, though distinct in style, resemble Fuller's. First, Dworkin's account is strongest when viewed as a description of the American legal system, with which he is most familiar. It is weakest if viewed as a conceptual theory about the meaning of law.

Second, the most prominent features of the descriptive aspect of the theory are those that emphasize the reasoning process by which judges ultimately justify their decisions, reaching well beyond the brute reality of current convention to the purposes and ultimate political principles that justify convention. Indeed, the empirical evidence for the description Dworkin provides consists almost entirely of views expressed by litigants, judges, and lawyers, views that insist that the application of organized sanctions must be justified, not simply imposed by officials who accept their position of power. Dworkin, of course, goes further, reading the same evidence to show that justification must take a certain form— requiring judicial intervention only and always to protect determinable, preexisting rights. But that particular claim is independent of, and for my purposes secondary to, the description of the demand for justification and the response that demand provokes.

Third, the weakness of the conceptual claim derives again, as in Fuller's case, from the apparent attempt to link this process of justification and hence law with a particular outcome: one that accords with what the soundest political or moral theory would require. Although Dworkin is usually thought to be at his most ambivalent in indicating whether he is talking about positive or critical morality, that ambivalence may be a reflection of the problem, discussed above, of the distinction between outsider and insider (which is what the distinction between positive and critical morality amounts to) artificially distorting the nature of the process of justification. As seen by the insider, that process is believed to be guided by principles of critical morality, so that positive and critical morality from his viewpoint are never consciously divergent, however much their theoretical divergence may fuel the dialectic that causes prevailing morality to be continually reevaluated.

A THEORY OF LAW

One may draw all of these strands together by returning to Aquinas and comparing his definition of law, usually identified as a classical statement of natural law, with what has been extracted from Fuller and Dworkin. Law, says Aquinas, is "an ordinance of reason for the common good, made by him who has care of the community."[54] With a slight modification of the usual interpretation, this formulation conveys the essence of the theory of law I have gradually been sketching. Instead of interpreting the definition to limit 'law' to those ordinances that do in fact serve the common good, one interprets it instead to require only that legal directives aim at serving the common good, however wide of the mark they may fall.[55] Legal systems are essentially characterized by the belief in value, the claim in good faith by those who rule that they do so in the interests of all. It is this claim of justice, rather then justice in fact, that one links conceptually with the idea of law.[56] Thus, the differences between law, morality, and coercion may be represented in terms of the variables of force and the belief in value. Law combines the organized sanction with the claim to justice by those who wield the sanction. Morality makes the same claim but lacks the sanction. Coercive systems rely on the sanction alone, unaccompanied by any concern for justice.

Another slogan? Perhaps, but one distilled from a long tradition of legal theory, encompassing both the concerns of natural law and the core of the positivists' program. With the positivist one may agree that the actual justice or injustice of a system of norms does not determine whether the system is legal; with the nonpositivist one shares the conviction that a legal system is more than a set of effectively enforced norms, voluntarily accepted by officials and summarily imposed on subjects. One requires at least the reciprocal bond between rulers and ruled that is entailed by a good faith defense of the system as in the interest of all. In support of this view I have thus far shown only that any theory of law that lacks this feature will be unable to distinguish legal from coercive systems and will distort many of the persistent features of the normative attitude toward law that one finds among both subjects and rulers. In that sense the official claim to justice would be a necessary feature of a normative model of law even if description alone were the goal. But the more meaningful goal, I have said, is definition. Thus there remains the task of explaining why this feature is essential to the idea of law. Accordingly, Chapter III shows that the requirement of an official claim of justice is necessary and, in conjunction with a second condition, sufficient for political obligation. Chapter IV shows how this conclusion of moral philosophy connects with the conclusions reached here, thus making plausible the view that systems are 'legal' not just because basic ground rules are accepted but because such rules are also defended as acceptable.[57]

POLITICAL THEORY

III

I POSED and then postponed in the last chapter the question that is central to this one: how to justify the difference in response to the gunman and the tax collector. To say that there is a difference, of course, is not to say that people believe they should always obey the law; nor is it to suggest that people should so conclude. The example of citizens deciding that conscience demands disobedience rather than compliance is a familiar one. And the suggestion that one has a moral obligation always to obey—with the consequence that the record of civil disobedience is also a record of immoral action—runs counter to the common perception that obligations can and do conflict. Promises are justifiably broken in order to comply with a greater duty to save human life; duties to family are rightfully breached in order to fulfill more pressing, unforeseen obligations; honesty is not always a better policy than, say, kindness or compassion.

One could, of course, structure an inquiry to ask what law must be if it is to obligate absolutely; but the only way such an inquiry could possibly conclude would be with a theory that by definition counts as law just those directives that prove morally superior in all situations of conflicting duties. Such a theory forces one to do the moral calculation first, with law reserved as a label to indicate the outcome of the moral inquiry. It is for this reason that the classical natural law slogan is so useless. Construed as a legal theory, the slogan pretends to ground moral obligation in law when in fact, by equating legal and moral obligation, it grounds, or underscores actually, only the latter.

These considerations explain why most recent theorists prefer to talk about prima facie rather than absolute obligation. The difference in response to the tax collector and the gunman from this perspective can be described, roughly, by saying that other things being equal, one has an obligation to obey the former but not the latter. This shift in focus leaves room for occasions of justified disobedience (when other things are not equal) while still positing an initial moral response toward the tax collector that is absent in the case of the gunman.[1]

Terminology

The language of obligation raises problems beyond those involved in distinguishing between prima facie and absolute senses of the term. Some think, for example, that obligation is a narrower concept than that of the morally correct. Thus an argument showing that one *ought* to obey the law does not necessarily establish an *obligation* to obey. To further complicate the matter, consider another member of my quartet of persons pressing demands for money: the beggar. In what language shall we describe the appropriate response to his request? To this question one can find at least the following answers in contemporary moral philosophy:

1. Some will say that if the sum demanded is trivial and the boon to the beggar immense, then morally one ought to give the requested alms, though one has no obligation to do so.

2. Others, denying the distinction between obligation and the morally correct result, will conclude, for example, that the net increase in satisfactions that results from giving the alms makes it both one's obligation and the morally correct thing to do.

3. Still others will suggest that one may have a duty to aid those in need but not an obligation, for obligations arise from consent or other voluntary actions, whereas duties arise naturally from circumstances not of one's choosing.

4. The most commonly held view probably is that one is under no moral constraint—of obligation, duty, or otherwise—to give alms. Giving alms is an act of charity, above and beyond the call of duty; moral praise may be appropriate, but moral blame is not.

5. Finally, one may eschew the terminology of "obligation," "ought," and "duty" altogether and talk instead of reasons for action. It may be urged that one has a moral reason to aid the beggar but other reasons (self-interest, aesthetics) not to. There then remains only the problem

of explaining when and why moral reasons outweigh other kinds of reasons for action.

These variations in terminology suggest that one faces a difficult task in explaining what political obligation means, much less in showing that it exists. Fortunately it is unnecessary for present purposes to choose among these linguistic approaches, for the simple reason that the puzzle I am trying to solve is more basic than any of the problems that these more refined analyses of moral language may plausibly be seen to address. The common response to the tax collector's demand I described as one of respectful attention. It is a fact of everyday experience that most people concede to the law a moral legitimacy, however weak, that is wholly absent in the case of the gunman. One may conclude on reflection that the moral claim is spurious, weak, or overridden by other, stronger claims; but all such descriptions point to a process of practical reasoning that is never undertaken at all in the case of the mugger. Where the mugger is concerned, practical reason weighs only the gravity of the threatened sanction and the likelihood of its imposition. It is this contrast that provides the question that guides this inquiry: what is it about law that justifies any degree of moral respect at all, however slight?

Three comments are in order about this way of putting the question. First, I do not believe that anything substantive hinges on the choice of terminology. The sense of the question is equally well conveyed by any of the formulations described above. Thus, one could just as easily ask what law must be to entail a moral reason, however weak, or a prima facie obligation or duty, however weak, to obey it. What is essential is the idea that one is seeking to ground even the most minimal attitude of moral respect for the law. I shall continue, then, to talk about obligations and moral reasons for action, with the understanding that these ideas are meant to be interchangeable with each other as well as with the concept of minimal moral respect.

Second, it is worth noting that the question put here is at the other extreme from the question ascribed earlier to the natural law slogan. Instead of defining law to ensure that it always obligates, one seeks an account that explains why it has any tendency to obligate at all. In this way an independent concept of law is preserved, distinct from that of morality, while at the same time room is left for the intuition that law has some moral authority, though it is not absolute.

Third, I anticipate the objection that the virtue just described is also a vice in that it seeks too modest an account of the moral authority of law. Political obligation, the objection would continue, is a much stronger bond than minimal respect and thus an account that grounds the latter does not approach the problem of grounding the former. To this, two replies suffice. First, to provide even a minimal basis for the moral authority of law is an accomplishment that escapes current legal and political theorists.[2] Second, once it is conceded that the political bond is not absolute, the only problem that remains concerns how much weight to accord the obligation, a nuance that, like the choice of terminology itself, may be allowed to escape us as it has escaped the attention of most of the traditional literature. Moral philosophy, after all, is notorious for its inability to assign weights to, as opposed to characterizing the form and ground of, the normative requirements of life.

Illustrating the Problem

Lest it be thought that I have too quickly dismissed the charge of making my task too easy, I shall begin with an argument designed to establish minimal moral respect for the law that does not succeed. Explaining why it does not succeed demonstrates why even the seemingly modest task I have set presents a problem for political theory.

The argument that does not succeed has been formulated in a variety of ways by a variety of theorists. M. B. E. Smith, for example, characterizes the argument as a utilitarian defense of obligation that proceeds as follows:

1. Legal systems, by providing minimal protection for life, liberty, and property, are preferable to the alternative of no law at all.

2. No legal system can survive in the face of widespread disobedience.

3. Therefore one has a prima facie obligation to obey the laws of any legal system.[3]

That the conclusion does not follow from the premises is almost too obvious to justify the amount of attention this argument has received. The premises assert a connection between widespread disobedience and a loss of the benefits provided by legal systems, whereas the conclusion is about the obligation to obey each specific law of any legal system. To justify the conclusion requires a different and unstated premise, positing that any act of disobedience threatens the legal system. But laws can be and are regularly broken without entailing either widespread disobedience or disintegration of the system.

The invalidity of the argument is not solely the result of the implausibility of this unstated premise. Robert Paul Wolff points to a more basic problem in considering a version of the same argument that relies on the analogy of a captain giving orders for manning the lifeboats on a sinking ship:

I may decide that under the circumstances I had better do what he says, since the confusion caused by disobeying him would be generally harmful. But insofar as I make such a decision, I am not *obeying his command;* that is I am not acknowledging him as having authority over me. I would make the same decision, for exactly the same reasons, if one of the passengers had started to issue "orders" and had, in the confusion, come to be obeyed.[4]

The reason the argument does not succeed, as this passage suggests, arises from an important constraint on any proposed solution to the problem of political obligation. What is required is a justification of the obligation to obey law in general—just because it is the law—not because of some independent argument for compliance based on considerations applicable only to particular laws or in a particular context. Circumstances may, after all, indicate that it is also best on the whole to obey a particular mugger's command, but few would thus conclude that there is a prima facie obligation in general to obey gunmen's directives. So too in the case of laws, disobedience sometimes has overall undesirable consequences, but sometimes it does not. As long as it is the independent calculation of consequences that determines the appropriate response rather than some feature of law itself, one has not produced a solution to the problem of political obligation.[5] In terms of the hypothetical inquiry, What must law be to obligate? the utilitarian argument just described could be successful only if law were defined to include just those directives whose disobedience on particular occasions would lead to more harm than good. That would leave us with a definition strikingly similar to, and just as arbitrary as, that of the natural law slogan.

The utilitarian argument probably derives its appeal from its tendency to explain as a matter of psychological fact why there is a difference in response to the gunman and the tax collector. The regime that backs the tax collector does much more than issue isolated orders to hand over money. Legal systems also offer protection and provide services through a complex of rules and institutions that people are likely to find beneficial on the whole. This positive attitude toward the system in general can easily lead to the internalization of a rule of thumb that checks one's inclination to resist particular laws in a way that finds no parallel in the case of chance encounters with strangers wielding weapons. The point to stress is that this psychological explanation, however valid, is not the explanation that theoretical inquiry demands. The problem of political obligation confronts one with a case in which by hypothesis all other arguments for compliance are unavailing: the act required by the law is not one that would produce the best consequences in any event, nor is it one required for other moral reasons, as in the case of a law against murder. In such a case the utilitarian argument cannot distinguish the tax collector from the gunman: subtract the threat of force in either confrontation and there is no longer any reason to comply. That is what I seek: a theory of law that gives a generally applicable moral reason to comply apart from the sanction.

It would be a mistake to conclude that this refutation of what has been called a utilitarian argument proves that no utilitarian solution to the problem of political obligation is possible. All that has been shown is that no utilitarian argument can succeed that depends on a posited connection between any single act of disobedience, however minor, and the undesirable consequence of general disintegration of the legal system. It is the empirical implausibility of this connection that makes the argument untenable in whatever form it is cast. Thus the rule-utilitarian cannot claim that the rule, Never disobey the law, is better than a more precise rule that excepts cases where disobedience will not be disastrous and may even be beneficial. Similarly, the relevant question for the utilitarian generalizer is not what would happen if everybody always disobeyed the law but what would happen if everyone disobeyed only in certain carefully defined circumstances in which disobedience would not be disastrous and might even be beneficial.

As long as the argument one develops for political obligation does not rely on the implausible equation of the effects of individual instances of disobedience with the effects of universal disobedience, it may prove consistent with a utilitarian analysis. Indeed, the theory I shall develop is not meant to depend critically on the position one takes with respect to the dispute between consequentialists and deontologists or the internal disputes among consequentialists about the correct form of utilitarianism. Moreover, I shall generally avoid these standard ways of characterizing moral theories, with the single concession of indicating, once the theory is developed, how it might be made to fit into either the deontologist or the utilitarian framework.

In addition to the constraint of generality, it is sometimes thought that the problem of political obligation must also satisfy a requirement of specificity. That is, whereas generality refers to the source of obligation, requiring it to be found in the nature of law per se, specificity refers to the object of the obligation—the country, for example, to which one is tied by the political bond. To suggest that there is a requirement of specificity in this sense may mean that the problem of political obligation requires demonstrating a special obligation to one's own country, distinct from whatever obligations are owed to countries one visits or in which one temporarily resides. Or it may refer to the idea that even within a single country, one must distinguish for purposes of political obligation between citizens and others—resident aliens or tourists, for example—with the consequence that the problem of political obligation becomes logically tied to the problem of defining citizenship. Finally, it may mean to exclude as solutions to the problem of political obligation any argument that has the consequence of creating obligations to more than one country or legal system at a time. Thus, for example, a theory that purports to show that there is an obligation to support just institutions or just governments would not count as a solution because it would entail an obligation of support toward all such governments in existence at a given time.[6]

This last interpretation is one that may be accepted without elevating the specificity requirement into an independent constraint on the problem of political obligation. As the example illustrates, the constraint of generality is violated by a theory that derives obligation from the duty to support just institutions rather than from the nature of law per se. Such a theory does not differ essentially from one based on an alleged utilitarian obligation to perform the best possible acts, which, as we have seen, does not always entail an obligation to obey the law.

The first two interpretations, suggesting that one must show a special bond between a country and its citizens, can also be rejected as at best tangential to the central inquiry, and at worst quite misleading. The attempt to account for the obligation to obey the law starts with a specific confrontation with force, with the de facto power of the tax official or gunman to subject one to sanctions if one fails to comply. It may turn out that this de facto authority is legitimate only in certain contexts, for example between a country and its citizens. But there is no need to prejudge this issue by insisting on a specificity constraint in advance of the attempt to distinguish those situations of effective force that are legitimate from those that are not. Indeed the common intuition is probably that there is an obligation for the visitor to obey the laws of a foreign country. One advantage of the theory developed here is that it accounts for that intuition while at the same time taking note of factors that might make the obligation toward one's own country different in weight, though not in kind.

The Problem of Method

Problems of method are indirectly problems of proof. What counts as a demonstration that one has solved the problem of political obligation, or for that matter as a demonstration that no solution is possible? Recent moral philosophy responds to this question most candidly when it concedes to "considered judgments" the linchpin role in moral argument.[7] With self-evident propositions confined at best to the field of logic, one can only rely in moral argument on an appeal to conclusions widely shared by men of common sense, commonly concerned about issues of justice and ethics. In this respect, this study shares with political theory the tendency to start with paradigms of obligation in other contexts—for example notions of promise or consent—without digressing into the question of why promises are thought to be binding in the first place.

Where this study parts company with recent political and moral theory is in the source to which I look for paradigms and consensus. Moral philosophers seldom cast beyond the ingenuity of their own hypotheticals for the arguments with which to unsettle or reassure considered judgments. In political theory, for example, the paradigms of obligation that dominate the discussion are those of consent and fair play. Arguments to show why these paradigms fail in the political context are developed by comparing the essential features of the paradigm with the features that characterize confrontation with the law. The conclusion that essential features of the paradigm are missing in the political confrontation rests ultimately on the persuasiveness of the claim about what is and is not essential to the paradigm case. These essential features turn out to be remarkably similar to those developed by another source, the common law, in its centuries-long development of principles governing the creation of legal obligations among strangers interacting in society.

That philosophers should pay no heed to the paradigms used by judges and lawyers is hardly surprising in light of the specialization that has led even such closely related fields as legal and political theory to ignore each other. Indeed, one may even sympathize with a philosopher's skepticism that the time-bound principles of a particular culture's jurisprudence, developed to settle and regulate the squabbles of ordinary citizens, should be an authoritative source for fundamental questions of ethics. It is the moral philosopher after all who must validate the legal result, not *vice versa*. But when validation depends for its persuasiveness on consensus, this dismissal of the insights of the philosophically uninitiated borders on hubris. Whatever else the common law may be, enough evidence exists for the view that it represents the efforts of people of intelligence and good will to find through reason general principles of fair dealing in society to justify its role as a source of insight into moral problems.

FAILURE OF THE STANDARD PARADIGMS

In the following pages I shall examine the standard devices for grounding political obligation using paradigms familiar to every lawyer: promise, estoppel, and unjust enrichment. Each of these sources of legal obligation finds a parallel in political theory's suggested sources for political obligation. Moreover, the explanations that political theorists give as to why these paradigms fail to ground an obligation to obey the law turn out to be straightforward applications of the law's statement of what is necessary for the paradigm to yield a legal claim. From one perspective, then, this approach provides additional confirmation for the conclusions reached independently by political theorists. From another perspective, it enables one to avoid elaborate independent arguments concerning what is and is not essential to obligation. Finally, this approach has the advantage of letting me rehearse in a somewhat unfamiliar form what is otherwise a familiar story as background to the alternative theory and paradigms for obligation that I shall develop.

Promise

When Jones, in apparent seriousness, agrees to buy Kafka's cabbages for a stated price, he becomes obligated by his express promise whether he meant what he said or not.[8] When Jones allows Kafka's delivery boy to unload unsolicited cabbages priced at a stated amount, Jones also becomes obligated to pay. Accepting delivery under such circumstances speaks every bit as loudly as words, though nonverbal indications of agreement may be distinguished from verbal indications by calling the former promises tacit.[9] If unsolicited cabbages are left on Jones's doorstep while he is away Jones becomes obligated to pay the price only if he uses them, providing he could easily have avoided doing so. But he cannot be deemed to have consented just because he fails to take unusual or even slightly onerous steps to make his nonconsent apparent. Thus one does not have to speak up to avoid being bound by offers of unsolicited merchandise, no matter how slight the effort.[10] Liability for promise, in short, results either because one consents in fact or because one has acted in ways that can reasonably be taken to imply consent.

It is not difficult to see why the paradigm of promise fails to provide a basis for political obligation. Some people, in taking oaths of office, for example, may expressly promise to obey the law; but most do not. For that matter the hypothetical question about what law must be in order to obligate cannot be answered by proposing that legal systems require oaths of allegiance from everyone, for in that case duress would then vitiate the promise. That leaves political theory with only the following possibilities for finding tacit in place of express consent:

1. The idea that one can be deemed to consent because one chooses to remain in the country rather than leave it warrants mention only because of the frequency with which the argument is raised and demolished in the literature. In the first place, legal systems do not generally present residents with this explicit choice, which is what the promissory analogy would require. Second, if a society did suddenly give residents that choice, the burden of moving might be sufficiently coercive to vitiate the apparent expression of consent in "choosing" to stay put. Finally, even for those for whom moving would not be troublesome, it would be at least as much trouble as speaking up in order to avoid being bound; if failure to do the latter cannot justify an inference of consent, *a fortiori* neither can failure to leave the country.

2. A variation on the above argument suggests that those are obligated who not only remain but also accept the benefits of the country in which they find themselves. But if benefits can be refused only by leaving the country, the argument is not essentially different from the preceding one. Even returning unsolicited merchandise creates enough of a nuisance to permit use and thus acceptance of the benefits without liability in most jurisdictions.[11] As for benefits that could easily be refused, such as welfare or other social services, these are not normally offered on the understanding that acceptance implies a promise to obey the law. If they were, those who knowingly accepted under such conditions could be deemed to have promised; but that would not cause others not in such a position to incur a similar obligation.

3. Political theorists who try to derive a promise-based account of obligation from the act of voting in a democracy face a difficult task. If the vote is significant and a right of citizens qua citizens, then it cannot be viewed as an implicit promise to obey. If the vote, on the other hand, is expressly conditioned on taking an oath of allegiance (or by convention comes to be so understood), then the "right" to vote is no longer as unqualified as liberal democratic theory usually assumes. Moreover, even if an oath given under such conditions would not count as "coerced," those who decided to forgo the vote rather than take the oath would still have no obligation to obey (nor, of course, would those who live in undemocratic regimes).

One can generalize from these examples to the following conclusions about any promise-based theory of political obligation:

1. Few people give actual consent.
2. One must thus rely on analogies that bind people to agreements

because they give objective indications of consent from which reasonable persons could infer actual consent. In this respect estoppel begins to emerge as the ground of the obligation rather than consent.

3. Promissory language not resulting from distress and apparently seriously intended is always a reasonable basis for inferring actual consent; but again most people do not take oaths of allegiance.

4. That leaves only nonverbal acts from which to infer consent; but these must be acts that one performs knowing of the inference that will be drawn and that one could easily and conveniently have chosen not to perform.

Under these constraints, no general account of obligation binding on all citizens can be given, which is exactly what one should expect. For the essence of promise-based obligation lies in the voluntariness of the undertaking, whereas the essence of the problem of political theory is to explain how obligations can arise despite the absence for most of voluntary choice of country or place of residence. The only promise-based accounts that saddle people involuntarily with contractual obligations are those in which people are careless in the signals they send to others. The careful citizen, seeking the ground for his obligation to obey in the absence of actual consent, will not find it here.

Estoppel

Repeated patterns of behavior can create expectations of regularity that lead others to rely on a continuation of the pattern. Similarly, announcements of an intention to take future action can lead to expectations of performance, even though one should know that relying on people not to change their minds is risky business. Sometimes such reliance is reasonable; sometimes it is not. If one knows or should know that others have reasonably come to rely on a course of conduct or statement of intention, one may have an obligation not to deviate from the expected course of action.[12] If Kafka knows that Jones has come to rely on Kafka's annual gift of cabbages in order for Jones to make his famous annual batch of Christmas sauerkraut, then Kafka may have an obligation to continue the annual gift unless he warns Jones in time that he should seek an alternate source. Doubt about this conclusion will center around the reasonableness of Jones's relying on behavior that is purely gratuitous and not locked in through contract. If the doubt is lessened when Kafka announces that he will supply the cabbages for free, it is because the statement of intention adds to the reasonableness of Jones's reliance. If Kafka's cabbages also gain in reputation and value through incorporation into Jones's sauerkraut, the case for seeing Jones's reliance as reasonable is stronger still, even though no formal contract governs the now mutually beneficial exchange.

I have already suggested that promise-based obligations, created because people carelessly signal apparent consent on which others rely, resemble estoppel-based obligations. Indeed both "sound in negligence," the former because of the careless use of conventional signals, the latter because of the careless inattention to the consequences of a sudden change in behavior after having created conditions (nonconventional signals) likely to lull reasonable people into a sense of security. Thus it is not always easy to distinguish independent, estoppel-based arguments for political obligation. One example of such an argument that differs from the promise-based arguments already considered is suggested by Peter Singer.

> By voting in a democracy I am announcing an intention to obey the laws that result from the democratic process. Others may rely on this apparent expression of intention. Or others may rely on my behavior in voting, coupled perhaps with my record of past compliance, to form expectations that I will continue to obey. In such cases I am obligated not to suddenly defeat these expectations by failing to obey, even though I have never agreed expressly or otherwise to do so.[13]

One defect in this argument, pointed out by Raz, is that people do not generally form expectations about a person's likely willingness to comply with the law from the mere act of voting or even from a past record of compliance.[14] Moreover, even if such expectations were formed, it would be difficult to defend them as reasonable for the same reasons that it is difficult to turn voting into an act of tacit consent. There are too many other reasons for voting, as well as for complying with the law, to justify the inference that such acts indicate a respect for law per se on which others may reasonably rely in the future. There is, however, an even more fundamental problem with the argument. Even if reasonable reliance on an apparent respect for law were to arise, it is difficult to see how sudden deviation could result in anybody's detriment. That is because the advantages of participatory democracy and the prudential reasons for compliance contained in the legal sanction are sufficient to induce continued participation by others regardless of how much one may have misled some or all of them into thinking initially that one's own participation was based on respect for the law.

This last observation points to the basic flaw that infects any estoppel-based theory of political obligation. Such theories are likely to be variants of the following scheme of argument:

1. The cooperative enterprise that is law involves sacrifices that no one would undergo unless one could rely on others making similar sacrifices.

2. If I mislead others into relying on my cooperation, then they will make sacrifices they would otherwise not have made.

3. In such a case I am under an obligation to follow through and do my expected part when it is my turn to make a sacrifice.

The first premise, even if true, misses the point. Even if the creation or stability of legal systems depends on our being able to rely generally on the cooperation of others, that cooperation can be quite effectively secured through threatened sanctions alone. If one did count on a moral attitude of respect for law only to be disappointed in discovering later that we are all "bad men," the enterprise would still work well enough—indeed that was precisely Holmes's point.

Similar reasoning shows the second premise to be simply false. Even if others have been misled into thinking that I am cooperating for moral reasons, it is not true that when I clarify the situation they are then left holding the bag by having made sacrifices they would not otherwise have made. They would have made these sacrifices anyway, relying on the sanctions as sufficient prudential reason to make the scheme work.

Estoppel arguments, it seems, are likely to be valid, if at all, only in the case of voluntary schemes that do not rely on sanctions. To use a familiar example, if everybody's cooperation in installing a pollution control device on his or her car is needed to secure the benefits of better air quality, and if others have voluntarily installed such devices only because I have misled them into thinking that I would too, then it may indeed be the case that I have an obligation to do my part as well. But apart from the problem of whether any single nonconformist can really jeopardize the enterprise—a problem that undermines the argument in the free-rider context—in law the rides are not free. I pay for my refusal to go along with my money, my freedom, my life. Once again, the brute fact that law is at least force, whatever else it also is, stands in the way of the attempt to ground political obligation.

Unjust Enrichment

If Jones mistakenly overpays Kafka for cabbages he has agreed to buy, Kafka is obligated to return the additional amount though he made no promise to do so and was not responsible for Jones's mistake.[15] To retain the benefits of such an overpayment when it clearly was not intended as a gift would unjustly enrich Kafka at Jones's expense. Although the vagueness of such a standard, which creates obligations based on benefits conferred only when retention of such benefits would be unjust, complicates the task of specifying precise conditions to govern application of the paradigm, some cases at least are clear. If Kafka, without being asked, paints Jones's house while Jones is away, Jones has no obligation to pay for the benefits even though he may be delighted and enriched by the result, and even though Kafka may not have intended to confer a gift. The law in such cases brands Kafka an officious intermeddler,[16] partly because Jones cannot easily return the benefits thrust on him but also because Kafka has deliberately avoided the obvious means of first ensuring through contract that the exchange was desired. In contrast, the doctor who renders aid to an unconscious victim expecting to be paid may recover for his services on the assumption that it was reasonable to think that actual consent would have been given, though under the circumstances it could not have been secured in advance.[17]

The idea that political obligation might also be based on the benefits received and enjoyed within a legal system is at least as old as Socrates' defense of obligation on these grounds in the *Crito*. Recent discussion of the idea focuses on the argument from fair play, developed by John Rawls as follows:

> Suppose there is a mutually beneficial and just scheme of social cooperation, and that the advantages it yields can only be obtained if everyone, or nearly everyone, cooperates. Suppose further that cooperation requires a certain sacrifice from each person, or at least involves a certain restriction of his liberty. Suppose finally that the benefits produced by cooperation are, up to a certain point, free: that is, the scheme of cooperation is unstable in the sense that if any one person knows that all (or nearly all) of the others will continue to do their part, he will still be able to gain from the scheme even if he does not do his part. Under these conditions a person who has accepted the benefits of the scheme is bound by a duty of fair play to do his fair part and not to take advantage of the free benefits by not cooperating.[18]

It is easy to confuse this argument with the previously considered estoppel argument, particularly in light of the emphasis on taking advantage of the sacrifice of others. If the fair play argument is to serve as an independent paradigm for obligation, one cannot assume that others have been misled into relying on everyone's cooperation in making sacrifices necessary to establish the enterprise. The critical claim is that the enterprise, once established for whatever reasons, generates obligations on the part of those who affirmatively choose to partake of the benefits.

It is also important to note how the fair play argument differs from promise-based theories that might also be thought to depend on the acceptance of benefits. The latter theories require a conscious decision to accept benefits that could easily be rejected as well as reason to know that such acceptance implies a promise to reciprocate. To avoid collapsing the fair play argument into a tacit consent argument at least one of two conditions must be assumed to fail. That is, it must be assumed either that the benefits cannot be easily rejected or that it is possible to accept the benefits in a way that cannot conventionally be understood as implying a promise to pay. In the context of political obligation the first assumption is probably justified. Most of the benefits of society are conferred in ways that do not allow one to avoid them easily. Some benefits, like police and fire protection or education, may even be paid for, in a sense, through taxes. Others, including the benefits that result from the submission of other citizens to the law, are public goods. They are part of the package deal offered by the country in which most people involuntarily find themselves. That is a major reason why promise-based accounts of obligation that focus on benefits fail, and it poses a similar hurdle for theories of unjust enrichment.

We have already seen that Jones incurs no liability to the officious intermeddler who benefits him by painting his house. But neither is Jones liable to his neighbors for the increased value of his house when his neighbors paint theirs, thus increasing neighborhood real estate values. Presumably (if this is not meant to be an estoppel argument) Jones's neighbors have self-interested reasons for their venture that do not depend on Jones's willingness to pay even though he indirectly benefits. To be obligated to play fair, one must first be a player. Jones cannot be forced into playing—participating, cooperating—merely because he cannot be excluded from enjoying the benefits of a venture that will proceed with or without his cooperation.

The major case in which doubts arise in the law about the obligation to pay for benefits thrust on one involves cases of mistake. If Kafka makes an honest mistake in painting Jones's house instead of the one he was supposed to, the case for requiring Jones to pay for the value of what he receives is strengthened and may even be conclusive if Jones himself was partly responsible for the mistake. But it is difficult to see how a theory of obligation based on the mistaken conferral of benefits can be applied in the political context, where the benefits are not the result of a mistake but are largely the incidental by-product of a self-serving enterprise that cannot exclude free riders.

If the benefits in question could easily have been rejected but are instead accepted, it is important to distinguish the resulting argument for obligation from ordinary promise-based arguments. If Jones accepts the cabbages proffered by Kafka's delivery boy, he becomes obligated to pay the price however clearly he may declare that he is not consenting to pay for them.[19] One does not need theories of unjust enrichment to explain why actual consent is irrelevant to the obligation to pay when one snatches goods that are excludable and that have been made available only on the condition that a price be paid. Theories of theft (conversion) or imputed promise will suffice, and such theories fail to explain political obligation for reasons already stated: the excludable benefits of society are few; they are not ordinarily offered with an accompanying price tag of obligation; and even if they were, most people would find it easy to avoid being in the position of having grabbed such benefits from those whose efforts went into making them.

What one must imagine in order to distinguish unjust enrichment from promise is a case in which benefits are seized that are not the excludable property of others but are nevertheless made possible only because of the efforts of others. Assume, for example, that Jones and Kafka are left property under identical provisions of a disputed will. Jones, but not Kafka, pursues the disputed point in litigation and succeeds in defending an interpretation that ensures that Kafka will now take his share without the need for further litigation. Is Kafka, in accepting these benefits that are clearly his, obligated to share the expenses of the litigation with Jones? Can Jones's attorney collect an additional fee from Kafka who, after all, is not his client and never agreed to litigate the matter? These questions unfortunately bring us to the usable limits of the method I have chosen to provide paradigms of obligation, for the legal conscience is itself troubled about the appropriate result in such a case. Lawyers, for example, increasingly do recover from strangers for benefits produced through proceedings never requested by them.[20] Whether such special treatment for lawyers represents a defensible exception to the general rule or marks instead the beginning of the rule's demise is a matter of academic speculation.[21]

Of course this area of doubt could be dismissed as irrelevant to the problem in any event, because these cases involve unsolicited benefits that are happily seized, whereas the benefits of the rule of law are not the sort that one can decline short of exiting the country. Indeed, this involuntary, passive stance of most of those who benefit from a legal system has led Rawls to conclude that the argument from fair play grounds political obligation only for officials and others who affirmatively assume valuable positions or roles, not for the populace as a whole.[22] But one cannot comfortably dismiss the unjust enrichment claim just because benefits were unsolicited and unreturnable. If, in order to develop his land, Jones drains water from a swamp thereby inevitably draining Kafka's swamp as well, the question whether Kafka, who can now develop his own land more profitably, should share the expenses of the drainage does not seem all that different from the question posed in the case of the will. The fact that Kafka cannot refuse to accept the drained land may make us cautious in determining the extent to which he actually values the improvement. Indeed in this case the general legal result, perhaps for this reason, still gives Kafka his free ride.[23] There are nonetheless exceptions to the general rule. To explore the exceptions with the aim of trying to show how they do or do not apply in the political context is to place too much strain on my method, which already bears the burden of a difficult analogy between the general benefits of society and the more particular benefits that give rise to unjust enrichment claims in the law. It is enough to note that the exceptions underscore the possibility that here at least the moral issue may not coincide with the legal result. One is dealing, after all, with cases in which the producer of benefits had self-interested reasons for his actions, even without forced contribution from incidental beneficiaries. That may be reason enough for the law not to intervene, however valid the moral claim for contribution. Both the strength and the weakness of the moral claim are aptly summarized by John Dawson:

> The underlying assumption, which at times seems almost to rise to the level of a moral judgment, is that self-serving enterprise, which claims the privilege of defining its own incentives, should make its own way and is not entitled to subsidies. Discussion could end at this point if it were not for the source of the subsidy sought. If awarded, it would be drawn from those who themselves have gained without effort or contribution of their own and who can offer no more persuasive reason for refusal to contribute than: "We never asked for it." So there is always present that underground spring of resentment that was so successfully tapped by Henry George with the polemic phrase "unearned increment," and even more successfully, long before, by the Book of Matthew, which described as a "hard man" one who reaps where he did not sow.[24]

One must not, then, reject out of hand the possible application of the unjust enrichment idea to the issue of political obligation, even in the case of unsolicited and unreturnable benefits. There is another set of objections to benefit-based theories of obligation, however, that is even

· 73 ·

more problematic than the objections based on the application of the paradigm. These objections concern the content of the obligation that the paradigm is supposed to yield, even assuming its applicability. I have been rather loosely assuming that the obligation generated by benefits received from a legal system is the obligation to obey the law. In fact, however, the paradigm suggests only that the obligation is to return a proportionate share of the benefits received. Since not all submissions to law are beneficial, one does not necessarily find oneself faced with a general obligation to obey the law even if the paradigm applies. Instead, one is faced only with the narrower obligation of obeying whenever it is beneficial to others to do so.[25] The paradigm, in short, fails to satisfy the constraint of generality.

Although the application of the paradigm is left in doubt, one can at least draw a few conclusions from this discussion to guide the attempt to develop an alternative theory. The strength of the argument from unjust enrichment depends largely on the motives and actions of both the benefactor and the recipient. The argument is weakest, indeed fails convincingly, when the benefactor acts officiously to confer benefits precisely in the hope of charging for them without first securing consent. The argument is strongest when the benefactor has made a mistake not easily chargeable to his own negligence. In between are the problem cases involving benefactors who are independently motivated by reasons of self-interest. On the recipient's side, the argument is weakest when the benefits can't be rejected and are not even desired in the first place, in which case it is probably a mistake even to call them benefits. The argument is strongest when the recipient indicates through word or deed that he values the benefits, is happy to have received them, and indeed would probably have taken steps to secure them himself, even though that conclusion cannot be put to the test where the benefits are literally unreturnable or unrefusable. It is this last observation that probably explains the appeal of the fair play argument. The appeal derives primarily from the plausibility of the claim that most people concede that there are more benefits than burdens in the rule of law. This is the same claim previously identified as the first and more plausible premise in the utilitarian argument.

In the remainder of this chapter I shall develop this idea—that legal systems are on the whole beneficial—into an argument for political obligation that does not, however, rely on the benefits-conferred theory of unjust enrichment. In that way one preserves the appeal of the fair play argument while avoiding the objections that theory encounters in application.

AUTONOMY AND AUTHORITY

There are other routes to establishing political obligation than those that begin with standard paradigms. Some discussions of the problem, for example, appeal directly to an intuitive understanding of the concepts of autonomy and authority in an effort to determine whether these ideas are ever compatible. Recasting the problem of political obligation into the problem of reconciling autonomy and authority helps explain, in fact, the failure of two of the standard paradigms. Consent and estoppel both generate obligations structured in some sense around actions that could have been avoided. This structure confronts the individual with his responsibility for the situation in which he finds himself, thus reducing to some degree the clash between authority and autonomy. The theories fail in the political context because the confrontation of the individual with the legal order is not the product of willful or negligent action at all.

Willful Assent and the Paradigms of Complicity

For some this lack of complicity in the creation of the state forever dooms all attempts to reconcile autonomy and authority. Wolff, for example, argues that only the decisions of a direct democracy, requiring the unanimous votes of all for each decision, could yield political obligation.[26] Even this conclusion, of course, rests on a theory of obligation that is not defended but simply assumed. It is not clear, after all, why a prior vote in favor of a legal directive should override a dissenter's subsequent change of mind. A vote, as we have seen, is not the same as a promise to be bound. If one makes autonomy a concept so strong that it prevents legitimating submission except to laws one has legislated for oneself, then it will also prevent legitimating submission to laws one has repealed for oneself.[27]

Pointing to voluntary or avoidable choices is not, however, the only way to mediate between autonomy and authority. Consent reduces the clash between the individual and external demands for submission by showing how the demands are causally connected to choices one has willfully made. Another way to reduce this clash, a way that is older than the attempt to mediate through consent and that ultimately underlies the consent idea itself, is the way of reason. By advancing arguments sufficiently plausible in the connection they make between the situation, the demand for submission, and one's own values, one may yield to authority not in acknowledgment of one's complicity but in acknowledgment of the rationality of the argument and the shared normative commitment.

This direct appeal not to the autonomy implicit in consent or will but to that implicit in reason or value is a familiar feature in both philosophy and law. In philosophy invitations to enter an original position or to become an ideal observer or to consider how one might legislate in a kingdom of ends are ultimately appeals to acknowledge the rationality of the moral claims that are being advanced. In law the contrast between tort and contract is in part a contrast between duties defended by appeal to what reasonable men should do and duties defended by pointing to actual choices willfully made.

That the appeal to reason is more fundamental than the appeal to consent or will should also be clear. I have assumed for simplicity's sake that showing consent or promise to be bound by law would solve the problem of political obligation. This assumption, of course, takes for granted an extensive literature on why and whether promises themselves obligate. Promisors, after all, change their minds too. The literature that explains why obligation can override such change of will without violating autonomy is a literature that can avoid an infinite regress only by relying on the rationality of the explanation rather than on consent to be bound by promise.[28]

I stress this distinction between will and mind for several reasons. First, it makes clear that the inability to demonstrate complicity in the creation of the state does not doom all attempts to ground political obligation but at most only one kind of strategy for assuaging the apparent insult to autonomy. This much should have been implicit in the earlier consideration of the utilitarian argument. Though ultimately unsuccessful, the utilitarian argument depends not on complicity but on a direct appeal to reason. Second, the distinction helps explain a suggestion made earlier, again in connection with the utilitarian argument, concerning the relative strength of the stated and implicit premises of that argument. The first premise—that legal systems are preferable to the alternative of no law at all—is much more plausible than the implicit premise connecting any act of disobedience with the disintegration of the legal system. If the first premise is acknowledged, and if that premise can be connected to the situation that confronts the individual in a legal system in a more plausible manner than does this particular utilitarian argument, then a connection will have been made between the demand for compliance and the acknowledgment of minimal legitimacy derived from an individual's own values and reason.

This partial resolution of the conflict between authority and autonomy is equivalent to showing a minimal basis for moral respect for the law. To try to do more, to try to reconcile the conflict completely, is doomed to failure as much as is the attempt to show that law obligates absolutely. The right of the individual to dissent, to conclude that the obligation to obey is outweighed by other obligations, is the irreducible core of autonomy which authority can never invade. Autonomy collapses if de facto authority must always be followed; authority collapses if it is defined de jure to include only those demands that are legitimate as measured by the autonomous calculation of ultimate obligation.

Rational Assent and the Paradigms of Respect

I have indulged in this brief description of the phenomenology of autonomy and authority as background to the argument to be developed in this section. Having examined and found wanting the complicity-based paradigms of obligation, I shall construct an argument by directly appealing to the beliefs and attitudes of rational individuals in situations analogous to the situation confronted in the case of law.

For most people, this confrontation with law and the question of its legitimacy occur relatively late in life, as measured by the passage of time between consciousness of oneself as a political being and the much earlier consciousness of oneself as an independent being in general. The child evidences increasing maturity in part by replacing inclinations toward automatic conformity with an insistence on evaluating things for himself. The opportunities for developing and evidencing this awareness arise long before one encounters anything so complex as the laws of the political community, which are, after all, aimed primarily at adults. So too, long before coming to grips with the question of civil disobedience or the obligation to obey the law one must previously have come to grips with the question of filial disobedience and the obligation to obey one's parents. At first glance this situation resembles those features of the political context that make the reconciliation of authority and autonomy so difficult. One does not choose the family into which one is born, nor can one be charged with complicity in any other sense for the situation that leads to the confrontation with parental authority.

That the family is a possible source of analogy for political obligation is hardly a novel idea. Socrates in the *Crito* personifies the laws and has them speak in a tone which, if the matter were not so serious, would sound unmistakably like the original stereotype of the guilt-inducing mother confronting her thankless child: "Are you not grateful to those of us laws which were instituted for this end, for requiring your father to give you a cultural and physical education? . . . We have brought you into the world and reared you and educated you, and given you and all your fellow citizens a share in all the good things at our disposal."[29]

More recently commentators have both defended and attacked the concept of filial duty as an analogy for political obligation.[30] But defenders and attackers alike center their discussions on an analysis that depends once again on benefits conferred. This preoccupation with duties arising from benefits makes it difficult to distinguish the alleged debt of gratitude from obligations based on unjust enrichment. Indeed, one recent summary of the necessary conditions for a debt of gratitude coincides remarkably with the conditions necessary for legal recovery on a theory of unjust enrichment in such cases as those of the doctor rendering aid to the unconscious victim.[31]

This focus on benefits still leaves unsolved the problem of deriving the specific content of an obligation to obey the law. (A debt of gratitude may require one to pick up the phone now and then and call but not to drink up the hemlock and die.) More fundamentally, the focus on benefits seems to miss altogether the relevant aspects of the confrontation of child with parent. Consider what it is that lessens the impact of the parental directive on the child's increasing sense of autonomy. What is it that distinguishes the parent's directive from that of a playground peer or an adult stranger who happens to be momentarily in a position to enforce his command?

It should not be difficult to see plausible answers to these questions that do not depend on showing specific rewards reaped from belonging to a family. The confrontation of two personalities, one demanding compliance, the other resisting, is too specific and basic a clash to be mediated by the appeal to benefits—particularly since the good done by a parent is usually motivated by feelings of benevolence or by the immediate rewards of parenting rather than by expectations of future repayment. (The debt, then, never arises in the first place, or has long since been repaid.) More likely, mediation occurs because there is something about the confronting parent that unites child and parent even while the conflict repels. And what unites? At the extreme it is love, which may be biologically based and which may reflect notions of gratitude. If those I care about, for whatever reason, demand my compliance, then my concern for them, not for what they have done for me, is one reason to comply, one reason to consider along with the other reasons produced by my independent evaluation of the action on its merits. But love is only the extreme, if utopian version of the appeal that accompanies the demand. At the other extreme the appeal need be only to the child's recognition of the value of some family, some parent or guardian, compared to the alternative of none at all. That concession lays a basis for respecting the kind of enterprise that a family is, the kind of values and functions it serves in terms of the child's own normative structure. To this basis for respect for the general enterprise one need add only one additional requirement in order also to lay a basis for respect for the particular person and particular enterprise: the requirement that the parent is trying in good faith to act in the interests of the child by acting in the interests of the family as a whole.

These two features of the situation, sufficient to lay a rational basis for moral respect, are most simply reflected in the following general reaction to the confrontation with authority:

1. Here is a job—directing an enterprise—that I concede someone needs to do.

2. The person who happens to be in charge is trying to do that job in good faith, taking my interests equally into account along with the interests of others who also find themselves part of the same scheme.

3. That effort deserves my respect and provides me with a moral reason to go along, though at some point this reason may be outweighed by the seriousness of the error I think is being made.

One could be more explicit about the ultimate source of this attitude of respect by connecting this reasoning to themes in moral philosophy that stress the virtue of empathy (how would I want others to respond if I happened to be in charge?) or to themes in philosophy and literature that emphasize the dangers of hubris (I could, after all, be wrong about what ought to be done). But at some point "proof" in ethics cannot go beyond putting an account in a way that rings true in light of experience and reflection.

Consider, then, a second example: the lifeboat. Like the family, the idea of the lifeboat also recommended itself to political theorists as a source of analogy long before the image came to be applied metaphorically to the earth as a whole. The source of its appeal is basically identical to that of the family. Here is another situation, less commonly experienced but easily imagined, in which one confronts demands for compliance unmediated by complicity in creating the situation. Indeed, Hume uses the boat analogy to parody arguments seeking to infer tacit consent from residence: "We may as well assert that a man, by remaining in a vessel, freely consents to the dominion of the master; though he was carried on board while asleep and must leap into the ocean, and perish, the moment he leaves her."[32]

Assume, then, a variation of Hume's case, omitting the element of abduction. One awakens, following a shipwreck let us say, into consciousness as into life and citizenship, confronted with someone in de facto control issuing orders. On what grounds does one have an obligation to obey? Answers to this question do not necessarily imply respect for authority *simpliciter*. As noted earlier, Wolff uses a similar example to show that one might obey the person in charge "since the confusion caused by disobeying him would be generally harmful."[33] The failure of this utilitarian argument contrasts instructively with the alternative account I am advancing here. On confronting the situation two things become obvious. First, somebody needs to be giving orders. A single boat and a single tiller require that conflicting opinions about the direction to steer to be resolved. Second, though I may have views of my own about the direction in which to sail, the forced submission to the opposing views of those in charge loses some of its sting if my views and arguments are considered and in good faith rejected. That provides a basis for respect in my acknowledgment that those in charge, after taking my interests into account, are acting no differently than I would if I were in charge. Of course, if I feel sufficiently strongly that the orders given will lead to disaster, I may decide I have no ultimate obligation to comply but should instead try to sabotage the existing leadership. The point is that this example suggests a basis for prima facie obligation that does not depend on asserting empirically false connections between disobedience and the success of the enterprise. What is relevant is not the impact of my decision on the venture but the impact on the person who stands in front of me trying to do his best to accomplish ends thought to advance the interests of the group as a whole, including myself.

A THEORY OF POLITICAL OBLIGATION

I have said enough by now to make fairly clear the features that should be sufficient to establish political obligation. Those features are (1) the fact that the enterprise of law in general—including the particular system, defective though it may be, that confronts an individual—is better than no law at all; and (2) a good faith effort by those in charge to govern in the interests of the entire community, including the dissenting individual.

I shall explore these features and strengthen the plausibility of the claim that they are sufficient conditions for obligation in three steps. First, I shall consider why it is that both features are necessary. Second, I shall consider how this theory of political obligation might be expressed in either utilitarian or deontological terms. Finally, I shall connect the theory with the discussion and conclusions of the preceding chapter.

The Value of Law and the Mutuality of Respect

By insisting that obligation exists only if legal systems in general are better than no law at all, one introduces a gap into the solution of the problem of political obligation. In essence one concedes that there is no obligation if the anarchist is correct in his claim that all legal systems are undesirable or immoral. To complete the argument one would have to show that the anarchist is wrong, but that is not a task that requires extensive discussion. First, the standard claims for the value of law in promoting security and stability are almost universally accepted. One need not agree with Hobbes that security is the entire raison d'être of the state in order to acknowledge that it is at least one very good reason for preferring organized society to the state of nature. Second, it is important to note how tiny the gap in the proof is and how starkly the conclusion reached here contrasts with the conclusion of current theorists, who are prepared to deny the existence of obligation whether or not anarchism is correct. It is, after all, hard to find a genuine anarchist among contemporary political theorists. Even those most critical of state intrusions on individual liberty remain persuaded of the legitimacy of the state, however "ultraminimal."[34] Thus the practical effect of the theory on the ordinary citizen who wants to know whether he has a duty to obey is not likely to be affected by assuming the falsity of the anarchist's view. Finally, as I have previously noted, the suspect premise in the utilitarian argument for obligation is the assertion of a connection between disobedience and the collapse of the legal system, not the claim that legal systems in general are valuable.

Instead of recounting familiar arguments for rejecting anarchism, it is more important to understand why it matters whether the anarchist is correct. The requirement that there be positive value in the type of enterprise an individual confronts stems from the need to accommodate the concern for autonomy. That the requirement accomplishes this much, at least where the individual himself acknowledges the value of the enterprise, is reinforced by the earlier discussion of the nature of autonomy as well as by the conclusions reached in connection with the paradigm of unjust enrichment. Recall that the strongest claims of unjust enrichment arise when the person benefited affirms as valuable the choices that others, for whatever reasons, have made. Thus this requirement—that the value of law be conceded—connects with the persistent and most plausible aspect of the appeal to benefit-based theories of obligation.

A more difficult question is whether the individual who honestly believes all law is bad has any obligation. Even if one assumes his belief is wrong, there is now no shared value between him and those in charge. The assault on autonomy must be assuaged by the appeal to reason alone rather than by the fact of a shared commitment. This difficulty is simply a variation of a familiar problem in moral theory. Individuals can only do what they subjectively think is right, even though objectively they may be wrong. The anarchist will conclude that he has no obligation; but if he is wrong about anarchism, he is also objectively wrong about his obligation.[35]

But why must one assume that the anarchist is wrong? Suppose he is right. Doesn't the theory suggest that an argument for obligation could be constructed in that case? I have stressed, after all, the link between obligation and the idea that people who have good faith disagreements about ethical judgments deserve respect as individuals equally concerned with the struggle to identify and defend value. Why not say then that the anarchist, even if he is correct in his views, has a minimal basis for respect for the law—a prima facie obligation to obey—based on the same dual considerations of equal commitment to the search for truth and humility about the correctness of one's conclusions?

This question illumines the dangers of moving so quickly between the concepts of respect and obligation. Though I shall continue to defend the decision to use these concepts interchangeably, it is important to stress that it is respect for the law that is in question. Though the theory developed here ultimately rests on an appeal to the respect that other moral beings deserve (as indeed any moral theory must if it is to steer clear of mysticism), it nevertheless remains a theory that links respect to law qua law. Respect for others may obligate the anarchist to listen to and consider seriously opposed views; but if the anarchist is correct about the lack of value of law in general, his obligation cannot extend even prima facie to require compliance except by undermining autonomy. However much he may remain connected to others in some respects—for example, in the commitment to the search for truth—as regards the dispute over the value of law the anarchist in the case imagined would not be connected to those he confronts either objectively through reason or subjectively through shared values.

It may now seem that I have defended the claim that obligation depends on the falsity of anarchism with an explanation that would apply as well in less extreme cases. One may, for example, admit to the value of law in general and yet deny the value of a particular legal system or a particular law. After all, what is in issue when it comes to the demand for compliance is this system, this law, not legal systems in general. If autonomy is strong enough to prevent obligation attaching in case there is no value to law in general, does a particular legal system that has no value also yield the requirement only that one listen, not that one obey? In some cases the appropriate answer to this question is yes. A particular legal system that has so deteriorated as to deny even the minimal security that makes the general enterprise valuable will not yield obligation. But the same conclusion does not hold just because a particular law is immoral or a particular system unjust, or socialist instead of capitalist.

The claim that there is a morally relevant difference between the value of the enterprise and the value of a particular law or legal system rests on the plausibility of distinguishing disagreements about what kind of legal system is best from disagreements about whether any legal system is defensible at all. The former disputes raise central issues in moral and political philosophy whose intractibility is reflected in stubbornly opposed theories of distributive justice and in conflicting political solutions to the problem of proportioning state power to individual prerogative. Arguments about these issues, like arguments about the merits of particular laws, are part of the process by which disagreement is resolved. Arguments about the legitimacy of the state, in contrast, are seldom heard outside of academic contexts. In one sense the choice between anarchy and law is both more fundamental and at the same time less open to individuals to affect than the choice of types of law or type of legal system. For these reasons, if the anarchist is correct, the only option consistent with his autonomy is moral escape from the obligation to obey the law. But for those who accept the value of law, the story is different. Disagreements for them are measured in degree, not kind. Coupled with the second requirement—good faith concern for the community as a whole—the possibility of persuasion appears both mutual and real in proportion to the merits of the case and the openness of the society.

Any other conclusion, of course, makes autonomy so strong a concept that by definition the problem of political obligation cannot be solved. There is just as much reason to suspect definitions that make the problem unsolvable as there is to suspect definitions that solve the problem by fiat, as in the case of the natural law slogan. If the persistent efforts of political theory are accepted as evidence that the phenomenon is real, then there is much to be said for a theory of obligation that depends on the falsity of anarchism but does not further depend on the correctness of the underlying political or moral principles of a particular society.

This discussion also helps explain the importance of the second condition for obligation. Acknowledgment of the value of law arises out of a rational appraisal of self-interest in the maintenance of a coercive social order. A system that ignores the individual's self-interest undercuts the basis for the bond between ruler and ruled. Respect, if it is owed, is also owing, and for essentially similar reasons: my acknowledgment that you are trying to do a job that must be done and that you think requires my compliance is mirrored by and dependent on your acknowledgment of my autonomy. In each case the specific content of the resulting obligation is determined by the nature of the interests of the person confronted. My respect for those in charge provides a reason for doing what these persons believe I should do: comply with the law.[36] Conversely, the rulers' respect for my autonomy in evaluating the extent to which law reflects my interests requires them at least to consider those interests in exercising their authority.

Standard Theories Compared

The last observation indicates how the problem of translating theoretical arguments for obligation into specific obligations to obey the law is met by a theory that focuses on the personal encounter with authority. We saw that a general utilitarian argument that focuses on the effects of disobedience would at best ground only an obligation to obey laws that require the best possible acts, not to obey all law. By contrast, a focus on those who seek others' compliance provides a reason for complying wholly apart from the overall effects of compliance on the enterprise. Similarly by dispensing with specific benefits received as the basis for obligation, one avoids the objection that the only obligation is to return those benefits, or at best to obey whenever it is beneficial to do so. While the benefits of law in general may play a part in the grounding of respect, it is a very different part from the specific conferral of benefits that underlies theories of gratitude and unjust enrichment. The content of my obligation is determined by what those I confront want me to do—namely comply—even though the basis for their right to such consideration may rest in part on a general concession of the value of a legal system.

This way of putting the matter may lead to the attempt to recast the argument in simpler utilitarian terms. Thus, if satisfaction of desires is a good thing, then the fact that by obeying I please the person who demands my compliance provides a reason to obey. There is therefore always a reason to obey the law simply because some good will result: that is, some people will be pleased. I must weigh this positive consequence of obedience against negative consequences in deciding my ultimate obligation.

Of course this argument makes the mugger and the tax man once again indistinguishable. Pleasing the mugger would also have to count as a reason to obey. Though I have tried to skirt the problem of explaining what a prima facie obligation or reason is, this example should caution against an interpretation that yields a prima facie obligation to perform any act, however obviously outrageous, just because some good effects would be realized along with the bad. As Smith puts it, one would hardly say that there is a prima facie obligation to kill the next person one meets just because that act would have some beneficial effect on the overpopulation problem.[37]

To see how one might cast the argument in acceptable utilitarian terms, compare the mugger again with the beggar. It is hardly implausible to suggest that the satisfaction the beggar receives from my alms is a good reason to heed his request, though it may be outweighed by the disutility to me of parting with the money. Indeed, some philosophers argue forcefully that utilitarianism requires giving relief to the severely distressed until one is left with just enough for subsistence. But suppose now that the beggar displays a gun beneath his coat and thus makes clear that if his appeal to conscience fails, he will resort to force to get his way. If the relative utilities of parting with and receiving the money remain unchanged, one might think that the gun is irrelevant to the utilitarian conclusion that one should still hand over the money.

This conclusion is completely counterintuitive. The beggar who displays a gun destroys whatever sympathy I may have had for his appeal to me as a fellow human in distress. In effect, the insult to my autonomy represented by the gun cancels out whatever moral, rational basis underlay the initial appeal for help. The utilitarian, of course, has devices for accommodating this intuition to his theory. He will shift his focus from the relative utilities within the transient encounter to those of the long run and the overall utility of muggers' demands being accorded moral sanction. In so doing he will quite plausibly suggest that more harm than good would result from giving money to muggers on the same basis as beggars. If one did not recognize the illegitimacy of the resort to force, one could expect an increase in muggings and a distortion of the calculation of relative utilities, resulting in a decrease in overall utility.

If this is what prima facie obligation means for the utilitarian, one can construct a similar argument for the theory of political obligation developed here. One begins with the same initial premise—the plausible premise—of the argument considered earlier: legal systems are better than no law at all. The second premise connects disobedience not to the disintegration of the legal system (the implicit, implausible premise) but, as a rule of thumb or steel, to the overall satisfactions to be gained by those who desire other people's compliance. This way of putting the argument brings to the fore the essential shift in the account I have given, focusing on the persons one confronts and their response to one's disobedience rather than on the effects of disobedience on the enterprise itself. Disobedience cannot easily be linked to societal disintegration; but it can be linked in an ascending scale to sadness, disappointment, concern, anxiety, and fear on the part of those who think the laws are important and my obedience desirable.

Recasting the utilitarian argument also reveals the role of the initial premise in the argument and the basis for its appeal. Recognizing the value of legal systems is necessary not to show that an admittedly valuable thing is endangered by disobedience but to counteract the insult from the threat of force that would otherwise cancel out any respect owing to those who require obedience. The premise thus serves to distinguish legal systems from gunmen and restores plausibility to the utilitarian argument that failed in the case of the mugger: the force that backs the legal demand for compliance is not an unwanted and ultimately counterproductive feature of the encounter but an aspect of a coercive social order which, by hypothesis, is admitted to represent an overall gain in utility.

The above sketch of how a utilitarian might recast the argument for political obligation is intended as an aid in understanding the features of the theory rather than as a claim that the theory is essentially utilitarian.[38] Indeed, it should be clear that the argument could just as easily be cast in nonutilitarian terms. In fact, the terminology I have used sits much more comfortably with the tradition that traces the source of all moral obligation to the respect that is due other equally autonomous, rational beings, mutually concerned for each other.

One final observation is in order. My effort has been to show that there is a prima facie obligation to obey the law, not to indicate how strong the obligation is or in what circumstances it must yield to conflicting obligations. But the theory I have developed has relevance for the latter problem by indicating what to look for in assessing the weight of the obligation. Smith has suggested, for example, that even if there were an obligation to obey the law, it would be at best trivial because "a prima facie obligation is a serious one if, and only if, an act which violates that obligation and fulfills no other is seriously wrong; and second, a prima facie obligation is a serious one if, and only if, violation of it will make considerably worse an act which on other grounds is already wrong."[39] Thus murder, which is already wrong, is not made significantly more so because it is also against the law. And morally trivial acts, like driving through a stop sign at 2 A.M. when no one is around, are not made serious because such acts violate the law.

The first thing to note about this attempt to trivialize the obligation to obey the law is that the same tests for seriousness likewise trivialize the prima facie obligation to keep a promise.[40] Murder is not made more reprehensible because one had promised not to kill. And a trivial act—running the stop sign—is not made seriously wrong because one had promised never to run stop signs. An argument that so casually dismisses a tradition that takes promise as the paradigm of prima facie obligation deserves to be met with some skepticism. But whatever one thinks about the strength of these two prima facie obligations, to admit that the obligation to obey the law is on a par with the obligation to keep promises is to solve the problem of political theory. Every theorist has assumed that consent-based theories would ground obligation in the necessary sense if only they could be made to fit the facts of the political context. There would be little reason to explore the defects of such consent theories (as Smith himself does in some detail) if, even with consent, disobedience is, in Smith's phrase, a "mere peccadillo."

The theory advanced here provides a key to the weight of the obligation to obey that does not trivialize it and that probably reflects common-sense conclusions. The seriousness of the obligation is directly proportional to the seriousness, as indicated by the severity of the attached sanctions, with which those who demand others' compliance will view disobedience. If I do not believe that abortion is wrong, the intensity with which others hold the opposite moral view makes the obligation to obey a law against abortion strong, outweighed only by an equally strong moral view of my own—not by reasons of mere self-interest or convenience. Conversely, if no one cares much about running stop signs at 2 A.M., the breach of the law will be easier to justify. Ultimately some such explanation probably accounts for the doctrine of desuetude: a law that nobody cares about anymore simply does not obligate, legally or otherwise. But any case in which I am potentially subject to conviction by implication means that someone cares, however slightly. What matters is how much it matters to others.

LEGAL AND POLITICAL THEORY REVISITED

The theory of law described in the preceding chapter shares a feature with the theory of political obligation developed here. Both require that

the substantive division over values between ruler and ruled be mediated by the good faith claim that the particular legal system serves the
interests of the entire community. That requirement, imposed on the
rulers of the coercive social order, is a necessary condition for law if law
is to include the idea of obligation and connote more than force; it is also
a necessary condition for political obligation. But there is a second condition for political obligation: it must also be true that law in general is
better than no law at all. That part of the theory I have left unfinished,
partly because it is generally the least controversial aspect of political
theory. It may seem that if this question is put aside, the solution to the
problem of political obligation becomes circular. If one grounds obligation only by assuming the legitimacy of the state, does one not beg the
very question at issue?

It *would* beg the question to suggest that an individual must first determine whether any particular directive is morally legitimate before
deciding whether the directive obligates and hence counts as law. But
that is not what I am doing. The initial question for the individual is
whether the basic concept of a coercive social system is justified—that
is, whether the centralized control of sanctions, the "enterprise of sub-
jecting human conduct to the governance of rules"[41] is to be preferred to
the situation of a state of nature in which there is no such monopoly on
force. The preanalytic phenomenon is that of force or power effectively
exercised over a group of people. The normative issue at this level concerns the choice between anarchy on the one hand and on the other any
of the theories from Hobbes to Nozick that purport to justify some form
of the state. The normative question of this chapter is the related but
separate one of the obligation to obey the law in a particular de facto
state.

This contrast between the general justification of the state and the
grounding of obligation within a particular state[42] can be further illustrated by returning to the problem with which I began: what justifies
the difference in response to the gunman and the tax collector? One can
answer that question now by imagining an attempt to apply the theory
of this chapter to the gunman. The moral response to the mugger's demand for money is hardly likely to change from indignation to respect
just because the gunman claims (in good faith, we shall assume) that the
"contribution" to his cause is ultimately in the interest of the contribu-
tor. Similarly the ideological beliefs of terrorists and gangsters can result
in a claim of justice comparable to that which I have insisted must ac-
company the directives of a legal system. That is why the claim of justice by itself is not enough to transform just any confrontation with
force into a legitimate demand for compliance. The reason such a trans-

formation does not occur is because the gunman represents an exercise of force that is not effectively and uniquely established. The critical value judgment on which the case for obligation depends is the desirability of a single, effective sovereign—which the gunman obviously is not, however sincerely he may believe in his cause. This value judgment, though I have elected not to pursue or defend it in detail, ultimately rests on the desirability of order and security which the monopoly of force entails. These values are not implicated in the case of competing sovereigns or self-appointed temporary sovereigns, effective only so long as they can escape an obviously superior force.

We thus return full circle to the passage from Kelsen discussed at the beginning of Chapter II. A gang of robbers becomes a legal system by effectively establishing control over a definite territory, though the gang must also issue directives sincerely believed to be in the interests of all—which may in effect distinguish them from what we ordinarily mean by robbers. But this Saul-Paul conversion from a gang of robbers to a legal system no longer depends on a mysterious presupposition or on the truth of a psychological proposition about the prerequisites for internalizing a norm. Rather, the new status derives from the truth of a proposition of moral philosophy about the value of the de facto state which first becomes instanced in the newly established, because now uniquely effective, regime. What in Kelsen remained entirely mysterious, or at best a stab at social psychology, turns out to be comprehensible only as a consequence of a substantive theory of political obligation.

One final observation: it may seem odd to suggest, where values are contested, that obligation is a matter of belief rather than of who is right in fact. But I do not mean in making this suggestion to imply that the skeptic is right in denying the existence of moral facts or objective values. The point is simply that the beliefs and attitudes of concerned people can be recognized as yielding valid obligations, while questions about the epistemological or ontological status of moral judgments continue to be debated.

The position thus reached with respect to the relation between belief and reality contrasts instructively with the position of the legal theorist described in Chapter II. The legal theorist makes the coercive order include the idea of obligation and hence count as legal just in case it is believed to obligate with no explanation of how belief can yield obligation in fact. Belief supercedes reality as the critical test for law in a way that makes the reality of obligation irrelevant in deciding whether a system is legal. The consequence is that insiders, whose search for obligation presupposes (if they are not relativists) a realm of real value, are left with nothing but an arbitrary distinction between law and force. This chapter in contrast connects belief and reality by showing that the former is part of the latter: real obligations arise from the beliefs of others, regardless of the ultimate correctness of those beliefs or the ultimate correctness of various metaethical theories about the nature of value judgments.

The consequence for legal theory is not so much that one corrects defective vision as that one gives meaning and vitality to that vision in a world in which all of us are and must inescapably remain insiders.

CONNECTIONS

IV

W HAT might one say to the person who concedes the argument for political obligation but who denies that 'law' is a term that refers only to regimes that obligate? What is the ultimate basis for claiming a conceptual distinction between law and force?

POLITICAL THEORY AND THE CONCEPT OF LAW

The answer to these questions takes us back to the problem of definition and the challenge of Austin. Theories that see no essential difference between law and force stake their claims about the meaning of law on the universal human interest in avoiding organized sanctions. A lawyer asked to advise a foreigner about the laws of our country would understand that what the visitor wants is advice about potential sanctions of a certain kind. The foreigner may have personal reasons for becoming familiar with strange customs and mores in order to avoid offending socially, but when he asks for legal advice, what he wants to know is what actions will incur a risk of organized retaliation. Thus the classical positivist has a strong case for the claim that the existing classificatory scheme uses the term 'legal system' to mark off regimes that are effectively and comprehensively organized to enforce commands or rules.

The modern positivist who suggests that there is another interest that needs to be taken into account—namely the interest in knowing what standards are accepted in society, regardless of sanctions—has a difficult time explaining why that interest is a key to the classification question. In contrast to the interest in avoiding organized retaliation, the interest in knowing what others expect is weak. One must explain why people might be interested in the expectations of others. If, for example, it can be shown that the expectations of others create prima facie moral obligations (see Chapter III), one will have connected the alleged normative element in the definition of law to a human interest at least as strong and persistent as the interest in avoiding sanctions: the interest of the moral man in knowing what he ought to do. The suggestion would be that, just as we divide the genus furniture into chairs and other items, so we divide the genus organized social system into legal systems, which entail prima facie obligation, and purely coercive regimes, which do not.

That is the claim. How does one test it? Presumably, the same way that one tests the claim about chairs. First one looks at standard cases (objects we are inclined to call chairs without much doubt) to see if the existing classificatory scheme more or less supports the claim about the important features for purposes of classification. Lots of things we call chairs do not have rockers, and they vary in color and comfort, but it is difficult to find a standard case of "chair" that does not accommodate a sitting person. Apply the same approach to law. Are there many organized social systems that we call legal that do not deserve any moral respect?

The theory of the preceding chapter suggests that the answer is no, and thus avoids the most cogent argument of the positivist against other attempts to link the concepts of law and legitimacy. The positivist sees, or can imagine, many regimes that are immoral in fact but that are nonetheless classified as legal.[1] A political theory that shows that moral authority exists wherever there is belief in justice, however, rather than justice in fact, provides the positivist with far fewer counterexamples to the alleged definitional connection. However easy it may be to find examples of legal systems that are immoral in fact—Tsarist Russia, South Africa, Nazi Germany—it is much more difficult to show that officials in these regimes did not even, at a minimum, believe in the justice of their regimes.

Two objections might be raised to even this weaker link between law and the belief in justice. In some respects, the argument of this study resembles what Raz calls "the derivative approach" to linking law and morality.[2] That is, my claim is not that 'law' is itself a moral concept, like 'justice', but that, like 'promise', it is identified by nonmoral features (supreme force and the belief in justice) which necessarily have moral worth. This connection makes it plausible to think that 'obligation' has the same primary meaning in both law and morals. To this approach, Raz raises two objections. First, he suggests, one cannot say that very evil laws still have some moral worth by virtue of their existence and their other nonmoral features. To be moral even in the prima facie sense, laws must have some actual moral worth, so that only "extraneous reasons like the occurrence of an emergency (for example, an earthquake or war)" can override the duty to obey.[3] But why, one might ask, should prima facie obligation function differently in the case of law than in the case of promise? The act required by a promise may also be very immoral in its content, but that does not mean that there is no countervailing moral obligation to weigh against the act.[4] Perhaps if the promisor knew the act was immoral when the promise was made, he could not appeal to the countervailing obligation to keep promises in order to justify his act. But that is not the present case. Citizens confront law that has moral worth despite immoral content because of the sincere belief of others that the law is moral; there is no deliberate misuse of the connection between law and morality to offset the taint of action known to be immoral.

Raz's second objection is that people disagree about whether there is a prima facie obligation to obey. He claims that the fact that we all use normative language in describing the law, despite so much disagreement about its moral worth, means that the explanation for our use of such language must lie elsewhere. "To explain the use of normative language [derivative theories] must show not only that all law is morally valid, but also that this is generally known and thus accounts for the application of normative value to the law."[5]

This objection is difficult to assess without a clearer understanding of what it is that needs explaining when normative language is used to talk about law. As we noted in Chapter II, 'legal obligation' means different things for different people. Some take it to mean nothing more than 'legal validity', and the only problem that needs explaining in this case is why such people use a term from moral language to make what is for them simply a statement of fact about pedigree or power. Raz himself is content to explain the normativity of law from the "point of view" of certain people: the judges who administer the rules. He does not claim that all people who use normative language share this point of view (or even that all judges do). If the explanation of normative language in law is to be more than simply a descriptive correlation of various uses of 'obligation' with various degrees of internalization of legal rules, then one cannot avoid the definitional problem discussed in Chapter II: which of these various meanings of 'obligation' expresses the central or key idea?

Finally, when Raz says that most people do not acknowledge the alleged connection between law and obligation, it is not clear that he is correct as regards prima facie obligation. Philosophers, after all, have only recently begun to argue against the existence of such obligation; most moral philosophers who have shaped Western consciousness, from Plato to Kant, seem to have assumed or explicitly argued for the opposite view. But it does not matter if Raz is right, for it is false that people never use language that presupposes facts, moral or otherwise, that are hotly contested or about which even they are in doubt. (Consider, for example, theology.) Suppose there were great doubt about whether promises obligate. The continued use of normative language in the sense of moral obligation, even by those who believe there is no such obligation, could be explained as a result of the continued search for an eventual proof that would show our doubts to be unjustified. Thus, even if the political theory advanced here is wrong, it will not necessarily mean that the legal theory too is wrong but only that one needs to think again about other possible solutions. Only when we give up on the problem of political obligation is it time to admit that continued use of the term 'legal obligation' is an anachronism, corresponding no longer to its primary meaning in morals.

So much, then, for the standard case of a legal system as a test of the claim that 'law' designates regimes that obligate. What about the borderline case and the "what if" question: what if an organized regime did not claim justice for its rule but simply relied on its superior power to enforce laws in the interests of the rulers? Is this still a legal system?

The borderline case is troublesome. The force of the classical positivist's theory is too strong to deny the possibility that some would see this system too as legal, despite the absence of any moral authority. Indeed, the example of the lawyer giving advice to a traveler provides intuitive support for the view that inquiries about law are best understood as inquiries about directives backed by organized sanctions. The so-called bad man's perspective is always a possible view about the essence of a legal system. That is why I used, in Chapter I, the analogy of the drawing that can be seen as a duck or a rabbit. One cannot deny the plausibility of the classical positivist's perspective. What one can do is show another possible meaning of 'legal system' that reflects an equally persistent human interest and that succeeds where no other theory has in defending an alternative to the coercive account.

In favor of this alternative view there is at least this to be said:

1. The moral interest that underlies the suggested classificatory scheme is at least as strong and persistent as the interest in avoiding organized sanctions and certainly is stronger than the interest in knowing

simply what others expect; indeed it explains why people might care about what others expect.

2. There are few actual borderline cases. In fact, when purely coercive systems are encountered or imagined (ad hoc sovereigns or primitive despotic tribes), we have seen that legal theorists disagree about whether to call these legal systems.[6]

3. The evidence provided by positivists themselves, who argue as a matter of description or observation that legal systems imply an official belief in justice, provides support for the theoretical claim; indeed only with the theory sketched here is it possible to explain or defend the positivist's claim.

The important conclusion is that there is *doubt* about the coercive regime, which is why such a regime is a borderline case. And doubt is all one needs to make plausible the definitional claim about the essence of the standard case. At the moment, then, I shall leave the matter at a stand off, content that the claim that 'law' designates only regimes that obligate is at least as consistent with the ordinary use of language, and a strong human interest that explains that use, as is the coercive view of law. I return to the possibility of resolving the stand off in the concluding section of the last chapter.

LEGAL THEORY AND THE CONCEPT OF OBLIGATION

I have provided an answer to the person who accepts the political theory but questions its bearing on the meaning of 'legal system'. Consider now the person who accepts the legal theory but not the political theory. Suppose one agrees that 'legal system' implies an official belief in justice but denies that such a belief necessarily results in moral obligation. Or suppose that one is simply unwilling to engage in the substantive moral philosophy which the political theory requires. Why not conclude that law exists wherever there is a belief in justice, without worrying about the implications of that conclusion for political theory?

Belief-Based and Reality-Based Concepts

This position, as we have seen, resembles that of both Kelsen and Raz. We have also seen that the position is untenable as a matter of description and unstable as a matter of definition: lacking explanation of the reason why belief in justice is important, one has no way of defending the alleged connection between law and belief. At most the connection is simply an inference about the unlikelihood of people acting toward others in a way they know to be immoral.

There is also a more subtle issue at stake in this dispute about the connection between legal and political theory. The positivist, after all, might try to fill the definitional gap in his argument about the connection between law and the belief in justice by building on the same psychological evidence that I have said trivializes his claim. He might say, for example, that precisely because legal systems are so powerful and potentially intrusive, people have made the connection between law and the belief in justice part of the meaning of law—unlike the case of social clubs and other lesser organizations that act mainly on consenting members or in less important spheres of life. (The positivist would still have to defend this claim conceptually, explaining what to say of regimes that do not believe in or openly deny the justice of their laws.) In this way the theory of law developed here can be accepted without accepting the political theory, just as I said one might accept the view that to promise means to undertake a moral obligation, without actually believing that such an obligation exists.

In order to appraise this final effort at maintaining the separation between legal and political thought, let us consider the analogy of a theorist defining religion as requiring, say, a belief in the existence of God. That analysis can be accurate without preventing the theorist, when he turns to the substantive question of whether God does exist, from deciding and arguing that the answer is no. Presumably, if the theorist in his substantive mode convinces everybody that there is no God, former believers will no longer have a religion. That leaves the meaning of religion intact—indeed it vindicates the meaning, for once the belief is shattered, the application of the concept goes with it.

Try now to apply the same analysis to law. If the positivist qua moral theorist persuaded us that there is no moral obligation to obey law qua law (that the political theory advanced here is incorrect), possibly we would no longer call all organized social systems (the preanalytic phenomenon) legal systems but would restrict that term to those regimes that do obligate morally. Thus, if only certain kinds of democratic regimes obligate, we might decide that henceforth only that kind would be called a legal system. This possibility admittedly seems remote, which is precisely why the positivist appears to be on strong ground in claiming that the ordinary sense of the term 'law' is one that refers primarily to effectively organized social systems rather than just to those that are moral. Of course, there is a second possibility. We might dispute the substantive issue of whether in fact most of the standard organized social systems do yield prima facie moral obligation. In that case we could still claim that the substantive moral question is an intricate part of what we mean by a legal system.

The difference between the case of religion and the case of law is that in the former I suggested a definition that depends on the belief in God, not on the truth of the proposition that God exists—a belief-based concept. In the latter case I propose a definition that depends on the truth in fact of the claim that a regime deserves moral fidelity—a reality-based concept. If the positivist claims that law is a belief-based concept, then he can maintain the distinction between legal and moral theory. Legal theory tells us that 'law' refers to regimes believed to be moral. Moral theory tells us which regimes are in fact moral. But if the concept of law is reality based, this division is impossible. If what we mean by 'law' includes only regimes that do in fact morally obligate, and not just regimes where that is believed to be the case, then the legal theorist cannot tell us which systems are legal without grappling with the very question that moral theory poses. Similarly, if what we mean by religion is something characterized not by the belief in God but by the truth of the proposition that God exists, then again the theorist cannot maintain the distinction between detached analysis and substantive theological debate. If he now argues that God does not exist, the fact that he persuades people to believe him does not mean that they no longer have a religion: that depends on whether they are right about God's existence. It is true that they will not think they have a religion, but they could be wrong.

So too in the case of law. If 'law' designates regimes that deserve fidelity in fact, then even if we are persuaded that a particular regime does not morally obligate, we still do not know whether it is legal until we know whether we have been correctly persuaded. Moreover, we might decide that as long as there is doubt about the moral issue, we should continue to call the regime legal. That is, establishing the connection between law and morality might be important enough to justify using a term that assumes the connection exists, even though it is in doubt, until the contrary has been conclusively established.[7]

The Reality of Belief

How do we know which view of law is correct: do we mean systems believed to be justified or do we mean systems that are justified in fact? If this is our question, it poses an independent task for legal theory. But the choice between these meanings has very different consequences for the ability of the theorist, after he has resolved this question, to keep his theory pure and free from substance. If a proper analysis of law reveals a belief-based concept, then one can apply and use the concept simply by taking account of certain social facts. (Where judges believe rules are justified, there is law. Where judges are all anarchists who openly admit that the belief is nonsense, there is not.) But where the concept is not belief based, it cannot be applied to existing regimes until one faces the substantive moral question.

Well which is it? There are good reasons to think that religion is a belief-based concept. A person who does not believe in God can hardly be said to have a religion, even if we assume that he is wrong in his belief and God does exist. But if judges do not believe in the justice of their regime and openly admit as much, even if they are wrong and the system really is just, can it be said that there is no legal system?

If one is to preserve any distinct concept of a completely coercive system (such as the troublesome borderline case of sovereigns issuing self-interested ad hoc decrees), one is not likely to decide that such systems are legal just because they accidentally achieve just results. One may approve of the result without acknowledging the authority of the ruler, just as one may agree with the substantive goal of a terrorist without acknowledging his authority to coerce participation in his cause. If official belief in justice is thus a necessary condition for calling a system legal, it seems at first glance to support the conclusion that law, like religion, is a belief-based concept: that is, neither concept applies in the absence of belief, regardless of the actual moral authority of the directives or the actual existence of God. In the case of religion, however, one could imagine that God exists even though a person does not believe. In the case of law, moral authority for the law qua law cannot be said to exist where the rulers do not believe that they are aiming at the common good—not if the political theory of the preceding chapter is correct. If it is correct, good faith official belief in justice is a necessary condition for moral authority. Thus every case that could support the belief-based interpretation of law and thus separate legal and moral theory turns out to be a case in which the reality-based interpretation would yield the same conclusion: that the system is not a legal system because the rulers are not sincere and thus have no moral authority.

To approach from the other direction, is belief also a sufficient condition for application of the concept? If a person believed in God, we would probably conclude that he has a religion even if we were convinced his belief was false. That conclusion supports the belief-based view of religion. What about judges who sincerely believe that what they are doing is just but in fact are wrong? Would we still say that theirs is a legal system? Yes, but the result is no different from the one reached under a political theory that makes good faith belief sufficient for prima facie obligation. The injustice of the system is relevant to ultimate obligation but not to prima facie obligation. This analysis suggests that the normal tests for deciding whether a concept is belief based or reality based are not available in law, if we assume that by making belief crucial to moral obligation, an adequate political theory partly collapses the distinction between belief and reality.

This analysis also helps explain why positivism might have overlooked for so long the essential connection with moral theory. Even where concepts are reality based, one has nothing more than beliefs about that reality, and the beliefs might be wrong. Because legal theory is supposed to be an analysis of meaning, it shies away from the substantive questions that the reality-based concept would force it to answer. Because every reality-based concept can be used only in the belief that it is being used correctly, there is a distinct bias toward concluding that one is dealing after all with only a belief-based concept. Finally, when one is dealing with morality it is easier to decide what people believe simply by asking them than it is to decide what is the case. All these factors explain the bias toward deciding that the concept of law is belief based: it is easier to apply. But the positivist's predilection for certainty when it comes to identifying laws (or rules or orders or norms) within a society cannot be carried over to this general level of legal theory as a reason to prefer whichever interpretation is easier to apply. Such a presumption would beg the question, unless one assumed that no concepts are difficult to apply, which is obviously false. To defend such a presumption one would have to explain why we might care that 'legal system' be used in a way that makes it easy to determine whether or not a particular regime is legal. If the answer is that we are interested in determining our moral obligations, one has no reason to worry about the vagueness of the concept of law, as long as it is no more uncertain than the concept of morality.

The important point is that whether we can and do tolerate uncertainty when it comes to applying the concept of legal system is entirely independent of the positivist's insistence that we distinguish within a social system those standards that are easily ascertained from those that are not. A source is critical for both the moral man and the bad man, which is simply a way of saying that the effectiveness of any system of social controls depends on efficient communication. But this practical interest in a certain guide to expected conduct does not apply to the broader question of whether in classifying the various means of ensuring compliance (coercive, moral, legal) one should use only concepts that are easy to apply. Indeed, if the argument here is correct, we have long been living quite comfortably with a concept of legal system that is as uncertain as the concept of the morally legitimate with which it is linked. The best evidence of that, as well as the best evidence that the two concepts *are* linked and are thus equally uncertain in application, is the unending debate about this very question within legal theory itself.

APPLICATIONS
V

TIME WAS when the premier puzzle of jurisprudence was the problem of explaining the relationship between law and morality. Today this puzzle shares center stage with a different but related problem: that of explaining the relationship between law and certainty.

To see how these problems are related and how the newcomer came to prominence one need only keep in mind the epistemological bent of modern legal theory. The theorist whose goal is to provide a model of legal validity must ensure that the model picks out just the legal standards in society. Other standards, such as moral ones, are to be included only if they can also be shown to be legal standards. But if the function of the model is epistemological (an aid in answering the question, What can we know?) the apparent uncertainty of moral standards will bias one from the outset against including them. Thus it is that the problem of law and morality leads to the problem of law and certainty.

LAW, MORALITY, AND CERTAINTY

Current positivist theory provides two distinct accounts of the relationship between legal and moral standards. The more recent and extreme account denies that moral standards can ever be a source of law. When a judge applies a rule that requires him to invalidate immoral contracts or to strike down statutes that violate due process, the standards the judge refers to in making his decision are not themselves part of the law. Presumably that is because if a standard is to count as a source of a decision, it must be rationally or causally connected to the decision in a way that allows a public check on the connection to determine whether it is right or wrong. If moral standards are too uncertain to allow such a check, they cannot qualify as legal sources. Classical positivism made a more modest claim: moral standards might be part of the law when expressly incorporated, as in the examples just mentioned; but since not all legal systems incorporate such standards, the connection between law and morality remains only a contingent rather than a necessary one.[1] I shall explore the problems raised by these alternative accounts by first reviewing the current debate and then considering how the matter appears from the perspective of this study.

Theory and Practice

Legal positivism, whatever its guise, has always cloaked a central claim: the ultimate source of law is a social fact, such as the human act of will. From the moral point of view, of course, the act of will, because it is simply another fact, must be evaluated like any other for its intrinsic or instrumental worth. This simple conceptual point has always been the positivist's strongest ally in defense of the view that there is no necessary connection between law and morality. Indeed, the point is so simple, so straightforward an application of the fact-value dichotomy, that it is easy to overlook the premise on which the point depends—namely, the assumption that human acts of will are the basic data of legal theory. Yet the premise is not an arbitrary one. Acts of will, whether seen in the issuing of commands or the acceptance of rules, are social facts that seem in theory capable of being observed and identified in ways that moral facts cannot. Moreover, an act of will always precedes the application of organized sanctions, even though the propriety of the sanction may be in dispute. Thus the act of will is a universal concomitant (and thus at the very least a necessary condition) of law. Together, both features— observability and universality—provide some support for the claim that social facts are also the exclusive source of law.

These considerations explain why a simple denial of the positivist's premise will not do. Simple denial only puts one on the arbitrary side of an apparently stipulative debate about how a concept is to be used—arbitrary because the positivist seems to have in his favor the point just made in connection with the problem of certainty. A theory built exclusively on observable social facts seems easier to apply and use than a theory that includes evaluative elements as well.

Because simple denial is so unsatisfactory, most nonpositivists choose another point of attack: the assumption that the fact of will is easier to identify and observe than the facts of morality. Note that this strategy depends on rejecting not the fact-value distinction, as many nonpositivists seem to think, but simply the idea that distinctions in theory count more than distinctions in practice in determining the nature of law. However separate in theory, the nonpositivist insists, in practice there is no way to avoid making evaluative judgments in determining what humans have willed. What, then, is the point in insisting on theoretical separation in a thoroughly practical world?

One must be careful not to dismiss this position out of hand as based on a misunderstanding of the theoretical nature of the definitional enterprise. The nonpositivist is making a claim about the theoretical inadequacy of a definition; he is not simply complaining about the practical difficulty of applying a concept, as might a bricklayer who is told to pay attention to Euclid's definition of a straight line. In geometry the utility of the ideal definition is apparent even though in practice one will never encounter a dimensionless object. Law, in contrast, is a practical rather than an ideal concept, and so an adequate definition must connect the concept, even in theory, with its most obvious practical function—that of guiding judges and litigants. If that function entails inescapable evaluative elements, then a concept that separates the two in theory is not a concept of law.

The point can be illustrated by imagining a definition of 'tool' that makes the concept separable in theory from the idea of actually using the tool. How can something be a tool, one is inclined to ask, if its use cannot be imagined? If we discover an elaborate artifact that has no conceivable use for us, we are entitled to call it a tool—a lever rather than a bar of iron—only because we assume that it had some such use for a prior society or person. So too we may construct models of law on a base of theoretically identifiable acts of will; but if only those acts of will that guide count as law, and if guiding requires interpretation and evaluation, then an adequate concept of law must reflect, even in theory, both processes—interpretation as well as identification.

This strategy of counterattack—emphasizing practice and the particular as opposed to theory and the abstract—characterizes much of Fuller's famous exchanges with both Hart and Ernest Nagel.[2] It also seems to represent in essence the strategy adopted by Dworkin in his descriptions of the role of moral and political principles in legal reasoning. That the counterattack leaves the positivist unscathed as respects his central conceptual point has already been noted. But the counterattack also fails as a challenge to the positivist's basic premise connecting law and will, for the positivist has at least two responses when faced with a demonstration of the merging of fact and value in practice. The first concedes the merger and the necessity of accounting for it but insists that the merger is itself the result of an act of will, thus leaving the core claim intact. This response is like that of the classical positivist who admits that law may sometimes incorporate moral standards but denies that it must always do so.

Alternatively, the positivist may admit that a conceptual point is at stake, as the tool example suggests, but proceed to turn the point against the nonpositivist. If law, a practical concept, must guide, then it does no good to point to evaluative elements in the process of interpretation and application, for the only such elements capable of providing guidance are those already fixed by convention or fiat—facts and will. Thus, measured by the nonpositivist's own test for conceptual adequacy, it is the positivist's theory, separating law from morals, that proves the more adequate. In what follows, I shall expand briefly on each of these positivist strategies for accommodating theory to practice.

Positivism muddled. The argument for the first strategy, which makes the fact of normative argument in law a consequence of the positivist's own theory,[3] begins by noting that some societies expressly choose moral concepts to control the decision in certain cases—as, for example, in the due process clause of the United States Constitution. Where this happens, moral principles become part of the law, but only because the positivist's theory, which makes human will the key to law, says they are. Thus, the discovery that any particular legal system relies on fundamental moral or political principles may actually confirm the positivist's insight, for the positivist is nothing if not catholic in his neutrality toward social orders capable of qualifying as legal systems. Rules of primitive tribes that ascribe meaning to totems or magic rites represent potential decision procedures capable of yielding legal systems, as long as belief persists in these phenomena as sources of meaning. What then are moral principles to these esoteric examples of human belief systems?

The nonpositivist, distressed at finding moral and political principles lumped together with, say, astrology or magic, may try to distinguish the two. Astrology, he may object, is a lost art, so much so that no litigant could possibly tell in advance how a case would be decided under such a procedure. But the positivist's reply is brutal and consistent: so much the worse for the litigant. Indeed, from the perspective of any citizen who does not share the insights behind the officially accepted belief structure, the judge (or priest or medicine man) will always seem mysterious, and legal decisions will be as impossible to determine in advance as those reached by throwing dice or flipping a coin. We must not forget that some people think the determination and application of moral principles is also a lost art; yet that does not prevent people, including judges, who do believe that morality guides from acting accordingly. If

one is willing to count such moral sources as legal despite the unverifia-
bility of moral claims, then one might as well count all sources—including the astrologer's—as legal, and for the same reason: that is, the
process of decision conforms to human-posited directions accepted as
authoritative by those in charge, however irrational or invisible the alleged connection between source of law and legal decision from the
viewpoint of the uninitiated. The critical point is that in all of these
cases the connection between law and morality or other legal source in
any society is entirely contingent upon what is accepted as a matter of
social fact.

Positivism purified. This imagined interchange between a classical
positivist and a neo-nonpositivist, such as Dworkin, leaves the former
vulnerable to a new objection, but one that comes from the positivist's
own camp, long notorious for harboring a variety of forms of positivism.
The objection is that nothing is law that is not reasonably ascertainable
or certain. A system that expressly incorporates moral principles as
guides to decision does not thereby convert those principles into legal
standards. Only those expressions of will that are reasonably precise
about the consequences entailed by specific acts may count as sources of
law.[4]

From one perspective this modern, extreme position represents a final
step in the purification of the positivist's program. Astrology and morality are alike consigned to the extralegal heap, not because of any preference for one over the other but because the moral and the magical are
equally infected with indeterminacy. The litigant's complaint must be
heeded. The nonpositivist's insistence on the guiding function of law
must be taken seriously, with the result that the tables are turned.
Sources of law must lead to reasonably predictable decisions or they are
not *sources* of law. Esoteric procedures are nothing but thinly disguised
lotteries at best and should be seen as such; there is no need to pretend
that there is any source behind the lottery that can causally or rationally
determine the outcome.

It may seem strange that both positivists and nonpositivists could
build divergent theories of law on similar observations about the connection between law and certainty. Fuller, for years the leading example
in American jurisprudence of a nonpositivist, made a similar observation central to much of his work: systems fail to become legal if they do
not provide, among other things, for a minimum degree of predictability.[5] But when Fuller made the point, he was met with the familiar positivist's response: predictability may determine whether the system
operates well but has nothing to do with its being legal. Just as dull
knives are still knives, however inefficient, so bumbling and inefficient

legal systems are still legal systems.[6] Given this consistent classical response, why do some modern positivists find themselves siding with Fuller in linking the concepts of law and certainty?

For the answer to that question we need to draw back once again and ask what practical point, if any, there is to these disputes. Two possible answers emerge. The first holds that the point is primarily epistemological. Law is a label to be pinned to the things we find in the world. Sources are legal if they systematically connect organized sanctions to specified actions. Any single such connection is an individual law, and the sum of all such connections, or more precisely the procedure through which all such possible connections may be identified, constitutes the legal system. In this way the predictability of the connection between source of law, action, and consequence becomes critical to the definition as well as to the identification of law.

This epistemological justification for insisting on the connection between law and certainty, reminiscent of the verifiability thesis of logical positivism, encounters both practical and theoretical objections. The practical objection is that neither outsiders nor insiders care whether or not we call regimes that operate unpredictably legal, though they may care a great deal about the consequences for planning and behavior on people living in such regimes. Predictability, stability, and order are values that can stand without an arbitrary stipulation about the meaning of law, particularly when legal theory itself is unable to give any but the most abstract and schematic tests for determining validity. Furthermore, to insist that sources, if they are to qualify as legal, must point with reasonable certainty to the connection between action and consequence invites a contradiction in application in the inevitable question, How certain is certain enough? Any standard that purports to tell a judge when he has left the "certain" area of law for the murky area of discretion will itself involve borderline cases that cannot be resolved with certainty. Thus unless, as seems unlikely, there is a quantum jump in going from core to penumbra, from easy case to hard, no theory that insists on completely eliminating uncertainty can provide a coherent account of the phenomenon under investigation.

A second, better justification for connecting law and certainty arises from asking the question that guides this study: what are the consequences for obligation in systems that distribute sanctions in haphazard and unpredictable fashion? It is this concern for the deterioration of the major value of law where stability and predictability are absent that dominates Fuller's discussion of the "inner morality of law"[7] (though that discussion is admittedly weakened by Fuller's failure to defend his claim conceptually).

Even this second explanation, although on the right track, remains incomplete. Nothing in the theory developed here suggests that a minimum degree of predictability is a sine qua non of the obligation to obey. If deciding disputes by the flip of a coin can be rationally defended as a way to resolve competing claims, then the good faith claim to justice that is a prerequisite to obligation is satisfied. And that one can rationally defend decision procedures that rely on lot and are hence unpredictable is obvious enough, at least in certain cases, such as when goods are insufficient to satisfy all equally situated claimants. Whether the rationale of such cases can be extended to embrace the resolution through chance of all disputes in complex societies is doubtful.

This last question will be explored in some detail in the following sections. For now it is enough to note the difference in approach that is suggested by the moral, as opposed to the epistemological, alternative. The moral approach turns the question of the relationship between law and certainty into a question of substantive ethics, exploring the justifications that might be advanced for demanding compliance with completely unpredictable decisions. The epistemological approach in contrast shuns uncertainty, not because of the consequences for obligation but because of the consequences for the task of identifying particular laws and legal systems.

The Legal Status of Moral Standards

The difference between these two approaches can be illustrated by reconsidering the dispute about the legal status of moral standards. As I have suggested, both sides in the dispute seem to assume that determining what standards are legal is primarily a matter of establishing the constraints that can plausibly be said to have been placed by society on behavior. The only dispute is over the extent to and the manner in which evaluative judgments enter into that determination. This study, in contrast, suggests that the search for law is a search in part for constraints that have some moral legitimacy as well as social pedigree.

From this perspective the views of both classical and modern positivists prove unacceptable. The classical positivist who concedes that morality is a contingent part of law wherever humans choose to make it so confronts a conceptual, not a descriptive challenge. For if the argument of the proceeding chapters is correct, no society may decide to make morality irrelevant and still remain a legal system. Directives must be justified to count as law, and so all societies must ultimately retreat to moral or political principles to defend the social facts that set constraints on citizens.

The modern positivist who denies that this process of moral justification is certain enough to count as law presents a different problem. It
will not do to contest his claim by trying to show that moral standards
are in fact determinable. Whether they are in some sense remains a live
issue for many people, but to debate this issue with the positivist is to
miss the point. The positivist need not claim that moral facts are inherently indeterminable or irrational. Indeed to do so would commit the
positivist to a substantive metaethical position which is inconsistent
with his pure stance as legal theorist. The dispute with the positivist
about the connection between law and certainty must proceed on another level. All the positivist need claim is that whether or not values are
in some sense determinable, they are, or at least seem, harder to determine than social facts. The question for legal theory, then, is whether
this perceived uncertainty is reflected in our use of 'law': that is, do we
identify as sources of law only standards that can be determined with
the same relative ease as a social fact?

Let us consider our answer in light of some of the more exotic cases
imagined above. Suppose, for example, that judges decided cases by
consulting astrological charts. Would the art of astrology be part of the
legal standards of the society, even though nobody could reduce that art
to a form that could be used to predict a decision? Would it be so even if
the judge's reading was mysterious to him too but was believed to lead
somehow to a decision causally connected to the "source"—that is, to
the configuration of the planets?

Of course if astrological charts did correlate with results in established, coherent ways, then they would amount to an easily determined
fact and would count as law even though there is nothing beyond the
charts that could be considered a source of law. But this focus on the irrational misses the point. What is relevant to law from the viewpoint of
this study is the justification for a decision procedure. What is there
about the configuration of planets that explains why these sanctions are
being imposed?

The claim that the standards used in justifying particular legal results
or procedures are themselves part of the law rests on several ideas. First,
without such justification the directives are merely coercive, not legal.
That is, the case for counting as law the reasons that underlie accepted
practices does not rest on the common epistemological suggestion that
one can understand what is wanted only by considering the justification
or purpose along with the directive. (One can certainly understand the
mugger's command, whether or not one knows his justification for giving the command.) The requirement for justification stems rather from
the fact that without it, the command is no different from the mugger's

and thus is not law. Second, by viewing the justification as part of the law, one brings into focus the means by which directives are changed, wills affected: namely normative argument and debate about the legitimacy of the underlying beliefs. Thus the connection between source of law and consequence for behavior is maintained, however irrational and indeterminate the particular decision-making procedure. The rational connection between the beliefs that underlie practice and the consequence for action exists not because the particular beliefs are necessarily rational but because normative argument about such beliefs is. Irrational beliefs can be shown to be just that—irrational.

What does the positivist have to say in defense of the other view, that justifying standards are too uncertain to count as law? Since he cannot take a metaethical position that declares them irrational (though many people mistakenly assume that legal positivism does incorporate this conclusion of logical positivism), he has to be open-minded on that issue; he has to be prepared to admit that normative argument might be rational and moral facts in some sense real and determinable. But then the claim about which sources count as law appears rather arbitrary. Instead of the clear distinction between sources and nonsources the positivist offers only a distinction between two kinds of sources: those that are clear and those that are not. As an explanation of what is meant by law, his is a difficult position to defend for two reasons. First, many social facts are also uncertain and hard to determine. (If 'cruel and unusual' punishment means 'thought to be cruel and unusual by most people', that becomes a social fact and a legal standard, although hard to determine.) Second, many people continue to think that moral argument is rational. Even if they are wrong, on the assumption that it is the meaning of 'law' for these same people that is at issue, the fact that they think that values are real and normative argument rational counts against the positivist's claim.

This strategy of contrasting the moral with the epistemological approach provides the theme for the remainder of this chapter. I shall examine a variety of problems in legal philosophy with a view toward indicating how the theory of the preceding chapters would restructure and resolve the inquiry raised by the particular problem.

COURTS AND LEGISLATURES

The problem of distinguishing courts from legislatures is important in modern legal theory for two reasons. First, the emphasis on validity—the criteria for identifying particular laws—implies that institutions could be designed that are capable of applying such criteria. Exploring the features of such institutions leads naturally to an examination of the concept of adjudication and the problem of explaining the difference between law-applying and law-creating institutions. Second, as one moves from theory to practice, from design to operation, courts are often observed to play a critical role in the transition from primitive to more mature legal systems. This observation prompts an inquiry into whether there is a necessary or logical connection between the concept of adjudication and the concept of law itself. Both questions—what counts as judging? and is judging essential to law?—lead to intractable issues.

The Traditional View: Courts as Adjudicatory Organs

Consider the first question. The essential difference between court and legislature consists in the constraint placed on the former, but not the latter, to reach decisions in accordance with preexisting standards. Judges find the law; legislatures make it. The glee with which realists brandished the apparently opposite opinion should not be mistaken for a disagreement about this conceptual point, for the realists' disagreement was over the practice and the facts rather than the logic of the concepts. Institutions called courts, realists noted, were in fact doing jobs that could not be described as constrained by external standards. Hence, courts in name were really acting as legislatures in concept. Indeed, it is only because the conceptual distinction is accepted that the realist's attack makes sense at all.

For all of the disagreement concerning the nature of the judicial decision that has followed the realists' attack, this basic conceptual point has remained unchallenged. Dispute instead has focused on subsidiary questions, all of which assume the underlying distinction. One such question asks whether it is possible, even in theory, to constrain an institution in a way that never permits discretion in deciding cases. The disagreement between Hart and Dworkin is largely a disagreement over this theoretical issue. Hart's view seems to be that no matter how simple the standard a court is required to apply (no vehicles in the park), borderline cases will always exist that leave the court no clear guidance, thus forcing a decision in a manner conceptually indistinguishable from the decision of a legislature. Dworkin, in contrast, insists on taking a broader view of the conventions and context available to supply meaning and guidance even in borderline cases so that a court's decision is never unconstrained. Thus described, the dispute centers as much on a problem in the philosophy of language and meaning as on a problem peculiar to legal theory.

Even if it is theoretically possible to constrain an institution so that it always acts as a court, the question remains how best to put that conclusion into practice. Are some tasks, for example, so incompatible with the role of a court that such jobs should not be given to institutions meant to be purely adjudicative? Much of Fuller's discussions of adjudication and of the difficulty courts have with "polycentric" questions bear on this issue, as do a variety of legal doctrines of justiciability (political questions, advisory opinions, and so on). Dworkin, in contrast, never explicitly addresses this issue, with the result that his claim that courts never have discretion becomes increasingly suspect. Either, it seems, one must claim that, by happy coincidence, existing institutions that we call courts have been assigned, or have accepted, only those functions that are compatible with the judging role, or one must claim that no tasks are incompatible with that role. An institution told to act as a court will find that every dispute that comes before it can be resolved by reference to preexisting standards that determine the decision.

The suggestion that all conceivable issues are theoretically justiciable leads to yet another question: what is the nature and source of the standards that constrain the court's decision and distinguish it from the legislature's? Legal theory requires that the standards be legal standards, not just any set of standards allegedly capable of generating a unique decision. One might, for example, admit that a utilitarian calculus could determine the best possible result in every dispute, whether it be the appropriate sentence for a convicted criminal or the appropriate allocation of heart-lung machines. But that admission is consistent with the claim that such a general, utilitarian calculus reflects at best moral but not legal standards. Reliance on such standards will not distinguish court from legislature because the latter too may be expected to operate against some such moral theory, enacting the best laws that can be devised by reference to that theory.

The point is again a conceptual one. To judge in general means to decide by reference to preexisting standards rather than personal whim. Courts represent a subset of the general concept, with judges of legal systems deciding cases by reference to external legal standards, just as judges of beauty contests decide by reference to aesthetic standards. Thus the court is doubly constrained: it must reach decisions that accord with preexisting standards (it must judge), and it has no choice about the standards to be used in performing that task (it must judge according to law).

It is here that the issues that divide positivists and nonpositivists resurface. The nonpositivist points to the fact that political and moral principles often are used by courts to decide cases as evidence that these standards are part of the law. The positivist, without denying the fact, may once again resort to either of his two standard replies, depending on the view taken concerning the connection between law and certainty: (1) either these principles are not law because they are too uncertain, in which case courts that rely on such standards are not judging but are behaving like legislators enacting laws; or (2) even assuming the standards are sufficiently certain to be used in judging, they are legal standards only because they have been implicitly designated as such by some legislative or constitutional act. In the latter case the nonpositivist is only drawing attention to one particular kind of legal system; he is not making a conceptual point about the relationship between law in general and moral or political standards.

It is here that matters currently rest. If the nonpositivist seems to get the worst of the exchange it is because of the nature of the claim he makes and the evidence on which he relies. The claim seems to be entirely descriptive and the evidence entirely compatible with the positivist's fundamental premise. What is needed if the nonpositivist is to engage the positivist at all is an explanation of how an adequate conceptual theory of law entails the normative practices of courts that the nonpositivist describes with such fascination.

To see how the theory of this study supplies the link missing from the nonpositivist's argument one need only return to the underlying conceptual distinction between court and legislature. That distinction, I said, opposes court to legislature as law finder to lawmaker. I also said that the distinction develops most comfortably out of theories of law whose centerpiece is the concept of legal validity and the epistemological problem of how to identify law. By shifting the focus to make the concept of obligation central to legal theory, one changes the distinguishing feature of the court. From this new perspective the court appears primarily as a justificatory rather than an adjudicatory institution; and the fact that much of the court's role involves judging proves to be the result of applying a particular underlying theory of justification. The prevailing view of the court as law finder will be seen to have mistaken a contingent, if dominant, function of an institution for its essential and distinguishing characteristic. In the pages that follow I shall set forth the argument that leads to this new perspective on the court and consider a variety of possible objections.

Another View: Courts as Justificatory Organs

The argument for this view, based on the conclusions of the preceding chapters, is easily anticipated. Legal systems, in order to impose obligation and avoid collapse into coercive regimes, must claim that their rules are just. But systems do not make claims; people do. In the case of legal systems it is the officials, whose acceptance of the basic rules makes the system effective and possible, who must defend the system against normative attack. While it is possible to conduct such a defense in an ad hoc manner as each law is passed, it is difficult to do so, because one cannot easily anticipate the variety of normative arguments or potential facts that need to be evaluated. It is natural then that there should arise an institution the primary function of which is to assume this responsibility of justifying the manner in which sanctions are imposed and disputes resolved. That institution is the court.

I shall elaborate on this argument by pausing briefly to consider the other question about courts that legal theorists tend to ask: how is the concept of a court connected to that of a legal system? The positivist's answer to this question contrasts instructively with the view just described. Hart, for example, sees the introduction of a rule of adjudication—along with a rule of recognition and a rule of change—as a step in the transformation from primitive to more complex legal systems. The rule of adjudication serves the purpose of settling authoritatively the question of which person or institution shall have the final say in declaring the law, as identified by the rule of recognition. Thus courts exist, in Hart's phrase, to end the interminable squabbles about what the law is. One might get along without courts and still have a legal system; thus the concepts are not logically connected. But the system would be primitive and inefficient.

The alternative view is similar but carries a different moral. Legal systems could operate without formal institutions to justify decisions, though formal institutions are likely to do so more efficiently than ad hoc devices. But the function of courts is not primarily to decide what the law is but to explain why particular sanctions and coercive orders are justified. Courts represent the most efficient way of demonstrating the good faith of the implicit claim of justice that distinguishes the legal from the coercive regime. It is with the acceptability of the rules rather than with what is accepted in fact that courts are primarily concerned. The objections to this view are also easy to anticipate. For the most part these objections result, as noted, from mistaking the dominant means by which courts justify decisions—namely judging—for the essential function. Thus one might object that judges do not think of themselves as called upon to defend the structure they administer; they simply do their job, which is to apply the law, and leave questions of the justice of the decision to the legislature. This view is so pervasive that it finds its way into anecdote, as in Learned Hand's tale of Justice Holmes's denial that "doing justice" was any part of his job.[8] What this view overlooks, of course, is the fact that a judicial reaction such as Holmes's may itself be based on a political theory that justifies a particular division of responsibility between court and legislature. Indeed, it is usually considered a hallmark of liberal political thought to ascribe as mechanical a role as possible to the court in carrying out the preference of citizens expressed in the legislative compromise.

I am not suggesting that an individual judge must bring his own moral and political theory into play in justifying each decision he makes. In this respect the obligation of the individual judge parallels the obligation of the citizen. The judge confronts the basic rules accepted by other judges, which constitute the system he is called upon to administer. Unless he is simply a henchman in a coercive regime, he also confronts a prevailing political theory which purports to show why the rules are acceptable. It is this prevailing theory, believed to justify the basic rules, that leads to a prima facie obligation on the part of each judge (apart from his promise to apply the law when he assumed office) which must be weighed against whatever obligations an individual judge may extract from his own political or moral theory.

The fact that courts often appear to be concerned only with applying, not justifying, individual laws is thus not counterevidence for the view that sees courts primarily as justificatory organs. The political theory that justifies the law-applying role, at least in liberal democracies, is so thoroughly a part of the background and tradition of judicial decision that the premises of that theory are implicit in the premises of every judicial decision. It is possible to see both Kelsen's "juristic hypothesis" and Dworkin's claim that judges must seek the "soundest political theory" that accounts for existing laws as ways of drawing attention to this underlying assumption. Indeed, just as Kelsen's conceptual claim about law appears plausible only when coupled with a normative theory of obligation, so too are Dworkin's descriptive and normative claims about the judicial process understandable only when seen as an aspect of a conceptual theory of law.

A second objection to the view that courts primarily justify rather than apply law focuses on the apparently counterintuitive implications of that claim. The implication is that courts ultimately determine the fundamental moral and political theory on which the basic rules of the system depend. As a result, a collective change of heart on the part of all or most of these officials would result in a fundamental change in the legal system, thus making an illusion of any permanent attempt to embody fundamental rules or their political justifications in constitutional or legislative documents. From the view that courts are constrained, we seem to have moved to the opposite view of courts as completely unconstrained. How does that view differ from the natural law slogan, and what, moreover, can be made of the persistent view which, in the United States for example, often insists that judicial decisions should be confined to the strict interpretation of a constitutional document?

First, this objection cannot lead to a preference for prevailing positivist theories of law over the view sketched here. Hart too insists that it is the fact of official acceptance that determines the basic rules of a legal system; if new rules are accepted, in disregard of constitutionally prescribed methods for change in the old rules, one can only conclude that a new legal system has emerged. While one may find interesting conceptual problems in distinguishing constitutional from revolutionary change in legal systems, the possibility of revolutionary change can never be excluded by fiat from a theory of law.[9]

As for theories of judicial review that preach the value of confining judicial discretion, such theories are exactly what they purport to be: normative theories. If they are viewed as correct and accepted as such by courts, then judicial recourse to novel political theories and fundamental values will be constrained. But in that case courts will once again be performing a role that is justified normatively by a larger underlying political theory. Theories of judicial review, in short, cannot be made self-executing by incorporation into a constitutional document which in turn requires acceptance and justification. Indeed, debates about judicial review are meaningful only on the assumption that the political theories on which they depend and the normative arguments they embrace are appropriate arguments for courts to consider and assess.[10]

This account leads to several conclusions concerning the dispute about judicial discretion and the nature of the judicial decision. First, there is no essential difference between the easy and the hard case as respects the kinds of considerations relevant to a legal decision. In both, existing ordinary legal materials must be seen as supplemented, implicitly or explicitly, by the prevailing political and moral theory that justifies using those materials to decide cases. The only difference is in appearance: in the easy case, the result required by ordinary legal materials is by definition clear, but so also is the theory that justifies a judge's imposing that result regardless of his moral or political views. In this case the premises of the underlying political theory are largely implicit; and a litigant who wants more in the way of justification than the response, "That's the law," would be referred to an elementary civics course. Dworkin, in short, is right about the inseparability of political theory and legal decision—not just in the hard case but in the easy case as well.

Second, the hard case differs from the easy case not only because the result required by ordinary materials is uncertain but also because the political theory about the proper role of the court in such a case is equally uncertain. Where the law is clear, liberal democratic theory justifies judicial constraint by viewing the judge as simply an expositor of the will expressed in the larger democratic process. This view of the judge's role follows from the premises of a theory of justification ultimately rooted in notions of consent expressed through elected representatives. These same premises, some critics conclude, prove liberal democratic theory a failure in the hard case, for then the judge, who is not a representative, must decide on his own, loosed from the principle of consent that legitimates his decision in the easy case.[11]

This attack, construed as an attempt to demonstrate inherent limits on the ability of liberal theory to legitimate the exercise of power, is far too unimaginative about the inferences to be drawn from that theory. If the judge really cannot help but decide on his own, how else is the decision to be legitimated? One might suggest that the dispute be sent back to the legislature for determination; but critics usually block that escape by claiming that in the meantime events will have changed and the dispute will no longer be the same.[12] Thus the dispute the court sees will be resolved de facto one way or the other: by default if the court does nothing or by the judge's decision, unrepresentative though it may be. If this account accurately describes the judge's dilemma, and if 'ought' implies 'can', then it should be clear that no one can fairly charge liberal democratic theory with the inability to legitimate decision in the hard case. The judge's dilemma itself becomes a legitimating reason for deciding in some other way, without direct recourse to the democratic will. Indeed, the dilemma provides a good reason for concluding that in these cases the democratic will can be seen as authorizing courts to make a legislative decision, in which case there is not even a need to modify the core legitimating concept of consent. Alternatively, the core concept can be modified by saying that this bit of unrepresentative decision making is legitimate—particularly since by hypothesis it cannot be helped—as long as the judge does the best he can, remains impartial, strives to reach the result he thinks the legislator would, and so on.

These are all familiar variations on a theme. What they show is not that liberal democratic theory is correct or is somehow connected to legal theory; rather they show only how easy it is to reach different conclusions about the proper role of a court in a hard case, even among people who otherwise accept the same underlying political theory and use it implicitly to justify decision in the easy case. It is the plausibility of these various views, the possibility that they might be advanced in good faith by those who have the power to make their normative views stick, that is relevant for the model of law developed here. Dworkin, in short, is wrong about the essential nature of the judicial decision in the hard case, at least as far as legal theory is concerned. Justification by reference to an underlying political theory is still required, but it need not be the particular method of justification (right answers and principles) suggested by Dworkin.

This last conclusion deserves elaboration. Note that I have not suggested that Dworkin's views about deciding hard cases are wrong as a matter of normative theory. On that issue one can imagine several plausible positions. First, one might believe, as Dworkin does, that virtually all cases involve preexisting rights which lead to only one correct result and that courts ought to try to find this result. Second, one might deny that there are correct answers and continue to defend judicial discretion with arguments such as those mentioned above. Third, one might argue that even if hard cases do have unique results in theory, in practice more error results from urging courts to try to find them than results from explicitly authorizing an unconstrained legislative decision.[13] Finally, one might make the reverse of this last argument: that is, one might believe that cases do not have uniquely correct answers and yet urge that judges will make fewer mistakes if they assume that they do.[14] These four positions represent the possible combinations that result from giving different answers to one pair of questions: (1) are there right answers, and (2) whether or not there are, should we tell judges always to look for them? Even if the first position is in some sense the best one, that fact is irrelevant to legal theory in the same way that the question of the correct political theory is irrelevant. Society must be open to debates about both kinds of normative issues: the moral principles that justify the basic rules and the no doubt related principles that justify a particular process of decision. But the implications for law and obligation that are at the heart of legal theory depend only on the good faith defense of whatever position officials take on these matters.

THE CLAIM OF ACCEPTABILITY

The plausibility as well as the utility of a theory that sees courts as justificatory organs and that links the concepts of law and obligation and the belief in justice will depend greatly on the content given to the last notion. What is meant by good faith belief in the justice of a coercive system? How is good faith demonstrated? If coercive systems obligate and are legal only if directives are backed by the claim that they are in the interest of all, have law and obligation been linked to a chimera?

Forms and Varieties of Justification

The suggestion that there is a meaningful concept of the public interest or the general welfare, endemic though it is in political theory, attracts as many skeptics and disbelievers as it does adherents. It would be a mistake, however, to interpret the present theory as requiring one to take a position on the question of the nature and existence of a concept of the public good. Indeed, it should be clear from the alternative formulations of the requirement in terms of a claim of justice that the essential element is belief in the legitimacy of the system rather than in a particular conception of legitimacy which the notion of the public interest may seem to imply. These ideas may become clearer if one considers the implications of the argument for various theories of legitimation.

First, though the argument finds respect for authority in the perception that the person issuing coercive directions believes them to be in the addressee's interest, I do not mean to suggest that all laws must convey some direct advantage on each and every citizen. Few laws do this. What is essential is that laws that appear to be to the disadvantage of particular individuals or groups be defended normatively. Officials must be able at a minimum to defend the imposition of sanctions as not unfair. One way to do this is to invoke a concept of the public interest that converts an apparent short-term disadvantage into a long-term advantage. Another is to invoke a conception of morality that legitimates the required sacrifice of some for the immediate gain of others in order to secure collective goods. That may be another way of invoking a larger concept of the public interest. But if the collective good is as abstract as the notion of a just society, there seems little to be gained in worrying about whether it is individual enlightened self-interest or a theory of justice that in the end provides the criterion of acceptability.

Second, the claim that a system is acceptable differs from claims about a public interest in that the former is compatible with pure process theories of justification. Particular substantive requirements of law that appear unjust on the surface may nevertheless be justified by reference to the process that produced them and that, presumably, is available to alter them. Indeed, such process justifications are likely to be a major element of the theory of justification in any complex society: it is the basic rules, authorizing procedures for lawmaking, that are defended as acceptable even though the process of following those rules may occasionally generate unhappy results. Theories that rely on such process justifications may in turn include both substantive and procedural standards for assessing the acceptability of outcomes; and just as substantive shortfalls may be overcome by procedural fairness, so too procedural defects may be found harmless if the substantive result is fair. In both cases some political or moral theory presumably provides the standards by which to assess the fairness of either the procedure or the result.

It is also possible to imagine a theory of justification that does not include any substantive standard for assessing the justice of outcomes or the fairness of the procedure. In that case the theory's sole legitimating value is order or security. It is illustrated in the extreme case by a Hobbesian justification of law that makes every coercive directive analogous to rules of the road: there are no substantive standards to dictate correct outcomes; all that matters is that some choice be made, that some order be imposed. This is the minimum form that a theory of justification can take. Though it is empirically implausible to imagine all rules being defended as analogous to rules of the road, it is nevertheless a justification that, so far at least, is conceptually consistent with the present theory. Indeed for the extreme skeptic or moral nihilist, it is the only recourse left for the justification of power that prevents collapse into pure coercion. It is the way that Justice Holmes is often thought to have taken in moments of extreme pessimism about the possibility of value defense. Though it remains a justification in the minimal sense, I shall show in the next and last chapter how difficult it is to avoid collapse into coercion when officials become complete relativists with only the value of order to justify the system.

Good Faith: Uses and Abuses

The major conclusion that results from the preceding discussion is that very little can be said a priori about the content of potential theories of justification in particular societies. That conclusion is consistent with the entire approach, which makes the sincerity of a belief rather than its accuracy the critical ingredient in generating respect and obligation. But if one cannot derive content from the requirement of belief, one may be able to derive something like content from the requirement of sincerity itself.

The importance of the requirement of sincerity or good faith belief is quickly seen if one considers the possible uses of the theory I have been sketching. Legal theory has long been preoccupied with questions such as whether or not Nazi Germany was a legal system. Such questions come to prominence as practical tests of a theory when the theory places primary emphasis on validity and identification. If one were to use the theory of law sketched here for the purpose of identifying which regimes are legal as opposed to coercive, one would quickly discover how closely the theory is tied to the sincerity of the officials of the regime in question. One does not need to read Machiavelli to appreciate that claims of rationality and justice are in the interest of even the most tyrannical governments. Indeed the greater the discrepancy between the social order and justice in fact, the greater the likelihood that officials will try to close the gap through the artful use of rhetoric. Even the most secure tyrant has little to lose by adding false claims of justice to his other means of control. In the modern world, where public opinion is carefully courted, the likelihood of encountering claims of justice along with the widest range of repressive measures is hardly less than when Machiavelli wrote. All of these considerations prove that legal regimes cannot be distinguished from coercive regimes on the basis of official *claims* of justice. In consequence the burden of distinguishing law from coercion rests almost entirely on determining whether such claims are made in good faith.

One can begin to elucidate the concept of good faith, or sincerity, by considering how a focus on obligation rather than validity affects these uses of legal theory. Such a focus raises questions not about whether an entire regime is legal, but about the prerequisites for imposing obligation on groups or individuals within a system of organized rules. That the obligation to obey the law may exist for some groups but not others within the same society should be obvious. For those who have no obligation, the system is indistinguishable from a purely coercive regime; for others, the system is legal in the sense of continuing to impose a prima facie obligation to obey. It is only the pure outsider, bent on the epistemological goal of verifying the existence *vel non* of a legal system, who has difficulty admitting to matters of degree when it comes to applying legal theory.[15]

Given this approach, what use is the present theory to the person or group who wants to know whether the regime that issues orders also obligates? I have already suggested that little in the way of substantive constraints can be imposed on the content of belief. The best effort along these lines would invoke the analogy to slaves or conquered peoples. Unlike dissenting citizens, such groups, as we have seen, lack obligation because no reciprocal claim is made that subjugation is in the interest of the group. This assumption, that force alone characterizes the relationship between ruler and conquered, makes the case an easy one. If one relaxes the assumption and posits now what history teaches—that justifications for the institution of slavery can be professed and sincerely believed—does one restore the case for fidelity?

Nothing in the theory necessarily prevents finding law and obligation for such groups. Disputes about what characteristics are relevant for purposes of disparate treatment of citizens are moral disputes that may be incorrect but are not conceptually inconsistent with the argument developed here. Officials who accept the beliefs that underlie such moral judgments are acting in the interests of justice and fairness as they see it, and in that sense in the interest of all (including the disadvantaged group which, from the official viewpoint, is being treated according to its deserts). Thus, tempting though it may be to derive a substantive constraint of equality from a theory that requires acting in the interests of all, the constraint is empty, as formal equality always is. Even slaves are being treated "equally" if one accepts the underlying beliefs that justify their treatment.

This conclusion is reinforced by the paradigm of the lifeboat and the argument for respect developed in that context. A dissenter who disagrees about the direction in which to steer the boat nevertheless has a basis for prima facie obligation to those in charge if they at least give fair consideration to his views. But *fair* does not mean equally weighted. If the dissenter has no experience at sea and those in charge do, that is a good reason for giving less weight to his views. All that fairness requires is potential openness to dispute. So too, if the dissenter is selected to do the rowing, his prima facie obligation to comply arises from respect for the honest belief that his selection was fair. That belief might be based on the view that he is the strongest oarsman or that he is less capable of performing other tasks in the boat; even if these views are erroneous, obligation results because, given the assumptions of those in charge, the rower is being treated fairly—that is, like everyone else.

Similarly, in terms of the paradigm of the family, one can imagine one child consistently being given more onerous tasks or less freedom than another because the parents believe that that child requires more discipline for the same return in character development. Numerous such justifications for disparate treatment can be imagined, all consistent with the view that the parents are acting in a manner they perceive to be equally in the interests of all. Disfavored children and galley slaves, in short, still face prima facie obligations as long as their positions are the result of an honestly held theory of justice. One may protest the assumptions of the theory and attempt to prove its inapplicability on the facts while still recognizing and respecting the human concern that attaches to the erroneous moral outlook. Kant's claim that good will deserves moral respect, despite all of the difficulties it encounters as a complete guide to morality, at least has force as a guide to the basis for prima facie obligation and respect.

There is one exception to this conclusion where the difference in manner of treatment becomes so great as to become a difference in kind. When the treatment accorded the disadvantaged group is so severe as to destroy the minimum security that law must provide, obligation is also destroyed. (See the next section for a fuller discussion of this issue.) Thus a systematic policy of genocide creates no obligation for the victimized group, however sincere the official belief in the justice of the policy. So too, policies short of genocide that nevertheless undermine minimal security leave the affected individuals or groups without obligation. But deprivation of liberty alone—forced indenture unaccompanied by life-threatening abuse—is not inconsistent with the need for protection that underlies recognition of the value of coercive regimes. This proposition may encounter dissent, though more typically in brave speeches ("Give me liberty or give me death") than in actual examples of the human preference for death over restrictions on liberty. If liberty is so important that no intrusion is justified, then no state or coercive system is justified: the anarchist is correct, and the case for obligation in any legal system collapses. If however only certain kinds of intrusions on liberty are unjustified, leaving questions only of degree to be settled through ordinary normative dispute, the situation still falls within the bounds of law and obligation.

Reluctance to accept this conclusion—that even slaves may have prima facie obligations to obey—may fade when one considers how difficult it is to decide which patterns of domination do and do not constitute slavery. For some, workers in capitalist countries are slaves; for near-anarchists like Robert Nozick, the citizen in the welfare state may be a slave.[16] That the paradigm case of slavery in the classical sense no longer exists demonstrates the empirical difficulty of justifying that particular form of the institution; but attempts to reach this result conceptually through legal theory alone seem doomed to fail and only invite an inflation of rhetoric in ordinary normative disagreements about how to realize the ideal of equality.[17]

Motivational Integrity: Conscious and Unconscious Aims

The present theory implies that the dominant motive of official action must be the conscious pursuit of justice or the common good. The pursuit of self-interest or of the interests of particular selected groups destroys the basis for obligation among the excluded groups and individuals, unless some larger theory justifies this selectively favorable treatment either procedurally or substantively. Where the claim to justice is a conscious, deliberate lie, masking real motives of self-interest, no obligation results. Indeed, such cases are paradigms of what is meant by insincerity or bad faith. Uncovering the lie may, of course, be difficult. That difficulty is one reason why propaganda and the conscious lie are favorite devices of regimes desirous of the benefits of fidelity to law but empirically unable to defend a theory that would connect acknowledged self-interest with a larger collective good. Such regimes prefer to deny the self-interested motivation, pretending that they are justified by a theory that is empirically defensible and makes no reference to self-interest.

Though the conscious lie and deliberate deception are obvious examples of insincerity, they are not analogous to what might be called instances of self-deception. Theories of false consciousness, whether Marxist or Freudian in inspiration, often suggest discrepancies between real and apparent motivation in ways that might be thought to raise similar questions about the credibility of official decisions and justification. But the relevance of such theories for issues in either legal or political theory is problematic. There is, of course, an initial problem in explaining just what is meant by unconscious motivation and how the notion of self-deception can be rescued from apparent paradox.[18] The more careful proponents of theories that see unacknowledged self- or class interest behind the avowed pursuit of public interest hasten to add that the influence of these hidden factors is not sufficiently controllable to warrant charges of actual malice or ill will. Indeed even charges of negligence may be unwarranted if it is as difficult to avoid class bias and the economic and social determinants of value as such theories usually assume.

Once these concessions are made about the sense in which the motivations at work are unconscious, the charge of discrepancy between real and apparent motivation becomes irrelevant. The paradigms of obligation developed here are generated by respect for people trying to aim at the common good. The more one insists on the endemic and unavoidable nature of the obstacles in the way of this goal, the less relevant the observation becomes. Empathy and compassion for the plight we all face generate respect for people whose normative views seem to us to be wrong. Nothing in the basis for such respect is altered by positing uncontrollable causal influences on the ultimate value choice. Indeed if the normatively blind deserve respect, a fortiori, it would seem, so do those whose blindness extends to the causes of their disease as well.

The relevance of theories of false consciousness to political and moral theory is equally problematic. Under one interpretation, theories that see ruling groups as pursuing their own self-interest disguised as the public good resemble theories of egoism in ethics which see pure selfishness even in altruism. On that level the claim is either tautological and uninteresting or false, as is the parallel claim of psychological egoism in ethics. If the charge is meant to entail more than a truism, then it must be capable of falsification. One must be able to imagine rulers confronted with a discrepancy between their own narrow interests and the interests of those they rule and choosing in the face of that discrepancy to pursue the latter. Such a choice results in law and obligation. But if the discrepancy cannot be brought to the level of conscious choice, then any theory of law or morality that makes good will central to blame or assumes that 'ought' implies 'can' can only take conscious belief and apparent choice as the morally and legally relevant fact.

Between the conscious lie and the uncontrollable springs of conduct there lies, of course, a vast domain. It is here that borderline cases of sincerity are to be found and that the teachings of psychology and common sense become useful. People can hide from the implications of belief, refusing to confront distasteful consequences of a theory because they find equally distasteful the prospect of abandoning the theory. Strategies for avoiding the most unpleasant aspects of experience and logic are common, everyday parts of life. We may turn from the beggar because we have a theory that justifies our comfort in the face of his misery. More likely we turn because we have no such theory and know that comfort can be maintained only by looking past facts and logic. More likely still, we turn without thinking at all, having worn by habit a place in our moral theories just large enough to accommodate the most obvious unpleasantnesses. Justification then takes the form of exceptions which, like all first principles, cannot be further justified; consistency is the only check, and that is a weak check in the absence of an objective theory of the good.

Are these and similar techniques of avoidance compatible with the concept of sincere belief? Do officials who employ such techniques forfeit respect and obligation and ultimately the claim to be administering law? The answer to these questions depends largely on the particular facts of particular cases. How serious are the facts they ignore? How fatal to the legitimating theory? Are there other explanations for avoidance (the pain of looking, knowing one can do nothing) that might still be consistent with good will and the effort to rule justly? As a general matter one answers these questions the same way one responds to the problem of false consciousness: the more one views these avoidance techniques as inevitable under the circumstances or as persistent aspects of the human condition, the less basis there is for loss of respect. It is the human struggle for good, not the efforts of imaginable psychological supermen, that generates in turn the human responses of empathy, compassion, understanding, respect.

As a practical matter the problem of whether claims of justice are sufficiently disingenuous to destroy the basis for obligation may not be a serious one. Where there is little conventional doubt about the immorality of certain practices—torture, slavery, wholesale denial of human rights to selected groups—one is not likely to conclude that regimes where such practices occur are best characterized as victims of their own self-deception. Either the case is one of deception pure and simple (political prisoners are tortured but officials' knowingly deny the fact) or the cases are morally more complicated than one supposed (apartheid is sincerely thought to be justified), at most a case of moral blindness, not self-deception. But the difficulty of uncovering degrees of deception and of distinguishing self-deception from mere moral blindness provides an unexpected possibility for deriving at least one important substantive right, apart from security, from the concept of law. To see how that might be done, let us first apply the present theory to another set of jurisprudential puzzles: the concept of rights in general and of natural rights in particular.

THE CONCEPT OF RIGHTS

The above discussion makes clear that one can understand and apply the concept of law as a general matter without first evaluating the official arguments used to justify a society's basic rules. Because it is good faith belief in these arguments rather than their correctness in fact that matters to legal theory, substantive appraisal may be left largely to other studies. With that much of the positivist's program I am in accord. The preceding discussion also suggests, however, a possible strategy for drawing conclusions about the content of legal systems and the nature of legal reasoning without engaging in direct evaluation. The strategy is to see whether certain kinds of rules or decision procedures can be characterized a priori as so implausible as to rule out the possibility of any normative defense in their behalf.

It may seem that this particular strategy is tantamount to engaging in substantive evaluation. Thus, if we condemn as implausible decision procedures that invoke magic or astrology, we simply evidence our own dissent from the beliefs that underlie such systems. Even if we prove that such theories could never plausibly be invoked to justify rules in most modern societies, such proof seems at best only a contingent attack on the possibility of an official claim that the system is justifiable and hence legal. This sort of attack is not without possibilities. The more we are able to show that an official theory of justification relies on premises so thoroughly discredited and unaccepted by most people, the harder it will be to suggest that the official defense is in good faith. But the approach remains primarily negative and empirical. It does not tell us what kinds of rules must be accepted if obligation is to result but at most indicates only that some justifications will not do. Moreover, the reason these justifications will not do is that we doubt the sincerity of the belief—and about that we could be wrong.

In contrast to this empirical approach in making a priori assessments of claims of acceptability is a conceptual approach, one that attempts to show that certain kinds of justifications—even if sincerely held—are inconsistent with the prerequisites for obligation developed here.

Preexisting Rights

This strategy can be illustrated by applying it to one aspect of the dispute described in a previous section: to what extent are courts necessarily involved in determining preexisting rights? I noted earlier that Dworkin's rights thesis, which claims that courts always resolve disputes by reference to such rights, is at best a normative and descriptive thesis. It is a claim about what courts should do and about what they in fact do in one particular society. Although Dworkin insists that he intends the claim to be a conceptual one as well, he does not mount a conceptual defense; that is, he does not show why a system that allows or requires judges to decide in some other way would no longer be a legal system.[19] I have suggested, in contrast, that a legal system need not recognize litigants as possessing preexisting rights and might even deliberately choose to instruct institutions to settle all disputes by legislating anew in each case. As long as such procedures can plausibly be defended, I have said, the consequences for obligation and hence for law are the same. The critical question, then, in choosing between these views is whether one can mount a conceptual attack on the attempt to defend a decision procedure that differs from that described by the rights thesis.

Let us start with an extreme example suggested earlier, by assuming that officials accept rules that require all disputes brought before a court to be settled by the flip of a coin. Assume further that the rules do not specify which disputes must be brought to court. Self-help remains permissible, though courts are ready to flip coins in any case submitted by any litigant. It is easy enough to imagine empirical attacks on the justifiability of such a system. The unpredictability of the legal decision will make life an extremely chancy affair. The value of life, liberty, and property will have to be discounted by the 50 percent chance that any stranger may be awarded them in a dispute. Indeed, descriptions of such a system will not differ much from standard descriptions of the state of nature. One may imagine protective associations coming into existence to provide the security that the state's decision procedure lacks.[20] But even these devices would have to prevent dissidents from taking their complaints to courts which, by hypothesis, would not be concerned about the preexisting terms of the pact or association. Given these and other clearly undesirable consequences, it is empirically unlikely that the officials of any society would actually embrace such a system, much less be able to proclaim its merits.

Empirical possibilities aside, the system is vulnerable to conceptual attack as well. Any citizen confronting the question of the obligation to obey the directives that emerge from the judicial process will discover that a crucial premise is missing in the argument for obligation: this system does not provide the minimal security and order that is presupposed by the premise that legal systems in general are better than no law at all, a premise that is essential to the obligation to obey the laws of a particular legal system. The conclusion that there is no obligation in such a situation parallels the conclusion reached in connection with a similar situation discussed at the end of Chapter III, where I concluded that isolated gunmen, though they may honestly believe in the justice of their demands, do not thereby create prima facie obligations to obey. That is because the citizens' belief in the value of legal systems in general is likely to rest at the very least on the desirability of order, provided by a single, supreme sovereign. Temporary sovereigns such as muggers do not implicate that basic value; but neither do permanent supreme sovereigns who exercise power so randomly and unpredictably that no appreciable trace of order or security remains. Such a system might be called Anarchist's Delight, differing from the war of all against all that Hobbes imagined only by the introduction of an artificial element of repeated and chance redistribution of goods under "state" coercion, with the consequence that even personal strength is made an unreliable ally in the battle. Indeed, this would not even be a case of choosing between the tyranny of the strong and of the state but a case of complete chaos.

This example illustrates how one might derive minimum conditions that any theory of justification must satisfy in meeting the requirements for a legal system. The theory must not only be capable of belief in fact (the empirical condition, which at best places culturally contingent constraints on what can be sincerely believed). The theory must also be consistent with the minimal basis for recognizing the value of legal systems in general. Anarchist's Delight fails to obligate not because it is a coercive system but because it is no system at all.

Of course the example is an extreme one. Let us modify the system slightly by denying citizens the right to take goods that are in the possession of others until a decision by lot has been reached. That is to say, let us assume that the state comes into being and places an immediate moratorium on the war of all against all by threatening sanctions against those who engage in self-help to settle disputes rather than seeking an official decision by lottery. Is the system now immune from conceptual attack? Can one imagine officials proffering (and believing in) a justification for the system that is not inconsistent with the minimal value of security that a coercive regime provides? At first glance, the answer seems to be yes. There is now at least that minimal justification of the state that Hobbes stressed: any orderly decision, however arbitrary, is better than none. But confidence in that answer turns to doubt when one asks what happens after disputed goods have been distributed by lot. May B, who has lost the toss to A, take the matter back to court and seek another toss of the coin? If so, then nothing is ever settled. Conflict and self-help are controlled, but expectations are still subject to the uncertainty of outlasting one's disputant in a never-ending dice game. If the first system is Anarchist's Delight, this is Gambler's Delight.

Still, to condemn this system as conceptually inconsistent with the premises that lead to obligation seems to require more discussion about the minimal value of a coercive system than I have yet provided. Gambler's Delight at least imposes some order through the control of private violence, whereas Anarchist's Delight does not even do that. Perhaps one could imagine this control of personal violence being so important that it would lead some people to view systems that did no more than this as better in general than anarchy. But that is likely to be a minority view. The value of order is largely instrumental; it makes possible the pursuit of private interests and the formation of expectations without constant fear of random deprivation. Yet random deprivation is precisely what occurs in Gambler's Delight, even though it is by "orderly" court mandate rather than by private violence. Thus even one who thinks that an increase in personal security is enough to make a system better than nothing should, on reflection, reject Gambler's Delight; for if all liberty and property, including what is necessary for subsistence, are continually up for grabs, personal security is just as gravely threatened as in the anarchist's world—indeed more so because one does not even have self-help or mutual protective associations to turn to.

By this process one arrives at the only conclusion that is left: once a

dispute is settled by lot, the winner must be seen as having an entitlement, a preexisting right that controls to some extent any future decision by the court involving the same dispute at least between the same
parties. Preexisting rights in the sense of some principle of *res judicata*
can be seen as an essential feature of a legal system, alterable at will only
at the cost of no longer obligating. But though A is now protected in his
entitlement against relottery by B, the resulting increase in security is
negligible if C, D, and the rest of the world may now take their
chance—particularly since the entitlement in issue is forever lost once
the toss is lost. That being the case, a similar process of reasoning leads
to the conclusion that some form of preexisting rights *in rem*—against
the world—must emerge in any legal system; that is, instructions to the
contrary cannot be issued to courts without destroying the basis for the
obligation to obey.

There is then a conceptual connection between the notion of some
preexisting rights which courts cannot ignore and the concept of law.
But the connection so far is limited in these ways:

1. Nothing I have said suggests that citizens have preexisting rights
prior to the court's initial decision. Once distributed, entitlements arise
and must be protected—just as in the case of legislation. But one could
not mount a conceptual attack on an initial decision to distribute all
goods by lot, for example, or to abolish all private ownership of goods.
In the first place, the empirical likelihood that people might hold views
justifying such a distribution is quite plausible: one has only to stress
the arbitrariness of the lottery that precedes the state's, namely the ge-
netic lottery and the accident of birth, fortune, and inheritance. Second,
any attempt to show a conceptual inconsistency between this justification and the grounds for obligation must fail, for though expectations
may be upset in a one-time redistribution by lot, the result is not a system permeated with insecurity. One kind of order is simply substituted
for another. Arguments about the fairness of the redistribution principle
may occur, but that still leaves us squarely within a legal system.

2. Nothing in this account suggests that courts or legislatures cannot
occasionally overrule past decisions and thus take back or redistribute
from time to time entitlements previously granted. It is only the systematic ignoring of precedent and previous entitlements that causes the collapse into chaos that is inconsistent with the concept of law. Where
expectations are upset only occasionally and haphazardly, the value of
security may still largely be preserved. (It is still necessary, of course, to
come forward with some theory that justifies these occasional upsets,
but that again presents at most an empirical, not a conceptual problem.)

3. It should be clear that no general conceptual constraint prevents a

court from acting on the basis of what Dworkin calls policy as opposed to principle.[21] It is conceivable that courts could be instructed explicitly to decide each case in a way most likely to advance collective goals, regardless of the impact on individual rights or entitlements. Empirically, it is again easy to imagine that officials might in good faith believe in a theory of justification that requires such a total subjection of the individual to the collective good. Indeed descriptions of societies organized around such a theory fill the pages of utopian literature and find historical flesh in the more extreme examples of socialist experiments. Moreover, as a conceptual matter, the resulting system differs significantly from either Anarchist's or Gambler's Delight. These systems also fail to recognize individual rights or entitlements, with the consequence of destroying the minimum value of security necessary for obligation. But in contrast to these systems, collective systems potentially offer a great deal of security for the individual. Instead of being subject to constant risk of loss through chance, property is now held subject to the calculation that the collective interest will be furthered by redistribution. That calculation in the name of collective goals is likely to be at least somewhat predictable. Indeed it is notoriously easy to justify on collective grounds even the seemingly paradoxical decision to make all property private. There is, in short, no a priori reason to think that collective systems that are justified entirely by reference to policy or collective goals will have any adverse effect on individual security.

Natural Rights

The conclusion reached above is a limited one. Courts must justify their decisions, but the only decision procedures this requirement rules out in advance are those that leave the individual essentially no better off than he would be without a legal system. The only preexisting right that courts must respect is the right to that minimum of security that underlies the judgment that any legal system is better than none.

In some respects this conclusion is a familiar one. Hart too, for example, concluded that legal systems must provide minimum protection for life, liberty, and property.[22] But in Hart's case the conclusion is contingent: without such protection no system is likely to remain viable for long. In the present case the conclusion is conceptual: without such protection no system, even assuming viability, could yield obligation. Moreover, I have indicated that the requirement applies as much to the state's duty to protect citizens from each other as from the state itself. Indeed, depending on the theory of justification, a state has considerable room to take entitlements from citizens (where private individuals might not) in the name of a greater collective good. As long as such takings do not occur so frequently and unpredictably as to undermine the general sense of security, prima facie obligation remains.

The question of whether one can derive substantive rights against the state beyond this Hobbesian right to minimum security is a question that current legal theory can only answer in the negative. The positivist must so answer because, as we have seen, he cannot distinguish legal from coercive regimes. Thus the only content he can derive is the minimum content implied by any system: there must be a minimum of order if there is to be a system instead of chaos. The nonpositivist, lacking a conceptual account of the connection between the normative practices he observes and the concept of law, cannot anchor the former in the latter except by fiat in the fashion of the natural law slogan. In that case the content is derived from moral theory, not legal theory. The argument of the present study, in contrast, offers a new possibility for finding rights against the state—natural rights, as I shall call them—beyond what is implied by the Hobbesian minimum.

Structure. If legal theory has become increasingly sterile, natural rights theory has become increasingly ambiguous. Part of the ambiguity results from the fact that legal theory continues to discuss natural rights even while announcing that all such discussion should be relegated to that other discipline, moral or political philosophy. Bentham, in his famous phrase about "nonsense on stilts," was at least consistent in this respect. Hart, in contrast, devotes a portion of his theory of law to a discussion of the minimum content of natural law and natural right. It turns out, as we have just seen, that the minimum content is only security, and even that is an observation not about morality but about the connection between the realities of human nature and the possibility of making any coercive system work. I have provided an additional conceptual support for this essentially Hobbesian insight: coercive systems do not obligate if they do not provide a measurable advance in security over the state of nature. There is nothing to prevent our calling this a natural right; but it is clear that it is less than the ringing affirmation of human dignity which that term is usually meant to convey. It is more a begrudging concession that, whatever else is important and valued in life, life must first be secured and is thus in that sense fundamental. Even the above conceptual grounding of this right is derived as much from the amoral concept of system as from the moral concept of obligation.

Natural rights theory is also ambiguous because, even as a moral theory about human rights, it is unclear what makes these rights natural. Historically the term was probably meant to distinguish those moral theories that base their conclusions on observations about human nature. One connects ethical principles about the good life with psychological and empirical propositions about the actual life of man. It is hard to see today, however, how this definition of a natural rights theory eliminates from the category any plausible moral theory. Utilitarians and Kantians have as much reason as any natural law theorist to think that their propositions about duty and reason and happiness are grounded in plausible assumptions about human nature. Natural rights theory, in short, seems to be just another name for moral theory, which may explain the tendency to use the terms *natural rights, human rights,* and *moral rights* somewhat interchangeably.[23]

One may also think of natural rights as distinctive in a third sense that assigns them to a particular subset of all moral rights: namely, those against the state. Locke, for example, is thought to have defended a theory of private property based on natural rights that precede and take priority over the state's interest. But again it should be clear that nothing essentially distinguishes such an argument from any moral argument that purports to establish individual liberties that the state must respect. All such theories are normative arguments about the legitimacy and limits of state power. If a state invades the area of individual interest described as protected by the moral theory, its action is immoral according to that theory; but unless we equate law and morals in discredited natural law fashion, the state's actions are still legal. In short, there is nothing in the concept of natural rights construed as a theory of rights against the state to distinguish arguments about such rights from ordinary normative debate about the legitimacy of law.

This last conclusion points to a final interpretation of what might be meant by natural rights; such rights, we might say, are rights against the state which can be invaded or ignored only at the cost of losing the title of law. In the terms of this study, directives that ignore or invade natural rights—if there are any—are directives that cannot impose even prima facie obligation. Thus the concept of natural rights is connected with legal theory in a way that makes the latter relevant to the discussion and at the same time distinguishes the rights at issue from the moral rights that any normative theory might entail.

The principles of natural justice. Are there any rights that fit the above description? So far I have based my attempts to answer this question on only half of the theory of this study. I have focused on the value of law in general as a prerequisite to obligation and then pursued the implications of that prerequisite for the content of legal systems. Because the argument for the value of law is largely Hobbesian, it is no surprise that the minimum content derived from this half of the theory is also Hobbesian. But there is a second requirement for obligation in the theory, and that is the necessity for good faith belief by officials in the justice of the system they administer. This requirement opens up a similar possibility for empirical and conceptual conclusions about the content of legal systems.

We have seen that to require belief in justice does not by itself require much in the way of content. At best the requirement yields only a right to formal equality which cannot, without further substantive criteria, distinguish among the wide variety of normative judgments that can be invoked to justify disparate treatment. We have also seen, however, that the critical factor in applying the present theory is the ability to distinguish sincerely held beliefs from insincere beliefs. I have been willing, for example, to assume that even the most odious moral views may nevertheless be held by men of good will, thus resulting in obligation. But at the same time I have insisted that the relationship between ruler and ruled must be reciprocal, resulting in mutual respect, as if officials must engage in something more than unthinking invocation of the prevailing theory of justification. The more the case for obligation rests on respect for the fact that people may have divergent moral views, the more critical becomes the demonstration of sincerity: nothing erodes respect as quickly as dissembling and lip service. It is this problem of demonstrating not that beliefs are right but that they are sincerely held that makes it possible to derive the only rights, other than security and formal equality, that deserve the name "natural" from the perspective of legal theory.

The process for deriving such rights can be illustrated by considering one set of substantive constraints thought to be found wherever there is law. Referred to as "principles of 'Natural Justice,' "[24] these constraints require rules to be applied consistently and impartially, usually by an objective or disinterested judge. It would not be difficult to defend such requirements as a matter of moral philosophy. To see how they might also be derived from the concept of law itself, one need only consider the tension that results if one tries to ignore these constraints while still claiming that the rules are being administered in the interests of all.

People can change their minds and believe tomorrow in theories of justification that yield very different outcomes from yesterday's theory. But constant vacillation on fundamental moral principles is sufficiently unusual in stable societies to make one suspect, where it occurs, that the motivating impulse is one not of securing justice for all but of serving the shifting interests of a particular group. Thus consistency in deciding cases becomes an important check on the sincerity of the claim of justice. So too it is possible for one to judge disinterestedly in his own case.

But the increased likelihood of bias, particularly where a disinterested judge could have been secured, heightens the suspicion that the claim of justice only masks self-interest. Thus impartiality and objectivity are also important checks on the sincerity of proffered justifications.

These arguments for the principles of natural justice are, it must be conceded, only empirical. They are not logically entailed by the concept of sincerity because it is not logically impossible for one to be sincere but erratic in one's views of justice, or to be sincere about ignoring an obvious conflict of interest when judging in one's own case. But the process just illustrated, and the suspicion created when one does ignore the principles of natural justice, point to another natural right that is conceptually linked to law. That right is sufficiently important and different in substance from those discussed so far to justify a separate and somewhat lengthier treatment.

THE RIGHT TO DISCOURSE

All of the preceding attempts to extract substantive moral rights from the requirement of sincere belief in justice confront a basic problem: respect for good will, on which the theory of obligation is based, overlooks honest mistakes—in value judgments as well as in judgments of fact. But how does one know that a mistake is honest, that a belief is sincere? I have continually referred to one basic ingredient in all of the imagined confrontations with effective power: the fact that those in charge are prepared to respond to normative challenge with normative justification of their coercive orders. The implication is that here at least is one right that cannot be ignored if the basis for mutual respect that underlies law and obligation is to be maintained. Dissenting individuals must be assured of a right to discourse, a right to insist on evidence of the bona fides of belief in the only form in which sincerity can be tested: communication, dialogue, exchange, debate. In the pages that follow I shall develop the argument for recognizing such a right, then define somewhat more precisely its scope and content.

Derivation

Several of the factors that point toward a natural right of discourse are implicit in the preceding discussion of the importance of good faith and the difficulty of determining when it exists. First, people can believe almost anything; that makes it difficult to rule out a priori any particular theory of justification. It also makes the sincerity of a belief critical in calling forth respect for the effort, however wrongheaded it seems to be. But sincerity in this context can only mean that the exercise of power reflects a basic commitment to a theory of justice rather than an unthinking response to inherited tradition or to the dictates of self-interest. In short, the very inability to rule out substantive theories means that sincerity as the critical test for obligation cannot be shown simply by invoking any theory that happens ex post facto to rationalize the result. It means revealing, to the extent one can, the process of reflective judgment and value formation that makes an abstract theory into a personally held world view. It means responding to the dissident on the level of normative debate rather than merely saying, "That's just the way it is."

Second, good faith places at least contingent restraints on claims of justice, making it difficult to avoid filtering such claims through procedures designed to produce consistency, impartiality, and objectivity. One could ignore these procedures and still be sincere, but it is highly suspicious to keep changing one's mind or to make allegedly disinterested choices in the face of obvious self-interest—so suspicious that explanation seems called for if the assumption of good faith is to be maintained. But explanation is another form of discourse. Thus, a right of discourse is more than contingent: it is either a by-product of applying and following the principles of natural justice or, where those principles are not followed, it is a prerequisite of continued respect that one give some justification for not doing so. The more unbelievable or implausible the empirical basis for thinking action is sincere, the more good faith requires explanation.

Third, it is common for people to confuse self-interest with public interest and conceal from themselves the facts and implications that would require honest resolution of that conflict. Though one must not brand all such techniques of avoidance as instances of insincerity, it is easy to see that respect in such cases often depends on the willingness to confront and deal with apparent discrepancies between what is practiced and what is preached. This fact too supports the case for recognizing a minimum right of discourse as the only check on self-deception.

A second set of arguments for a right of discourse can be constructed by considering the basis for respect revealed intuitively in the paradigms of obligation in Chapter III. The child confronted with the demands of the parent develops respect for the latter's wishes despite substantive disagreement because of two factors: recognition of the value of family, and the perception that the parent is honestly attempting to act in the child's best interests. Increasing maturity erodes both factors. The value of continued family shelter and protection diminishes as the child grows increasingly self-sufficient until the point is reached when the child makes in essence the parallel decision to the anarchist's: family, in the sense of a coercive social order, is no longer better than the alternative of complete autonomy. Before this point is reached, however, the child's growing intelligence and independent values will considerably strain the second requirement for respect: the perception that the parent is acting in the child's interests. Strain results first because of the child's recurring confidence that he is so obviously right on the merits that the parent's adamancy must be disingenuous—a case of face saving in not admitting that the child is right. Second, even if the child is wrong, or the parent's judgment is conceded to be in good faith, the justification for imposing the parent's will on the child weakens with maturity—partly because one sometimes learns best from one's own mistakes, partly because it becomes less clear who is to decide what counts as a mistake. In short, the case for paternalism as a justification weakens long before the value of the family as a coercive order expires. Together these increasing obstacles to justifying parental authority lead to a correlative increase in the child's insistence on discourse and explanation as a basis for continued respect.

Evidence for these observations may be found in a number of commonplace experiences. Few parents who have raised children will continue to doubt what they may have doubted when very young themselves: namely, the legitimacy of the response, "You'll understand when you're older." Most parents dealing with older children can testify that few responses are better guaranteed to outrage.

As a paradigm for obligation and respect in human society, the analogy with the family requires some tinkering but still supports the conclusion that a right of discourse is a prerequisite for respect. First, there is no reason to think that the perceived value of the coercive social order declines in proportion to age and maturity; if anything the opposite is true. Thus, whereas the child may eventually escape obligation by becoming an adult, the citizen does not. As a result, the second test for obligation—the sincerity of the attempt to rule in the other's best interests—becomes once again the critical test for the citizen even more so than for the child.

Second, with rare exceptions, the justification for particular laws is not paternalistic. More likely justification appeals directly to the good or to various forms of consent or to procedural devices supposed to ensure fairness. Thus the explanation that cuts off discourse in the case of the child on the grounds of assumed incapacity to understand is not available in human society: the citizen whose obligation is in issue is an adult. Paternalistic legislation can be defended and will generate respect and obligation if such defense is based on the merits of the case for paternalistic treatment: what is excluded is the refusal to listen to objections on the ground that those voicing them are not fully competent and cannot understand.

There is a problem in this last conclusion similar to the problem confronted in a previous chapter in considering possible grounds for obligation to the "enlightened" terrorist or gunman. By stressing perceived good will as the basis for respect, it is possible to argue that even the gunman who sincerely believes his cause is in his victim's interest presents his victim with a prima facie obligation to obey. I rejected that conclusion because it left no room for the concept of autonomy. The citizen in society at least shares a basic normative value with the officials he confronts. That shared commitment provides a basis for respect in the individual's recognition that if he were in charge he too could do no other than seek the common good according to his own lights. Empathy for the difficulty in securing value agreement, respect for the sincerity of the effort of those in charge, and hope that the respect, being mutual, will lead to one's own views eventually being acknowledged—all these factors play a role in the argument for obligation.

Similarly, in the case of groups sincerely treated as incapable of discourse, one might suggest that the sincerity of the belief still justifies respect and obligation, pending enlightenment. But the last two words give us the rebuttal: the most obvious means of enlightenment, available in the normal case of the dissident who is fairly heard but found unpersuasive, by hypothesis does not exist. One may respect the good will of those who treat one as incapacitated; but again, not every argument for respect in the ordinary sense of the term can be equated with an argument for prima facie obligation. What is missing is the mutuality of respect that autonomy demands if obligation is to result. The shared commitment to the value of a coercive order will of course remain; in that sense the unheeded citizen differs from the gunman's victim. But the demands of autonomy are felt in both parts of the test for obligation. The victim may concede that the terrorist is sincere and that he (the victim) is respected even as he is ordered about; yet the victim escapes obligation because he does not concede the value of erratic, nonmonopolistic exercises of force. The citizen, in contrast, may be fully persuaded of the value of monopolized coercion in general, exemplified in the official regime he confronts; yet he escapes obligation if the regime treats him as not worth heeding in arguments about the particular form society should take. When that happens, autonomy responds in kind: if I am not worth heeding then neither are the laws of society in the prima facie sense (just because they are the laws of the society; of course both the victim and the ignored citizen may have other reasons for obeying).

One final case needs to be considered. I have discussed the case of societies that attempt to skirt the right to discourse by claiming citizen incompetence or incapacity and concluded that even if that claim is made in good faith, it is inconsistent with the requirement of mutual respect that leads to obligation.[25] What though of the society that denies discourse on ideological grounds—not because citizens or groups are deemed incompetent but because discourse is too effective, too dangerous, too likely to detract from the official, sincerely held theory of justification? Is there still a case to be made for respect and obligation if such views about the dangers of discourse are held in good faith?

One's initial response might be to view this case as indistinguishable from the previous one. However honest the view that discourse is dangerous, the case for mutual respect and obligation is built in part on the hope that normative errors can be corrected through challenge and response. With that possibility denied, one of the olive branches that can be held out to insulted autonomy is missing. But the two cases also differ in important respects. Discourse is now denied on substantive grounds, not on grounds that impeach equality or suggest citizen inferiority. If respect and obligation derive from acknowledging that people of good will can disagree about values, why should the case collapse just because the disagreement is about the value of speech or discourse itself? Certainly it is easier to defend as empirically plausible the belief that speech is dangerous than some of the other beliefs I have imagined as capable of leading to obligation if sincerely held.

One might try to avoid resolving these competing arguments by suggesting that discourse must be available at least with respect to the value of discourse itself. Thus a state could prevent discourse about most aspects of its underlying theory of justification except that aspect which purports to justify the prevention of discourse. As to that, challenge and response must occur; the justification for denying discourse in other substantive areas must be open and continuous.

There is much to be said for the view that this modification is sufficient to restore the case for obligation. Unlike the case where all discourse is resisted, there is now at least some room to persuade officials of the error of their views about the dangers of discourse; if successful in that effort, one can then debate the merits of the rest of the prevailing theory of justification. Though one admittedly introduces an additional step along the road to potential normative consensus through discourse, that road is at least still theoretically open. When that possibility is coupled with the previously noted fact that disagreement here is substantive, rather than the result of implied disrespect, it is no longer easy to see why one should reach different conclusions about the basis for obligation. In practice, however, this theoretical defense of a truncated right to discourse may collapse, for it is difficult to see how one can debate the value of debate without concrete examples—without discussing various theories of justification, including that of the state in question—in order to show how those theories might be improved through discourse. To be fully open to argument about the value of discourse, in short, may require permitting discourse about things besides discourse.

There still remains the case of complete prevention of discourse. Although it may in theory be sufficient for obligation to allow debate, at least about the value of debate, is it necessary? That question may now be somewhat easier to answer. A state that prevents all discourse must still justify that policy, even though it does not brook challenge. I have mentioned the most common justifications for restricting debate—justifications that seem to follow from what might be called positions of extreme or over-sincerity. This situation occurs when official commitment to the underlying values is so strong or the received state position is so clearly the "true" position that dissent or challenge is prevented precisely because it distracts from received truth or because it annoys or enrages believers. These justifications impugn the assumption of mutual respect based on tolerance for value disagreement. That is to say, whereas dissenters are urged to consider how difficult consensus is and to tolerate official normative error, in such a regime as this a like tolerance for the normative error of dissenters does not exist. Moreover, if we try to imagine what possible justification can be given for not allowing debate at least about the value of debate itself, we are left with the strong implication that the only justification resembles the parent's response that the child cannot understand and thus explanation is useless. Combining this implication with the one-sided expression of tolerance seems enough to undercut the basis for mutual respect and hence obligation.

This conclusion can be reinforced by considering what a state that prohibits all discourse must be like. Historical examples of religious or quasi-religious states that brook no dissension from doctrine are common enough to make empirically plausible the view that debate and open challenge to doctrine are evils not to be tolerated. Such views, however, are not likely to be defended or justified by claiming that debate is inherently evil. That is, debate is perceived only as instrumentally related to more basic values rather than as an inherent value itself. Where this is the case, a state that believes that the instrument can only have pernicious effects on the inherent values being debated should have no reason to discourage debate about debate: not being an inherent value, the instrument only destroys itself and proves the state's view.

But debate can be viewed as intrinsically good, or conversely as intrinsically bad. Thus it can be part of doctrine to disallow all dissent, including dissent about the value of debate. But the image of the state that results is one of total social conformity; it is the organic political body par excellence, in which individuality as to ideas as well as conduct is totally suppressed. What is this but another way of describing authority in a way that leaves no room for individual autonomy? However sincere the official belief in such doctrine, the equally sincere dissenting belief has no outlet at all. Persons in such regimes, even though they concede the value of law in general, have no prima facie obligations.

Content

Thus one may derive from legal theory a positive right, beyond security and formal equality—a right that is natural in the only sense in which that term has meaning in legal theory. States that do not recognize that right do not impose obligation and in that sense remain coercive rather than legal systems. But the enthusiasm with which one uses this conclusion to label regimes as legal or not must be tempered by a note of caution concerning the scope and content of the right. I have called it a right of discourse in part to avoid the inference that there is built into legal theory the full-blown liberal theory of rights to free speech and press to which it bears an obvious resemblance. Indeed some justifications for freedom of speech and press are identical to those I have explored for the right of discourse. It is important, however, to note how the latter right differs from rights urged as essential to a particular legal order such as a liberal democracy.

One difference is already clear. I have suggested that regimes do not become coercive even though debate is prevented over a wide range of substantive matters—indeed over the entire range of matters encompassed by the underlying theory of justification—as long as they do this while still allowing meaningful debate about the justification for the preclusion of debate. That is a result inconsistent with the application of free speech theory in liberal democracies. Thus the scope of protection provided by legal theory is quite small in comparison to what might be thought of as required by a complete moral or political theory.

The content of the right even in the area where it does apply also differs from the content of most free speech theories because of the difference in the reasons that underlie recognition of the natural right. The natural right, as opposed to the right derived from liberal political theory, is a consequence of the requirement of sincere official belief in justice. The concept of sincerity as I have developed it has two components: honest belief in fact and respect for the possibility of dissent. Admittedly, to suggest that both of these are components of sincerity does some violence to ordinary language, which is usually content to find sincerity in honest belief alone. That is why difficulties arose in my consideration of the limiting case of sincere intolerance. One is tempted to ask which is the more important ingredient in the argument for obligation: sincerity or mutual tolerance? If we keep in mind the original argument for obligation and recall that 'sincerity' is shorthand for 'good faith', we should have little trouble seeing that the answer is that both are important. Discourse is necessary to ensure that belief is honest, particularly in light of the ease with which self-deception is possible. But discourse is also necessary because the reason that honest belief deserves respect stems from the individual's recognition of and tolerance for value disagreement; if that recognition and tolerance is not mutual, obligation again does not result.

The consequence of this rehearsal of the grounds for the natural right of discourse is the exclusion of a great many of the values and theories of justification to be found in free speech theory in general. In particular, discourse is not required as a means of enhancing individual personality. Nor is it required as a means of ensuring individual participation in the governing process. Moreover, even the "marketplace of ideas" metaphor, which stresses the relationship between diversity of views and truth, plays a truncated role in informing the content of the right of discourse in legal theory. Although I placed some emphasis on the marketplace idea in holding out hope for a dissenter's ultimate vindication, I do so less as a means of sifting for truth than as a means of soothing wounded autonomy. It is peace and mutual respect, not truth per se, that the marketplace metaphor serves in the present theory, even though it may serve the former only because individuals believe it serves the latter.

To see clearly just how these differences in theory yield differences in content, let us consider a few illustrative applications. First, the natural right of discourse does not require that every individual be able to express views about the basic theory of justification underlying the legal order. It is enough that the challenge an individual might mount is already adequately represented by someone else. This means that in most cases the obvious alternatives to prevailing fundamental ideologies— socialism, democracy, monarchy, aristocracy—have already been implicitly confronted in the state's defense and justification of its basic structure. The right to discourse is not a personal right to proselytize in an attempt to gain control by revolution or personal charisma; it is a right only to ensure that the other side of the normative issue has been fairly considered by officials in an attempt to gain control through the rational influence of ideas. In contrast, free speech theories that stress personal development or that stress marketplace and truth above all else presumably would not tolerate such truncated rights.

Second, the right to discourse has little to do with the literary, artistic, and commercial aspects of speech that constitute a significant branch of free speech theory in some liberal democracies. The core value of the natural right aims at the justification of the basic political structure, which may or may not recognize the various forms of personal expression found in liberal democracies. In some respects the basic value that informs the content of the natural right resembles what one scholar of First Amendment theory in the United States calls the "checking value": a guard against and means of exposing governmental abuse or misconduct.[26] Indeed, one might find the sharpest contrast between the right of discourse, on the one hand, and free speech rights, on the other, in the general idea that the former gives citizens the right to have the state speak, whereas the latter gives citizens the right to speak themselves. This distinction, however, must not be pressed too far. The state's "duty to speak" is in fact a duty to respond to normative challenge about the use of force and thus implies that something more than monologue is required.

Third, as the last observation suggests, the word 'discourse' cannot be taken literally. To require more than monologue is not to require full and open dialogue. Just as no individual has a right to try his hand at personal persuasion of officials or other citizens, neither does he have a right to demand that any particular official or judicial decision be prefaced by a full discussion of what justice demands. We have already seen that fundamental theories of justification are found largely in the implicit premises of easy judicial decisions; explicit wrestling with normative argument occurs only in hard cases. Moreover, even this much elaboration and justification is only one way of maintaining the sense of discourse, for it is the sense that is important, rather than direct official response to every debater's point raised in a citizen's dissenting brief. What is important is the credibility of the official posture that society is open to new values and plausible challenges to accepted visions as they emerge. Thus there are empirical checks on the individual's right to demand discourse, just as there are empirical checks on the range of plausible official theories of justification within a given culture. The more outlandish the individual's normative disagreement as measured by conventional views, the less need there will be for direct official response. Put another way, the more outlandish the normative objection, the more likely that the response will be found implicitly in the basic theory of justification without the need for official reiteration. Convention and tradition, in short, will always play a strong role in justification, either because tradition itself is sometimes a reason for continuing a practice or because convention creates a heavy presumption that a dissenter must overcome in explaining why everyone else is wrong and only he is right. (The mistake of much of legal and moral theory is to equate this obvious role played by convention in the justification of norms with the very idea of a norm itself.)

Lest it seem that I have now taken back all that seemed promising in the search for natural rights, let us recall that it is legal not moral theory we are pursuing. The right to discourse is a minimal right, just as is the right to security and equality, insofar as either can be derived from the concept of law itself. Such results are consequences of framing the present study at all points to seek minima: the minimal basis for respect, for prima facie obligation, for distinguishing law from coercion. A full political or moral theory would undoubtedly add a good deal in the way of flesh to these bones. Even so, it is a matter of some importance to know that whatever rights are recognized in the political theory of a particular society, the structure described here must form the core of those rights if the regime is to obligate as well as coerce.

DEATH AND TRANSFIGURATION

When legal theorists turn to the pathology of legal systems,[27] the problems they discuss and the solutions they find to those problems are predictable consequences of the preoccupation with criteria for validity. The continued existence of legal systems, we are told, depends on two factors: continuity in the basic rules that are officially accepted, and effective overall enforcement or general obedience. The first factor enables us to tell whether a regime that is effective over a continuous period is the same legal system throughout its history. Thus one may say that the English legal system has persisted for centuries; but certain former colonies of England have become new legal systems by virtue of unchallenged acceptance of a new ultimate source of basic rules, even though there has been no discontinuity in the handing over of the coercive reins. The second ingredient ensures that the content of the legal system, as identified by the basic rules, corresponds in fact to a real entity: a functioning, effective system. Thus the legal system in the Soviet Union today is not that of the Tsarist regime, even though there may be

Tsarist "officials" in exile continuing to claim allegiance to basic Tsarist rules.[28]

Breakdown and collapse of either ingredient results in collapse of the legal system. Sometimes the death of one system is but the preface to the birth of a new one, as in the peaceful transition from colony to independent state. At other times competition for effective control plunges the state into civil war, revolution, or war against another state, leaving the question of which legal system exists to be answered only when the dust clears and the key empirical issue of effective control is settled.

The puzzles for jurisprudence presented by these familiar phenomena deal largely with the borderline cases that result when either of these ingredients is missing in varying degrees. My interest is not in these particular problems but in the general schema itself and the alterations in that schema necessitated by the perspective of this study. It should be clear that the pathology of legal systems must now take account of an additional ingredient that can collapse or disappear: namely the good faith official claim to justice. When that occurs, what results is no longer a legal system but a coercive system that cannot impose even prima facie obligation on its citizens. That a change this drastic belongs to the study of the pathology of legal systems follows from the recognition that this issue, as a practical matter, overwhelms the interest in legal validity or the criteria for identifying legal systems.

This new possibility for legal disintegration can be contrasted with the possibilities already mentioned by playing on the analogy with human health that the pathology metaphor suggests. Abrupt, unconstitutional change in the basic rules yields a new legal system, just as abrupt, "unconstitutional" changes of personality may be said to yield a new individual. Chaos and disorder mark the collapse of the legal system into anarchy, just as bodily disintegration marks the death of the individual. The third possibility is change into something altogether different—not a person but a beast; not a legal system but a coercive regime. Though more likely the stuff of science fiction in the case of individuals, the Jekyll-Hyde phenomenon in the case of social orders is all too familiar.

The new problems created for jurisprudence by this additional possibility for the death of law are fascinating and familiar aspects of contemporary life. The most obvious borderline case is that of martial law, a phrase that hints at the contradictions exposed by ordinary speech at the boundary between coercive and legal regimes. The prototypical case of martial law is the suspension of ordinary rules and normal legal process in order to preserve the minimum value of security in the face of threatened chaos and general disorder. Such a regime remains legal if there is good faith belief in the existence of the emergency. Indeed, as we have seen, the minimum theory of justification that a legal system can invoke is the Hobbesian idea that stresses the value of order above all else: all rules are justified not directly on their merits but indirectly like rules of the road. Such a theory combines two claims: first, that any rule is better than none; second, that necessity (or, in the case of true rules of the road, indifference) obviates any finer calculation and comparison of the merits of alternative rules.

But the legal system is martial because all fundamental values that underlie the requirement of justification have been temporarily collapsed into the basic value of coercive systems in general. The modifier 'martial' qualifies the claim that the directives are 'law' for two reasons. Empirically the claim is likely to rest on the plausibility of the claim of emergency. One cannot rule out a priori the possibility that officials believe in the brute Hobbesian justification for all rules. But in the modern world few will be able to defend empirically the idea that no other fundamental ideas exist by which to test the justice of a system other than the degree to which order is maintained. That is why military juntas commonly rely on claims of emergency to justify temporary suspension of other values. The qualifier 'martial' thus points to the temporary nature of the change that has taken place and underscores the risk of collapse into pure coercion as the factual basis for the claim of emergency erodes. Second, because the case for law in these situations rests critically on the factual evidence for the claim of emergency, the sincerity of the claim is somewhat easier to challenge. The dispute is not over fundamental values that lead to different theories of justification but over the proper characterization of an issue of fact: is the emergency such as to preclude finer calculations of the merits of various commands?

Emphasis on the relationship between law and the belief in justice allows one to account not only for a new kind of death but also for the transformation of law into various utopian ideals of political thought; for if legal systems can degenerate into coercive systems, they can also evolve into systems that appear at the opposite end of the spectrum of possible social orders. Such systems are characterized by so complete a consensus in the nature and content of the ideal of justice that the need for force and coercion disappears. There may still be a need for coordination through law, even in a society of angels.[29] But the problem of grounding obligation in the face of normative dissent no longer remains. This vision of complete harmony, of a withering away of the state, is the counterpart in the present theory to the purely coercive regime. In each case one of the two essential criteria for law is missing. The coercive regime lacks the official belief in justice and serves only the self-interest of those in charge. The utopian society, in contrast, has made such progress toward value consensus that it no longer needs coercion. The question that guides this study—is there an obligation to obey?—is answered in the negative in the former case and does not even arise in the latter. In both cases, then, there is a basis for concluding that what exists is no longer a legal system.

The historical record, of course, suggests that death is much more likely to occur than transfiguration. (In that respect the analogy with the individual remains intact.) But it is more than just a lack of historical examples that leads to pessimism about the possibility of utopia. Utopian theories suffer from a bad press for very understandable reasons: the assumption of value consensus on which such theories depend appears too inconsistent with what experience teaches us about human nature.[30]

Complete transfiguration thus remains largely a motivating ideal. Yet the ideal makes itself felt within legal systems in ways that lead to new puzzles for jurisprudence. One such puzzle concerns the place for mercy in law. The power to pardon is by definition a power to dispense with the requirements of justice in the sense that the pardon is not morally deserved. Moreover, the demands of equality seem likewise suspended when mercy is exercised: one cannot complain that mercy is granted to some but not others identically situated. This conclusion is difficult for some to accept. I do not intend to explore the problems in moral philosophy posed by these issues but only to note how the present theory places these problems in understandable perspective. We have difficulty providing a formal place for mercy in law precisely because we cannot easily reconcile it with the requirement that officials act impartially in the interest of all. But we are unwilling to conclude that all such exercises of mercy are but guises for self-interest or displays of official favoritism. That unwillingness reflects the ideal of a transfigured society in which humans are judged by nonhuman standards. Though we cannot realize such a society in practice, we are sensitive to the normative ideal that such a society suggests. At the same time we are also sensitive to the ease with which the standardless exercise of power turns into tyranny. The latter unease prevents formally incorporating a place for mercy into law; the former ideal prevents exorcising it completely. Thus its exercise becomes rare, as in the case of presidential pardon, or hidden, as in the case of jury nullification.

The problems of legal mercy and of martial law are then examples of problems best understood against the backdrop of a theory that recognizes the additional possibilities for legal pathology discussed here. Undoubtedly there are other such problems. One in particular, however, seems unique and sufficiently characteristic of the modern era to warrant additional discussion. That is the problem of the collapse of belief in justice or value altogether—the problem of nihilism or the more extreme versions of moral relativism.

I have assumed that exposing the insincerity of the official claim of justice or the falsity of the military junta's claim of emergency exposes the true, self-interested motivation behind the exercise of power and thus the true coercive character of the regime. But exposing self-interest or class interest as the guiding motive is not the only possibility. It is also possible that officials simply believe in nothing—that the idea of justice or of reasoned discourse leading to value discovery or consensus is dismissed as misguided or meaningless. In that case, of course, nothing remains but power itself, and the only issues left to discuss are those that concern the effectiveness of coercion and the most efficient means of securing the only value that may be left—that of order. The implications of this collapse of belief in value deserve brief consideration in a separate and, perhaps appropriately, final chapter.

IMPLICATIONS
VI

I HAVE SAID that law dies when officials pursue self- or class interest rather than the common interest. A comparable metaphor for the collapse of belief in all value might be that of disease. In this final chapter I expand briefly on the metaphor in considering the implications of disbelief for the present theory. I also show what might turn on the question left open in Chapter IV: whether to count the purely coercive regime as a legal system.

NIHILISM AND OTHER MALADIES

Consider the difference between a state characterized by official nihilism and a state characterized by official belief in the minimal Hobbesian justification for law. In the latter case officials justify the legal structure by reference to a single value: order. That justification is sufficient to yield a legal system and a minimal basis for obligation. Official nihilism, in contrast, does not entail defense of the state's coercive apparatus even in the name of order and security, for those values for the true nihilist do not exist. In the nihilistic state there is no official defense of power at all but only an acceptance of whatever power structure happens to exist. Believing that value inquiries are meaningless, the true nihilist no more worries about justifying the power structure that supports him than about justifying the color red. The nihilist, we might say, is to the Hobbesian as the atheist is to the agnostic.

But the nihilist also differs from the tyrant who pursues, whether openly or in disguise, his own self-interest. The tyrant, we may assume, acknowledges the tension between self-regarding and other-regarding impulses and chooses to follow the former. He may do so out of weakness of will, or he may do so because he honestly believes he can justify taking the selfish point of view over the moral point of view. The question, Why be moral? is sufficiently difficult to answer so as to forestall accusations of irrationality just because one decides there is no good reason to prefer the moral to the selfish point of view. There is no obligation in such a system, but that is not the same as suggesting that the officials of such a system are misguided or clearly wrong in the choice they have made. Machiavelli and Nietzsche made that point long ago. It is because it is so difficult to refute the point that social systems balance so precariously between legal and coercive regimes.

The nihilist, in contrast to the despot, does not pursue self-interest any more than he pursues order as a value in itself. Beyond the tautological sense in which we are all psychological egoists, the nihilist is as atheistic toward his own values as he is toward those of others. The peculiar subjective urgency of his values is what make them his; but he does not attach any particular ethical importance to the fact that they are his in making decisions about what to pursue. All is accident, nothing is defensible. That the nihilist may have various motives for continuing to exercise and maintain his position of power is not inconsistent with this attitude. The acceptance of his position of power need not be an affirmation of self over others but only an affirmation of the ultimate meaninglessness of all attempts at value defense. The source of the nihilist's vision is not Machiavelli but Dostoyevski: requests to justify patterns of domination, whether exhibited in the beating of a horse or the persecution of a slave, are met with the shrug rather than the fist, with "all is permitted" rather than "my will be done."

We thus arrive at a picture of the nihilist that also highlights the single most neglected aspect of the theory I have been developing. The nihilist believes that demands to justify normative attitudes are meaningless because justification presupposes objective standards or a process of reasoning unavailable where values are concerned. This view invites one to explain in contrast what might be meant by the justification of a political structure. One thing that cannot be meant is that justification requires demonstrating, in any ordinary sense of the term, that the underlying values of the legal system are correct. Nothing I have said is inconsistent with the view that ends and ultimate values are in some sense unprovable. Indeed I have made clear that it is the belief in value, not the ability to ground that belief or to persuade others, that is critical to law and obligation. At the same time, however, I have stressed the need for justification and dialogue, as if to say that reason has more than a purely instrumental role to play in the formation and defense of value.

This emphasis on the role of reason is partly a consequence of the assumption of basic equality among human beings and of the corresponding empirical constraints which that assumption places on the otherwise infinite number of possible beliefs. Beliefs are not formed in vacuums free of all contaminating connections to reality. Common experiences and common human responses to painful and pleasurable stimuli provide minimum Archimedean points from which to assess claims about what is in fact in the interests of all. That one cannot prove who is right in the case of value disagreement is not proof that the concept of truth in ethics is meaningless. And the belief that it is not meaningless, however indeterminable, is what ultimately distinguishes the officials we have been considering from the nihilist. The nihilist's response when challenged to justify coercion is to take refuge not in values that may be ultimately unprovable but in the judgment that there is no meaningful sense in which even he can assert that some values are preferable to others.

What are the implications of this attitude for law and obligation? Though I have distinguished the nihilist from the tyrant, the implications are the same in both cases. From the perspective of the dissident who asks why he should obey the law, there is little to distinguish officials who exercise power in their own interests from officials who exercise power with no interest in view at all. Indeed in the latter case, if the nihilist really does believe that all values are equally untenable (or equally tenable), it is hard to understand why he does not hand the reins of power over to someone who does care about how they are used. His refusal to do so, though I have tried to distinguish it from the simple pursuit of self-interest, is likely to appear as a choice of self over others and thus destroy the basis for obligation just as surely as in the case of the tyrant. Also missing in the case of both nihilist and tyrant is the minimal bond between ruler and ruled entailed by the concession that the common interest is to be pursued, leaving disagreements about what that entails to be worked out mutually. The tyrant denies that he should be just; the nihilist denies that there is any such thing as justice. Both attitudes prevent the possibility of agreement through dialogue.

The case for concluding that there is no obligation where official nihilism prevails becomes conclusive when we recall the suggestion of an earlier chapter about how to assess the weight to be given to the obligation to obey the law. Because the obligation is based on respect for the views and honest efforts of others, its weight varies with the intensity of the conviction that accompanies the belief. What matters is how much it matters to others. But then the nihilist who cares about nothing cannot care about disobedience either. Thus the strength of the obligation is nil.

Why not simply conclude, then, that nihilism is the equivalent of death rather than merely disease, that legal systems become purely coercive when the belief in justice disappears, regardless of whether it is the fist or the shrug that displaces the belief? I do not, of course, intend to substitute the metaphor for analysis, and as far as the ultimate question that guides this study is concerned, there is no difference between the tyrant and the nihilist. But I have used the metaphor to draw attention to a particular feature of this process of death through disillusion that distinguishes it from simple tyranny. The extreme version of nihilism that I have sketched is not likely to be an accurate description of the official ideology of actual states. That is because ideology by definition connotes a structure of normative belief, not a total absence of belief. Thus to ask for examples of the nihilistic state is to ask for examples of states with no ideology at all. Such examples are difficult to find. Any power structure that persists over time is likely to generate justifications for the structure that appeal either to the interests of the power holders, which is tyranny, or to the interests of all, which is law.

Distinguishing between these two kinds of justification, particularly in light of the possibility of self-deception, is the major problem for legal theory that I have discussed so far in considering the concept of sincerity. But once one has determined whether the claim of justice is made in good faith, the question of the existence of prima facie obligation—though not the matter of its weight—is settled. Good faith is not a matter of degree even though—indeed precisely because—it consists of components that do allow for degrees. Thus one may still conclude that officials are sincere even though their claims of justice are accompanied by (1) a good deal of self-doubt; (2) a wide variation in the mix between conscious and unconscious motivations; and (3) a healthy dose of unavoidable self-interest. Yet the tendency toward nihilism does appear in degrees. Nihilism points toward the strength of the conviction that underlies the value commitment in a way that the distinction between good faith and bad faith does not. Since the extreme case of nihilism is seldom found, what one most often finds are legal systems that exhibit varying degrees of nihilism. It is this possibility of infection with a process that can lead ultimately to death that explains my use of the metaphor of disease.

Now let us abandon the metaphor and state the problem directly. The problem of nihilism is the problem of the degree of conviction that underlies the official commitment to the basic values of a legal system. The weaker the commitment, the weaker the basis for obligation, a conclusion consistent with my earlier suggestion for determining the weight of the obligation to obey the law. In the extreme case there is no obligation because officials care about nothing. At the other extreme particular values are thought to be so important to justice or to the preservation of society that only countervailing obligations that one believes to be equally weighty, or nearly so, will outweigh the obligation to obey. In between are various states corresponding to the degree of importance attached by officials to the values protected by law or threatened by disobedience.

What makes nihilism a problem for legal theory, rather than simply another way of drawing attention to the fact that beliefs can differ in strength as well as substance, is the fact that the theory developed here can itself be viewed as harboring tendencies toward nihilism. I have built the case for obligation out of seemingly inconsistent strands. The stronger the value commitment of society, the greater the resulting obligation. Yet at the same time the case for obligation depends critically on the notion of tolerance for the dissenting views of equals. These strands combine poorly. The stronger one's conviction, it would seem, the less likely one is to pay attention to dissenters. Conversely, the more tenuous one's commitment to a particular value, the easier it may be to consider an opposing view.

This tension between conviction and tolerance is a familiar one in moral philosophy.[1] In the present case the tension produces not logical inconsistency but a variety of empirical tendencies that explain a variety of phenomena concerning the felt sense of obligation toward law. There is no logical inconsistency because in considering the tension between commitment and tolerance I have made the former the important ingredient for obligation. Strong and sincere commitment by officials creates a strong case for obligation, even though official tolerance for the dissenting view may be less in the sense that it is harder to change the official view. It is true that the dissenter's tolerance for the fact that people can hold different views—and can hold them strongly—helps ground his obligation; but the only corresponding requirement of official tolerance is that entailed by the right of discourse. Though one thus avoids theoretical inconsistency, it is not difficult to see the empirical consequences of applying in practice these ideas about the basis for obligation. Several phenomena that seem to undermine the sense of obligation can be explained. For example, to suggest that the degree of commitment is always positively correlated with the degree of obligation may be wrong in the extreme case. The image of passion overwhelming reason in the individual has a parallel in the image of the rabidly fervent

state whose ideological commitment is so strong that it cannot see anything else. In that case one is tempted to say that the right of discourse is
not being honored; the emotional fervor is so strong that it prevents fair
consideration of competing ideologies.

In this sense there is a constraint on commitment parallel to the constraint on claims to be serving the common interest. Such claims are suspect as mere rationalizations when obviously self-serving aspects are
ignored. So too the claim to have fairly evaluated and rejected alternative ideologies may be suspect when passions are so strong that reflection and dialogue seem only pretense. Lip service, the first sign of
insincerity, can result from the failure to confront either the self-serving
nature of one's beliefs or the weakness of one's theory of justice—even
though the latter failure may reflect a kind of religious fervor.

The theme of alienation that constitutes a large part of the literature
on the bureaucratic state can also be understood as a response to a sense
of decreasing personal commitment on the part of officials. The modern
state is a far cry from the paradigms of lifeboat and family that I used
earlier to construct a theory of obligation. Indeed, one may wonder
whether the face-to-face confrontation that leads to respect in those
cases can be said to have a counterpart at all when the confrontation in
society is largely with institutions as impersonal as court and legislature
or administrative agency. But behind courts and legislatures and agen-
cies are people, and it is this sense that there are people who care about
the laws they enact that warrants extrapolating from the simple case of
personal to the general case of political obligation. This sense, however,
is impaired in proportion to the degree that structure controls rather
than people. The bureaucratization of the courts,[2] the unthinking invocation of standard ideologies, the conversion of response and dialogue
into ritual and rote—all these erode the sense of confronting people who
care and with it the case for obligation. If the rabid theocracy is at one
end of the spectrum of commitment, the faceless bureaucracy is at the
other. Both verge on death.

Between these extremes one may locate a wide variety of familiar examples: laws that are applied seemingly mechanically, without attention
to whether they reflect the purposes of caring people; disruption of trials
by litigants when officials appear to mock justice because their commitment to established values is so passionate that it hinders fair evaluation
of the litigant's claim; agency regulations openly flouted because they
seem to result from mindless process, a bureaucratic inertia that has out-
run its human controls. All of these are examples of alienating confrontations with law which are likely to invoke a common response: outrage.
That, of course, is the response to the mugger with which this study be-

gan. The present theory explains why it may sometimes seem an appropriate response to the law as well.

THE PROBLEM OF COMMITMENT

If nihilism is the disease, commitment must be the cure. That, at least, would seem to be the implication of all that has preceded. It does not matter what you believe; what matters is that you believe at all. Surely, though, this is a facile and dangerous slogan, as anyone will agree who has reflected on contemporary movements organized around a similar commitment to commitment for its own sake.[3] It is once again the solution of the outsider, whom I criticized in an earlier chapter for too sharply separating his perspective from that of the insider. Were one to apply this outsider's perspective to the theory developed here, the conclusion that all that matters is belief would be sound—at least as respects the inquiry into the basis for obligation. But for insiders that conclusion is as unhelpful as modern positivism's assertion that law viewed from the outside is normative. The sharp separation of inside and outside points of view once again distorts the reality we all experience as we continually mix subjective and objective perspectives in an uneasy but unavoidable tension.[4] Recognizing the power of commitment, in short, must be balanced by recognizing as well the problem of commitment. By the problem of commitment I do not mean simply the problem of grounding values. From the perspective of legal theory there is a unique aspect to the problem of commitment that both contributes to and arises out of the more general problem of grounding values. It is the purpose of this section to describe this aspect and, briefly, to note its implications.

Kelsen is thought to have been a moral relativist. His moral perspective did not hinder his characterizing law from the outside as essentially normative, grounded in basic value commitments by those wielding effective societal control. I have already explained how Kelsen's theory remains incomplete from the insider's perspective. Had Kelsen become a judge, he would have found his own theory of law useless: until he (and his colleagues) could "posit" the basic norm, the legal system would not exist. But how does a relativist forced to become an insider posit a norm in a way that makes statements of legal obligation anything more than reports of legal validity? He may draw obligation from his promise or the conditions of his office, if his relativism allows for extracting duty from voluntarily assumed roles; but the normative status of law depends on a more far-reaching noncontractual commitment by him and his equivalent officials to the basic values of the system. What then does the true relativist do as judge, given the modifications made here to Kelsen's theory?

If one searches for historical examples to answer that question, one is likely to hit on Holmes as the paradigm of the insider who must act as a judge despite tendencies to despair of the reality of values. This is not the place to recount the biographical accounts that would justify making Holmes such a paradigm case.[5] Many such accounts are in fact defective for such purposes, for reasons I have already noted. The despairing side of Holmes is usually thought evidenced by his judicial opinions and private statements that emphasize the absence of any objective check on values and the corresponding dominance through history of power and self-interest. This view is thought to have led to judicial opinions in which Holmes declared a willingness to uphold the will of the majority as expressed through Congress rather than invalidate a statute in the name of larger constitutional values (nonexistent in Holmes's opinion). This account, of course, does not quite yield the required paradigm. To embrace the values of the majority as a judge may be to accept a set of fundamental values, linked perhaps to a theory of democracy; it is not, at least not necessarily, the choice of one who believes that there are no fundamental values at all.[6]

There is another possible interpretation, however, of Holmes's retreat to majoritarianism, an interpretation that comes closer to indicating how the problem of commitment is related to legal theory. Lon Fuller made the point in contrasting two conceptions of democracy. The negative conception

is that which finds the justification for democracy in intellectual skepticism. There is no such thing as justice. Human reason is utterly incapable of regulating the relations of men among themselves. Some purely arbitrary principle of order becomes, therefore, necessary. Since power rests ultimately on the acquiescence of the governed, the most logical principle of government is that of majority rule, since this offers the broadest base for the order set up ... Majority rule is preferred not because it is most likely to be right, but because it is most likely to be obeyed. Democracy is rested not on an affirmation, but on a denial that government and law can in the end be anything but arbitrary.[7]

Fuller contrasts this conception of democracy founded "on a negation of the force of ideas" with a conception built "on a faith that in the long run ideas are more important than the men who form them ... By preserving a fluidity in the power structures of society, by making possible the peaceful liquidation of unsuccessful governments, democracy creates a field in which ideas may effectively compete with one another for the possession of men's minds."[8]

Fuller's negative conception of democracy calls to mind the descriptions given above of the nihilist. It also calls to mind the minimal Hobbesian justification for the state, which holds order to be the only value and embraces any structure that promotes order. Indeed the negative conception of democracy merely adds a refinement to the Hobbesian view by arguing for the efficiency of one particular political structure in realizing the goal of order. It is this affinity of the Hobbesian view for nihilism that explains the doubts I expressed earlier in accepting the Hobbesian justification as a minimal basis for law and obligation. Indeed, if the Hobbesian conception is negative in Fuller's sense—if order is sought because there are no other defensible values—the distinction between the Hobbesian state and the nihilist regime as respects the case for obligation may well disappear. Only if one interprets the Hobbesian conception as one that gives priority to the value of order, without necessarily denying the possible reality of other values (agnostic rather than atheistic), can one comfortably accept the conclusion that law and obligation result.

So far, though, it seems that we are dealing once again with the problem of nihilism. What has all of this to do with the problem of commitment? The answer is that the problem of commitment is never very far removed from the problem of nihilism. Consider what leads to the negative conception of democracy or to the negative conception of the Hobbesian theory of justice. The legal theory developed here contains an emphasis on process and dialogue that can generate either of two attitudes. The more one stresses dialogue, good faith, and belief as key ingredients in the grounding of obligation, the more vulnerable one is to the charge of having abandoned the realm of reality as a test for justice. The problem of commitment in legal theory is that legal theory cannot itself ground the commitment even though it shows that the commitment is essential to law and obligation. Thus preoccupation with the theory rather than with the business of actually forming convictions, beliefs, and judgments of value is ultimately self-defeating. In legal scholarship such preoccupation takes the form of a fascination with process for its own sake and with the worship of contradiction and ambivalence. But one can revel in dialectic and contradiction only at the risk of spreading the disease of nihilism and with it the death of law.

I have developed a theory that grounds the normative base of law, but I have not developed a complete political theory to ground the commitment that the legal theory requires as a precondition of law's normativity. In that respect it is possible to level at the theory a partial charge of insider irrelevance, similar to the charge I leveled earlier at existing theories of law. But there is a critical difference. The present theory at least explains how law can be normative and entail obligation despite value disagreement and despite official error in value judgment. To explain as much is to solve the problem of political obligation. It is also to make legal theory relevant to the insider in the only way it can be—not by replacing legal with political thought but by connecting the two to reveal the moral bond in society that subsists even while the jury remains out on the question of a definitive theory of the just state.

CHOOSING A VIEW

I have developed and defended an alternative to the classical view of law as force and have also shown how both modern positivism and classical natural law theories fail in their attempts to go beyond the coercive model. What I have not shown is that the classical view is wrong. The test case for the theory of this study remains the purely coercive system, the regime that fails to defend or claim justice for its power structure in the manner described here. What would one say if asked whether such a regime is a legal system?

There is no point in denying that our existing classificatory scheme permits calling such regimes legal despite the absence of moral authority. But it also seems consistent with the existing linguistic scheme to make the opposite decision—to call such systems coercive rather than legal. In favor of the former decision, as discussed in Chapter IV, is the view that the classification serves primarily to correlate a social entity with the universal interest in knowing about the risk of encountering organized sanctions. In favor of the latter view is the persistent claim that the concepts of law and fidelity are linked. The fact that one seldom encounters a purely coercive regime helps explain why we have not been forced to embody a permanent choice between these views in our linguistic scheme. The coercive system remains a borderline case and so explains why we might not know exactly what to say, just as we might not know exactly what to say if asked whether a stool is a chair.

Two possibilities remain. First, we could rest the case here, content with having provided a defense of the meaning of law in the standard case that invests the term with significance beyond that found in modern positivism or in the classical Austinian account. One could then deal with the borderline case on the level of description rather than definition, just as one surely would in the case of the stool's possibly being a chair. In that latter case one would no doubt try to find out what puzzles the questioner, explaining that a stool is like a chair in some ways (one can sit on it) but unlike in other ways and thus might serve purposes most chairs do not (milking cows, for example). So too the person who asks whether the coercive system is legal can be told that there is no basis for moral fidelity in such a regime, if that is what he wants to know, but that there may be clearly predictable sanctions attached to behavior which prudence suggests he should take into account.

A second possibility is to consider the implications of deciding (stipulating if you will) once and for all what to call the coercive system. Some positivists, for example, after arguing that there is no necessary connection between law and morality as we now use those terms, proceed to consider whether the term 'law' should be limited to exclude iniquitous regimes. The practical and theoretical objections the positivist raises to such a proposal have been noted elsewhere in this study.[9] Indeed those same objections prevent the positivist from excluding coercive regimes from the concept of law just as much as they prevent his excluding iniquitous regimes. But the theoretical and practical objections are less forceful when considered against the background of this study. The theoretical objection assumes that what interests us in the study of legal systems is a "specific method of social control." That being the case, it is artificial to carve out from the study of this type of social control those regimes that are immoral, particularly since "study of the use [of this method of social control] involves study of its abuse."[10] But why is it artificial to subdivide social entities according to the various types of social control? The method of social control that the positivist claims interests us is already a very special one: it is the coercive method of control in which rules are imposed by officials on others for any reason whatsoever. This study suggests that there are distinct theoretical interests in dividing the study of organized social systems into subcategories that reflect whether the type of social control is coercive or moral. With coercion as the key to the class selected for study, theoretical interest will focus on efficacy—the power and ability of rulers to enforce decrees and thus ensure compliance. With the claim to justice as the key to law, theoretical interest shifts its focus to the nature of the justification in society and its effectiveness, assessed either descriptively or normatively, in persuading dissidents and in maintaining voluntary allegiance.

The practical objection of the positivist to the proposal to eliminate iniquitous systems from the concept of law rests on the claim that moral inquiry about what one should do is aided by separating the question of what law is from the question of whether it should be obeyed. That argument is persuasive when the moral question concerns one's ultimate obligation—whether, all things considered, one should obey a law. The argument is less persuasive when the moral question concerns prima facie obligation. By connecting the concepts of law and prima facie obligation, one ensures that moral deliberation about whether to obey does not totally discount the moral claim of the law. If anything, it is the positivist's suggestion that these ideas are totally distinct that threatens to skew practical deliberations about one's ultimate obligation by inviting one to give no moral weight at all to the law (just because it is the law) in deciding whether to obey.

There is, however, a final factor to consider in deciding whether to count the purely coercive social order as a legal system. It is a factor that connects this definitional decision with the preceding discussion of the problem of nihilism. Modern positivists go out of their way to deny any connection between legal and logical positivism. That is to say, one's view about the separation of law and morals, it is claimed, does not entail any particular view about whether moral claims can be true or false.[11] I have already noted that the converse is not true: one's views about the status of moral judgments can entail, or be a good reason for, a view about the relation between law and morals. Thus if we were all persuaded that moral claims are meaningless, that would be a very good reason for settling the present question in the classical positivist's favor, for there would no longer be any meaningful moral interest to justify excluding coercive systems from the concept of law. Some positivists, we have seen, do seem to rely on just such a metaethical view about the status of moral judgments in claiming that moral standards are too uncertain to be sources of law. But the positivist who is careful to keep his theory pure of metaethics as well as of substantive ethics will leave this question of the status of moral judgments open.

Whatever one concludes about this question of metaethics, a final argument in favor of linking the concepts of law and morality can be built on two simple empirical claims: (1) that it is important to people to believe in the reality of value judgments; and (2) that one way this faith is maintained is by investing concepts that refer to the most basic social phenomena with a moral meaning. Organized social systems are ubiquitous and powerful. They cannot be avoided; indeed they claim the power to intrude into every facet of human life. If it is also true that people want to believe (or do believe) in the reality of moral value, it should not be surprising to discover that the concept used to designate such pervasive social phenomena is one that requires a similar faith in the reality of moral justification. The problem with classical positivism, in short, is not that it entails nihilism but that it entails aloofness from the question of nihilism.

This final argument can be illustrated by considering once again the parallel with religion. Suppose the question were whether to extend the term 'religion' to include humanitarian philosophies which embrace moral ideals identical to those of other religions but do not profess a belief in a deity. It is not difficult to see that one might decide to limit the term to exclude such organizations for reasons based on the same two empirical claims just mentioned. First, the belief in such a being is important to many people, and second, one way of evidencing this belief is to develop a concept for organizations that address humanitarian and spiritual needs and to link this concept by definition to a further requirement that such organizations profess a belief in God. Organizations with the same aim but without the belief cannot be considered religions.

The decision to view law as only force or as more than force can be viewed in similar fashion as a decision about whether the concept we use to describe a certain social reality should also be one that implies a commitment to some kind of moral reality as well. The view that sees an essential difference between law and force is a view that implies that moral argument is rational, however difficult it may be to substantiate value judgments. The view that is content to include the coercive regime within the concept of the legal implies that it is not important to reflect views about moral reality in a classification of social reality—at least not this particular piece of social reality. Such a view may not require one to abandon faith, but it does require one to abandon one particular way of demonstrating and announcing that faith.

It has not been my purpose to argue conclusively for one of these views over the other. In that respect the definition of law advanced here, if one insists that it is more than a hypothetical connection between certain social orders and obligation, remains incomplete. To complete it one would have to explain, for example, why it is important to care about the reality of obligation and to struggle to preserve moral as well as physical integrity—and why it is important to reflect these concerns in the concepts one develops to designate social reality. I do not doubt that this gap in the argument could be filled. I do doubt that it could be filled solely by analysis unaccompanied by an initial choice of position on the question of the reality of value. A stand on that issue must precede the search for particular values, if only because the difficulty of the search will otherwise quickly ensure its abandonment by those not committed to it in advance.

But this conclusion entails another. A stand on the question of the reality of value is one that theory can only confirm in the end, not provide at the start; at the start it can only be taken—or not.

NOTES

I. INTRODUCTION

1. See John Austin, *The Province of Jurisprudence Determined* (London: J. Murray, 1832).

2. See for example Glanville Williams, "The Controversy Concerning the Word 'Law,'" in *Philosophy, Politics, and Society*, 1st ser., ed. Peter Laslett (Oxford: Oxford University Press, 1967), p. 134. See also Judith Shklar, *Legalism* (Cambridge, Mass.: Harvard University Press, 1964).

3. Thurman Arnold, *The Symbols of Government* (New Haven: Yale University Press, 1935), p. 216.

4. See for example Ronald Dworkin, *Taking Rights Seriously* (Cambridge, Mass.: Harvard University Press, 1977), p. 35. Dworkin relies on the evidence of how lawyers and litigants think and talk about law in order to prove what law is. See Philip Soper, "Legal Theory and the Obligation of a Judge: The Hart/Dworkin Dispute," 75 *Michigan Law Review* 473, 506–508 (1977). This empirical or descriptive approach to resolving disputes about the nature of law only invites the charge that such disputes are verbal. What law is depends on whatever lawyers find it in their interest as advocates to say it is rather than on any more objective reality. Similarly, whether judges have discretion in deciding cases will depend on whether they think they do. See Rolf Sartorius, "Social Policy and Judicial Legislation," 8 *American Philosophical Quarterly* 151 (1971), noting that claims or denials of judicial discretion can become self-fulfilling.

5. The claim that legal theory is of little use to the anthropologist cannot be proved by asking whether anthropologists cite and talk about legal theory. They do, extensively. Moreover they even seem to be active participants in the debate about the nature of law, offering their own anthropological definitions. See Branislaw Malinowski, *Crime and Custom in Savage Society* (London: Routledge and Kegan Paul, 1926), pp. 55–59. On examination, however, the use

that is made of legal theory in such work proves to be purely descriptive. That is to say, descriptions of the various kinds of norms likely to be found in advanced societies are taken over from legal theory as guides to what to look for in a certain, usually primitive, society. See for example Stuart Schlegel, *Tiruray Justice* (Berkeley: University of California Press, 1970), chap. 7, on whether the Tiruray society can be said to have a "rule of recognition," "rule of adjudication," and "rule of change," thus constituting a legal system à la Hart. On the conceptual question of whether the presence or absence of some of these features is essential to qualify the system as legal, anthropologists have nothing to add to the debates of legal theorists and in fact seem able to get along without waiting for these debates to be resolved. (For the distinction between conceptual and descriptive theories of law, see Soper, "Legal Theory and the Obligation of a Judge," note 4 above, pp. 473–474.)

This general account of the relationship between anthropology and legal theory can be illustrated by considering the major conceptual dispute in the literature: namely whether custom should count as law. At the descriptive level there is little disagreement. Societal norms include some that are identified through institutionalized mechanisms and backed by organized sanctions and some that are not. Many anthropologists, like positivists, emphasize the importance of the organized sanction and the institutionalized method for determining the norm. See for example Paul Bohannan, "The Differing Realms of the Law," 67 *American Anthropologist* 33–37 (December 1965); E. A. Hoebel, "Primitive Law and Modern," 5 *Transactions of the New York Academy of Sciences* 31 (2d ser., December 1942). Others resemble nonpositivists such as Dworkin in stressing that an actual judicial attempt to determine the content of institutionalized norms requires going beyond the formalized standard to take account of more general, societal views about what ought to be. See Max Gluckman, *The Ideas in Bartose Jurisprudence* (New Haven: Yale University Press, 1965), pp. 17–26.

Now to "emphasize" or "stress as important" certain norms of society is to point to a particular purpose or function those norms serve and to identify the features that enable them to do so effectively. All of this can be done at the descriptive level. To go further and declare that law covers a broad or narrow range of such norms assumes what is in issue (or ought to be) in legal theory— namely the essential function of a legal system. If one believes that the function of law is to provide a reliable guide to official action, one is likely to side with the positivists; if one thinks its function is to legitimate the exercise of organized force, one may not. In either case, this conceptual inquiry is not advanced by the anthropologist qua anthropologist. Likewise, a theory of law that is truly conceptual cannot improve the anthropologist's investigative techniques, though it may in the course of its analysis suggest new descriptive categories to look for in analyzing a functioning society into its various parts. See also John Finnis, *Natural Law and Natural Rights* (Oxford: Clarendon Press, 1980), chap. 1.

6. The literature of sociology, like that of anthropology, is filled with references to definitions of law that suggest a connection to legal theory. But the situ-

ation here parallels the situation in anthropology: legal theory is useful at most for the descriptive features it provides of the various ways of effecting social control, not for its conclusions about what counts as legal. Indeed, some sociologists admit that the phenomenon they study, though called law, is simply "governmental social control," with the problem of explaining what constitutes the "distinctively legal" left as "a problem for jurisprudence, not science." See Donald Black, "The Boundaries of Legal Sociology," 81 *Yale Law Journal* 1086, 1092, 1096 (1976). It is possible, of course, to view legal theory itself as nothing more than "an essay in descriptive sociology," in the words of H. L. A. Hart, *The Concept of Law* (Oxford: Clarendon Press, 1961), p. xii. In that case one must concede that there is no point to the pursuit of the "distinctively legal" even in jurisprudence—a concession I hope the present study will show is unnecessary.

When sociologists do engage in what appear to be conceptual disputes about law, they array themselves in patterns strikingly similar to those displayed by anthropologists. Some show the positivist's influence in emphasizing the importance of coercion and an authoritative, institutional apparatus for norm identification and enforcement. See for example Max Rheinstein, ed. and trans., and Edward Shils, trans., *Max Weber on Law in Economy and Society* (Cambridge, Mass.: Harvard University Press, 1954), p. 13. Others insist on the equal importance of the ideal element in law—the moral ends or values which the coercive system serves or toward which it tends. See Philip Selznick, *Law, Society, and Industrial Justice* (New York: Russell Sage Foundation, 1969), chap. 1. In fact this question of the extent to which law must include a reference to the ideals that are pursued in an organized society divides sociologists just as the question of whether custom is law divides anthropologists. But the contribution sociologists make to this question as a conceptual matter is nil, as is the contribution legal theory makes to the sociologists' concern to provide a theory of effective government control. See Jack Gibbs, "Definitions of Law and Empirical Questions," 2 *Law and Society Review* 429 (1968).

The present study provides the conceptual connection between the ideal element emphasized by sociologists such as Selznick and the concept of law. In doing so I am admittedly engaging in the classical enterprise of definition rather than description—an enterprise that combines evaluative and factual elements in a manner more fully described elsewhere in this study. Thus sociologists who insist on limiting pure sociology to the study of factual statements about the techniques of effective social ordering will find their goals unaffected by this investigation. They may also find, however, that they face the same dilemma as the legal theorist who tries to remain disengaged from evaluation while still providing a useful and complete theory. If the ideal element is an important element in social ordering and in predicting legal effectiveness, it must be included in the sociologist's complete account. But attempting to include this element while still remaining a purely external observer (that is, describing but not personally evaluating the ideal) will prove impossible if the force of the ideal in society depends on a rational normative structure, and hence on the correctness of normative arguments about the content of the ideal. In that case, efforts to predict or describe the impact of such rational ideals in society will depend on one's ability to participate in (that is, predict the outcome of) these normative debates. That is just another way of saying that one must be prepared to evaluate the ideal. Thus the conclusion reached here about current legal theory—that it must content itself with being unable to distinguish law from force if it insists on remaining pure—has a parallel moral for the sociologist. To remain pure the sociologist must abandon his quest for a general theory of governmental social control and accept instead a partial theory of governmental control through force alone.

7. Equating the prick of conscience, the pointed finger of shame, and the pain of prison is a common method of debunking attempts to distinguish between moral, social, and legal norms. See Shklar, *Legalism*, pp. 51–55. For a sensitive analysis see P. M. S. Hacker, "Sanction Theories of Duty," in *Oxford Essays in Jurisprudence*, 2d ser., ed. A. W. B. Simpson (Oxford: Clarendon Press, 1973), p. 121.

8. See Rolf Sartorius, "Social Policy and Judicial Legislation," note 4 above, pp. 155–156.

9. See Rolf Sartorius, *Individual Conduct and Social Norms* (Encino, Calif.: Dickerson Publishing Co., 1975) pp. 201–202; Soper, "Legal Theory and the Obligation of a Judge," note 4 above, p. 509.

10. There is no contradiction between the charge of insider irrelevance and the claim that theory can affect insider beliefs and thus change the phenomenon under study. Current legal theory is irrelevant as a guide to insiders who want to know what the law is—that is, what directives are actually in force. The fact that insiders might react to a theory that shows law to be indistinguishable from force supports the premise of this study: the relevance of legal theory for insiders lies in the moral implications of a concept of law, not in its usefulness in determining legal validity.

11. See Shklar, *Legalism*, pp. 32–35.

12. See Anthony Quinton, ed., *Political Philosophy* (Oxford: Oxford University Press, 1967), p. 9.

13. One commentator suggests that this conclusion is "becoming more popular." Joseph Raz, "Authority and Consent," 67 *Virginia Law Review* 103 (1981). See also Raz, *The Authority of Law* (Oxford: Clarendon Press, 1979), p. 233; A. J. Simmons, *Moral Principles and Political Obligations* (Princeton: Princeton University Press, 1979); Anthony Woozley, *Law and Obedience* (Chapel Hill: University of North Carolina Press, 1979); M. B. E. Smith, "Is There a Prima Facie Obligation to Obey the Law?," 82 *Yale Law Journal* 950 (1973).

14. Hart, of course, in claiming that law must include the idea of obligation does not mean that it must actually entail obligation as a conclusion of moral philosophy but only that it must connote obligation; that is, law is to be classified among a society's rules of obligation, which may be the wrong rules according to moral philosophy. I argue in the next chapter that Hart's model fails even to do this, but at least the insistence on the connotational point is a start in the right direction.

15. Hart, *The Concept of Law*, p. 7. It is possible, of course, that a concept like that of an order backed by a threat—which does not connote obligation—might nevertheless entail obligation as a matter of moral philosophy. If, for example, such orders always happen to promote or entail moral value, then one may have an obligation to comply. See Joseph Raz, *Practical Reason and Norms* (London: Hutchinson and Co., 1975), pp. 165–166. Putting the matter this way, though, makes it even easier to see that knowing what law is must precede knowing whether it entails obligation. I argue in Chapter III, for example, that there *is* a morally relevant difference between the ordinary gunman and the gunman "writ large." The "large" gunman (the state monopoly on force) is a necessary but not a sufficient condition for obligation. In that respect, the claim in the text is overstated. One *does* have to engage in some discussion to move from the conclusion that ordinary gunmen do not obligate to the conclusion that "large" gunmen do not either. The point remains that political theorists' conclusions are incomplete if they end their analysis here without considering whether the changes that even positivists want to make in the gunman model of law might affect conclusions about the obligation to obey.

16. Compare Joseph Raz, *The Concept of a Legal System*, 2d ed. (Oxford: Clarendon Press, 1970), with his *Practical Reason and Norms*, pp. 147–148, and *The Authority of Law*, p. 155.

17. Raz, *The Authority of Law*, chap. 12.

18. As noted, Raz does seem to claim that assertions of legal obligation entail assertions of (moral) obligation and thus, from the viewpoint of judges who honestly accept the system, such statements have a dimension that sanction-based theories such as Austin's cannot capture. See H. L. A. Hart, *Essays on Bentham* (Oxford: Clarendon Press, 1982), pp. 153–161, 264–268, in which he discusses his disagreement with Raz on this issue; see also chapter II, note 32. Hart's own view is that there is no necessary moral component in the judicial attitude toward law—a view that makes Hart's model indistinguishable from Austin's as respects the implications for obligation.

I consider this dispute in more detail in the next chapter. But it should be noted here that when Raz connects law with the perception of obligation, he probably means that it is the content of the rules that is perceived to be morally binding. That is, judges think that the specific rules of their society are just, not that the rules obligate simply because they are law. So when Raz declares that law does not obligate in the prima facie sense, he is not necessarily undermining or weakening the attitude that his legal theory declares is essential to law. Raz's difficulties lie elsewhere: he is unable to defend his claim about the connection between law and the perception of obligation because, like Hart, he appears to have taken description as his goal rather than definition.

My views resemble these more recent and tentative suggestions of Raz's concerning the connection between law and the official belief in justice. See Philip Soper, "The 'Acceptability' of Law: An Analysis of the Concept of Law Based on the Legal Theory of Professor H. L. A. Hart," Ph.D. diss., Washington University, 1972. But I argue that this claim about the nature of law can be defended only by connecting legal and political theory. The strongest support for the legal theory claim, after all, is the opposite conclusion in political theory from the one Raz reaches concerning the obligation to obey.

19. See Dworkin, *Taking Rights Seriously,* chaps. 2–4.

20. See the sources cited in note 9 above.

21. Morse Peckham, *Beyond the Tragic Vision* (New York: George Braziller, 1962), p. 148.

II. LEGAL THEORY

1. See Joseph Raz, *The Concept of a Legal System,* 2d ed. (Oxford: Clarendon Press, 1970), p. 128.

2. H. L. A. Hart, *The Concept of Law* (Oxford: Clarendon Press, 1961), chaps. 3–5.

3. Critics of Austin's account of sovereignty often do claim that attempts to identify a sovereign empirically, without reference to an authoritative rule, involve a logical contradiction or circularity. See W. L. Morison, *John Austin* (Stanford: Stanford University Press, 1982), pp. 82–83, 106–107, 183. Hart raises a similar objection in *The Concept of Law,* chap. 4, but elsewhere agrees that legal systems could exist in which the exclusive source of law is a supreme legislator's will or command. See H. L. A. Hart, *Essays on Bentham* (Oxford: Clarendon Press, 1982), p. 144. The problem, according to Hart, is that this model does not accurately portray the typical case of legal standards that are accepted and enforced even though they are not traceable to the will of an identifiable person or group.

4. Hart raises four analytical objections to Austin's account (summarized in *The Concept of Law,* p. 77), of which I consider the two most obvious in the text—namely the claim that the coercive model cannot account for either the variety or the range of application of laws. Hart's other two objections are that: (1) the coercive model cannot account for the "mode of origin" of some laws, namely customs; and (2) the model cannot explain the continuity of law when one sovereign succeeds another, nor can it, for that matter, even identify the sovereign in many modern states.

The first of these objections about the status of customary laws assumes that one can identify customs prior to judicial enforcement—an assumption that Ronald Dworkin notes either commits the positivist to a model of law that no longer distinguishes law from (positive) morality or makes the positivist's test for law trivial (whatever is accepted as law is law). See Dworkin, *Taking Rights Seriously* (Cambridge, Mass.: Harvard University Press, 1977), pp. 42–44. The second objection—that one cannot account for the continuity of law with the simple idea of habitual obedience—is persuasive only because Hart takes 'habit' to mean an unthinking pattern of behavior, such as "going to the cinema on Saturday nights." Hart, *The Concept of Law,* pp. 54–56. But the coercive model entails not unthinking obedience but rational obedience prompted by the prudential interest in avoiding sanctions. In this respect Raz is correct to note that orders backed by threats are also norms in the sense of being rational guides to conduct. See Raz, *The Concept of a Legal System*, p. 128. Thus Hart's objection discredits Austin's terminology ('habit') but not the basic model: orders backed by threats *can* explain the continuity of a legal system. (When Rex I dies and is succeeded by Rex II, one does not have to wait to see whether a habit of obedience to Rex II will develop, any more than one has to wait to see whether hostages held at gunpoint will obey the next terrorist to pick up the gun after the gang's leader is shot.)

This conclusion leaves only one remaining objection to Austin's account: the problem of identifying and accounting for the legal status of sovereigns in modern states. But for all the analytical objections raised by Hart and others to Austin's account of sovereignty, none seems to affect the basic connotational claim that sanctions are imposed by a select group of people on others in a manner indistinguishable from the coercive commands of a sovereign. Hart simply replaces Austin's sovereign with "the officials" as the select group. Problems in identifying Austin's sovereign (whose will is the key to law) are simply transferred to the problem of identifying the officials, whose collective will, evidenced in the rules they accept, is also the key to law. It is true that Hart's officials do not directly will the content of the rules they administer, as does Austin's sovereign. But they do will to accept specified rules (their content already fixed or entrenched) to govern the imposition of sanctions. Even if this indirect exercise of control over content can be distinguished from direct control for some purposes (*who* is boss around here?), the distinction will not affect the connotational claim that law is essentially coercive (someone—or rule—is *boss* around here). To eliminate this coercive aspect requires one to say considerably more about the attitude of acceptance, as in this study.

5. Even one of Austin's strongest defenders, who calls for a "back to Austin" movement in other respects, Morison, *John Austin*, p. 142, hastens to disassociate himself from the definitional aspect of Austin's theory. Ibid., pp. 57–58, 146. In Morison's case, this retreat from definition results in a view of law admittedly designed to reflect not professional or ordinary understandings but the specialized interests of social scientists. Ibid., pp. 180–181.

6. Compare John Finnis's *Natural Law and Natural Rights* (Oxford: Clarendon Press, 1980), pp. 5–6, 267, with Hans Kelsen's *General Theory of Law and State* (New York: Russell and Russell, 1961), pp. 19–22.

7. See Hart, *The Concept of Law*, chap. I.

8. Ibid., p. 14. The approach to definition described in the text resembles Hart's in many ways but diverges here in claiming that we are looking for "the latent principle that guides our use [of the term 'legal system']." Hart rejects this possibility because he claims that there is no wider genus or "familiar well-understood general category of which law is a member"; ibid., p. 15. The text argues in contrast that there is a wider genus—namely organized social systems—and that we divide that general category into members distinguished by the type of social bond that makes the group cohere. The members of the genus and their associated type of social bonds are primarily: (1) coercive systems (force); (2) legal systems (*prima facie* moral obligation); and (3) moral systems (ultimate moral obligation).

9. There may be other plausible explanations for why one distinguishes chairs from couches. The text focuses mainly on function, but even with that focus 'chairs' may mean mainly one-seaters, while the larger love seat is a 'small couch'. One could also suggest that people map the world linguistically in response to certain natural ways of perceiving things, which might make relative size or shape as important as function. Thus a stool is neither a chair nor a couch, though it is also a one-seater. This suggestion could even use modern theories of cognitive psychology to buttress the "old-fashioned" idea of natural essences. Whatever the explanation, the model of what one is trying to do when one defends a "real" definition remains the same. See Richard Robinson, *Definition* (Oxford: Clarendon Press, 1954), pp. 16, 62, 149–151). One looks for the latent principle of the existing classification scheme by considering the human needs (in the sense both of function and of natural human responses to the environment) that the scheme appears to serve.

In the case of the concept of legal system, most modern theorists agree that it is function that provides the clue to the latent principle. See Finnis, *Natural Law and Natural Rights*, pp. 6–7.

10. Hart seems to concede that the potential frustration of desires makes it possible to accommodate power-conferring laws to the coercive model. See *The Concept of Law*, pp. 33–34. He relies on another argument to show that nullity cannot be treated as a sanction. Unlike criminal laws, where one can subtract the sanction and still leave an intelligible standard of conduct, Hart claims that one cannot similarly subtract the sanction of nullity and still leave a meaningful standard. "We cannot logically make . . . a distinction between the rule requiring compliance with certain conditions, e.g., attestation for a valid will, and the so-called sanction of 'nullity.' In this case, if failure to comply with this essential condition did not entail nullity, the rule itself could not be intelligibly said to exist without sanctions even as a non-legal rule"; ibid., p. 34.

This seems incorrect. One could uphold a will even though it did not have the requisite number of witnesses, all the while criticizing the testator for creating extra problems in proving his intent, which could have been avoided by getting witnesses as the rule stipulates. Power-conferring rules, in short, establish intelligible standards of behavior, even subtracting the sanction of nullity, as long as there is some reason or substantive purpose for the particular way in which the rule requires power to be exercised: some reason why contracts require consideration or wills require witnesses or drivers are required to pass a road test. The reason furnishes a standard and a basis for criticism even though we decide to uphold the will or contract (that is, subtract the sanction of nullity).

The only rules to which Hart's criticism applies are those that are purely constitutive—like the rules of a game. (One cannot allow a bishop to move like a knight while still retaining the rule about how bishops move.) Some legal rules are probably purely constitutive, such as rules defining court jurisdiction, which Hart also views as counterexamples to the coercive model. But purely constitutive rules can be accommodated to the coercive model in another way, as Hart recognizes: they become part of the defining conditions for the application of sanctions. See ibid., pp. 35–38. Hart's only objection now is that this model distorts the way the rule functions—for example by making it appear that laws are addressed to judges rather than citizens, or by making it impossible to distinguish a tax from a fine. These objections, however, do not seem to hold in the case of purely constitutive rules such as those defining court jurisdiction which are after all addressed to courts and which, being purely constitutive, can only be part of the definition (just as the rule about how a bishop moves can only be a definition of a bishop's move). Where the objection does seem to apply, as in the case of the tax and the fine, the claim that there is distortion begs the issue as to whether it is a distortion to ignore any point of view but that of the bad man in depicting the essence of law. Ibid., p. 39.

11. Ibid., p. 149. Hart suggests that this power of courts to make their (collective) will determinative of the law is limited to cases of "previously unenvisaged questions." But nothing in his model limits the theoretical power of courts to do the same in the case of settled rules as well, a "standing possibility" even according to Hart; ibid., p. 142. If officials accept new rules in violation of the Constitution, and are able to enforce their decision, we will have a new legal system. The fact that there may be empirical constraints that prevent officials from accepting just any rules does not distinguish Hart's officials on this score from Austin's sovereign. See also note 4 above.

12. Ibid., p. 39.

13. One must take care not to confuse the question of what is important about law with the question of what is important in deciding whether to classify something as law. Everyone may agree that comfort is the most important thing about chairs, but that does not mean that whether something is a chair depends on whether it is comfortable. For further discussion of this point see Philip Soper, "Legal Theory and the Problem of Definition," 50 *Chicago Law Review* 1170, 1188–1190, (1983).

14. The common assumption "that power cannot be exercised without some voluntary support" is criticized in Michael Polanyi, *Personal Knowledge* (Chicago: University of Chicago Press, 1958), pp. 224–226. Polanyi's claim that purely coercive regimes can and do exist seems to me correct, although I have obviously not conducted an empirical survey. In any event, the positivist who asserts a conceptual connection between law and the idea of voluntary (official) allegiance does not seem to deny the empirical possibility of a purely coercive regime. In that case the positivist must either explain why such a regime would not count as legal or concede that he is only describing a variety of important characteristics of most standard legal systems—an enterprise that makes it just as plausible to add the moral ideals that most standard legal systems also claim to embody. See also note 21 below.

15. See Hart, *The Concept of Law*, pp. 199–200.

16. Hans Kelsen, *The Pure Theory of Law*, trans. M. Knight (Berkeley: University of California Press, 1970), p. 8.

17. Ibid., pp. 47–48.

18. Graham Hughes, "Validity and the Basic Norm," 59 *California Law Review* 695, 702 (1971).

19. See note 14 above.

20. Hart, *The Concept of Law*, pp. 204–206.

21. It is necessary at this point to note an ambiguity in positivist legal theory about whether or not a purely coercive system—one that operates only through orders backed by threats—is or is not a legal system. Hart, of course, rejects this "Austinian" model because, like Kelsen, he insists on the importance of the additional normative element entailed in an attitude of acceptance of the system. But rejection of the coercive model may imply either a strong or a weak thesis. The strong thesis would be that no purely coercive system could count as law. (See Raz, *The Concept of a Legal System*, pp. 128–137, 149–150, where he says that orders backed by threats are norms but do not impose obligations in the same sense as laws.) The weak thesis would count such systems as law but would emphasize the additional feature of rule-acceptance because it is a pervasive characteristic of most complex systems.

For reasons more fully explained in the text, only the strong thesis is of interest. After all, if purely coercive systems are legal, what is the point in modifying Austin's account just because it neglects certain additional, but by hypothesis nonessential, features? If positivists such as Hart mean to embrace the weak thesis—that coercive systems are legal but lack some important additional features—then one might as well continue to add as many important features to the account as can plausibly be identified, including, for example, the features emphasized in this study. See also Finnis, *Natural Law and Natural Rights*, pp. 13–14. Either way, current positivist legal theory seems arbitrary in the features it chooses to include and exclude in its account of law.

22. A rare and excellent analysis of the textual contradictions in the *Concept of Law* may be found in Roscoe E. Hill, "Legal Validity and Legal Obligation," 80 *Yale Law Journal* 47 (1970). Hill correctly notes that Hart's description of the "idea of obligation" in Chapter 5 proves completely irrelevant to the picture of "legal obligation" that eventually emerges from the book. The best way to see this is to compare Hart's discussion in Chapter 5, Section 2 ("The Idea of Obligation") with his discussion in Chapter 8, Section 2 ("Moral and Legal Obligation"). The latter discussion takes back, in distinguishing law from morals, everything that was said in Chapter 5 about how to identify "rules of obligation" (laws no longer have to be "important," they can arise by human fiat, they do not necessarily imply moral blame, the distinguishing form of pressure is the threat of organized sanction). The consequence is that one is left with a description of law whose distinguishing feature is the same as that identified by Austin: the organized sanction. When one considers in addition Hart's description of the reasons for acceptance of the rule of recognition (see Hart, *The Concept of Law*, pp. 198, 226), only one conclusion is possible: the normative attitude of Hart's officials is indistinguishable from that of Austin's sovereign. After all, Austin's sovereign (which may be a group of people) will also have the same reasons for accepting his (their) position as power wielder(s) that Hart requires of his officials in their attitude toward the rules they accept.

The textual contradiction in Hart's account is also briefly noted in David Lyons's review of *H. L. A. Hart* by Neil MacCormick, 68 *Cornell Law Review* 257, 262 (1983).

23. Hart, *The Concept of Law*, pp. 83–85.

24. Ibid., p. 198.

25. For an illuminating analysis of this puzzle in Hart's account, see Gerald J. Postema, "Coordination and Convention at the Foundation of Law," 11 *Journal of Legal Studies* 165, 169–171 (1982).

26. In *Essays on Bentham*, p. 135, Hart discusses the relationship between statements of legal obligation and statements about the likelihood of punishment, arguing that these statements do not have the same meaning. In *The Concept of Law*, p. 83, Hart makes a similar argument about the relation between statements of legal obligation and the statement that there is "not the slightest chance of . . . being caught or made to suffer." As the text indicates, the example Hart uses in the latter case (escaping the jurisdiction or bribing the court) are not ones where all chance of being made to suffer can ever be ruled out empirically except by death. If by hypothesis it *is* ruled out, it is plausible to view as a contradiction the claim that there is still a legal obligation.

27. See Hart, *The Concept of Law*, p. 39, where this objection to Kelsen's view is raised. The point is also raised as an objection to probabilistic accounts of obligation in Hart, *Essays on Bentham*, pp. 133–134.

28. See Hart, *The Concept of Law*, pp. 10–11, 82, 143. The common assumption that predictive theories of law must be logically circular from the judge's viewpoint is forcefully challenged in Anthony D'Amoto, "The Limits of Legal Realism," 87 *Yale Law Journal* 468, 495–505 (1978). Hart's claim seems only to be that predictive theories are inaccurate descriptions of the judge's viewpoint, not that they are logically circular.

29. This is the point made by Hill in "Legal Validity and Legal Obligation," note 22 above. See also Note, "H. L. A. Hart on Legal and Moral Obligation," 73 *Michigan Law Review* 443 (1974). Neil MacCormick tries to rescue Hart from the accusation that he treats obligation inconsistently by suggesting that Hill's criticism exploits the confusion "between rules which themselves determine obligations and rules which for some reason one has an obligation to obey." MacCormick, *H. L. A. Hart* (Stanford: Stanford University Press, 1981), p. 59. If MacCormick means by this to place law in the category of rules which for some reason one has an obligation to obey, the positivist cannot tell us that they belong there without engaging in substantive moral philosophy, as in this study. But if MacCormick means only to defend Hart's claim that law should be classified among the rules that people *think* there is some reason to obey, he runs into the contradictions noted in the text when Hart describes the necessary attitude of acceptance of law so weakly. See also Hart, *The Concept of Law*, p. 226, where he claims that legal systems do not necessarily rest on a perceived obligation to obey the law.

30. See P. M. S. Hacker, "Sanction Theories of Duty," in *Oxford Essays in Jurisprudence*, ed. A. W. B. Simpson, 2d. ed. (Oxford: Clarendon Press, 1973), p. 131.

31. The oddity of suggesting a unique kind of legal obligation distinct from the moral can also be seen in the fact that such a view seems to entail the conclusion that there could be a legal discretion to disobey law. That is, the law it-

self might provide for the possibility that just because something is legally obligatory does not mean that one ought (morally) to obey but only that one ought (legally) to obey. This view seems to be advanced by Mortimer R. and Sanford H. Kadish in *Discretion to Disobey* (Stanford: Stanford University Press, 1973). The view is challenged as incoherent in M. B. E. Smith, "Concerning Lawful Illegality," 83 *Yale Law Journal* 1534, 1539-1546 (1974). Much of the strength of Raz's claims that law provides an "exclusionary reason" for acting and that, from the viewpoint of the judge, legal obligation is presented as consistent with morality derives from the oddness of thinking that there could be any other meaning to the judge's claim (unless it is simply a statement about legal validity). Those who issue law have already decided that, all things considered, the legal obligations are morally proper and they purport to pre-empt others from second-guessing that judgment. Thus law is presented as both "exclusionary" and as entailing claims of obligation that share the same meaning as moral obligation. See generally Joseph Raz, *Practical Reason and Norms* (London: Hutchinson and Co., 1975), chaps. 1, 5.

32. For those aspects of Raz's theory discussed here see generally Raz, *The Authority of Law* (Oxford: Clarendon Press, 1979), chaps. 4, 8. The specific dispute between Hart and Raz over how to describe the normative aspect of law can best be followed by considering Hart's recent defense of his view against Raz's in Hart, *Essays on Bentham*, pp. 153-161, 262-268 (citing Raz, *Practical Reason and Norms*, pp. 123-129, 146-148, 162-177; Raz, *The Authority of Law*, pp. 153-157; Raz, *The Concept of a Legal System*, pp. 234-238).

33. Hart, *The Concept of Law*, pp. 198-199.

34. See Raz, *The Authority of Law*, p. 155, n.13.

35. See Hart, *The Concept of Law*, pp. 112-113; 196-198.

36. Ibid., p. 199.

37. See Philip Soper, "Metaphors and Models of Law," 75 *Michigan Law Review* 1196, 1205-1209; John Noonan, Book Review, 7 *Natural Law Forum* 169, 176-177 (1962). The game analogy to law and the limitations of the analogy are frequently discussed in the literature. See for example John Ladd, "Legal and Moral Obligation," in *Nomos XII: Political and Legal Obligation*, ed. J. Roland Pennock and John W. Chapman (New York: Atherton Press, 1970), pp. 3, 17-24.

38. Hart's description of the features that identify rules of obligation and of the internal attitude toward rules in general has received considerable attention. MacCormick, for example, stresses the qualitative as well as the quantitative aspect of the social pressure behind rules of obligation. See MacCormick, *H. L. A. Hart*, pp. 65-70. MacCormick also stresses that the "internal viewpoint" that underlies the attitude of rule acceptance has both cognitive and volitional elements. Cognitive acceptance involves appreciating, or understanding, what a rule requires; volitional acceptance includes a willing endorsement of the rule. Ibid., pp. 34-40, 43-44. See also MacCormick, *Legal Reasoning and Legal Theory* (Oxford: Clarendon Press, 1978) pp. 275-292, and his "Legal Obligation and the Imperative Fallacy," in *Oxford Essays in Jurisprudence*, ed. A. W. B. Simpson, 2d. ed. (Oxford: Clarendon Press, 1973), p. 100. (This distinction be-

tween cognitive and volitional components seems to have been anticipated by Roscoe Hill; see his "Legal Validity and Legal Obligation," note 22 above, p. 57.)

The text follows MacCormick in arguing that the qualitative aspect of the pressure behind rules of obligation is more important than the quantitative aspect; indeed the latter is parasitic on the former. I also assume that volitional acceptance is the critical component in the official attitude toward the rules of a legal sysem. But unlike Hart, and apparently also MacCormick (see *Legal Reasoning and Legal Theory*, pp. 288–292), I do not believe one can willingly embrace rules for any reason and still distinguish law from force. The rules must be embraced because they are believed to be just.

39. See generally J. Raz, "Kelsen's Theory of the Basic Norm," 19 *American Journal of Jurisprudence* 94, 103 (1974).

40. Jean Piaget, *The Moral Judgment of the Child* (New York: The Free Press, 1965).

41. P. M. S. Hacker suggests that the failure to make this distinction between descriptions of group obligations, which merely report facts, and assertions of group obligations, which make normative claims, accounts for most of the confusion engendered by Hart's analysis of social rules and legal obligation. See P. M. S. Hacker, "Hart's Philosophy of Law," in *Law, Morality, and Society*, ed. P. M. S. Hacker and J. Raz (Oxford: Clarendon Press, 1979), pp. 153–157. See also note 38 above.

42. For an eloquent argument to the same effect, on the impossibility of separating descriptive and evaluative aspects of normative discourse, see Finnis, *Natural Law and Natural Rights*, pp. 357–359.

43. See MacCormick, "Legal Obligation and the Imperative Fallacy," note 30 above, p. 119, where he argues that strong social pressure is neither a necessary nor a sufficient test for group obligation.

44. See P. T. Geach, *The Virtues* (Cambridge: Cambridge University Press, 1977), p. 128, where he writes, "It doesn't matter whether you *call* them laws or not: the question is what consequences follow."

45. This interpretation of Aquinas is nicely developed in Finnis, *Natural Law and Natural Rights*, pp. 363–366.

46. See for example, Lon Fuller, *Legal Fictions* (Stanford: Stanford University Press, 1967), and Fuller and William Perdue, "The Reliance Interest in Contract Damages," 46 *Yale Law Journal* 52, 373 (1936–1937).

47. Lon Fuller, "Positivism and Fidelity to Law—A Reply to Professor Hart," 71 *Harvard Law Review* 630, 636, (1958).

48. See Fuller, *The Morality of Law* (New Haven: Yale University Press, 1963), pp. 145–151.

49. See Hart, review of Fuller's *Morality of Law*, 78 *Harvard Law Review* 1281, 1286–1287, 1296 (1965).

50. For a thoughtful appraisal of these criticisms of Fuller and a conclusion sympathetic to his claim about the relationship between reason and goodness see Rolf Sartorius, *Individual Conduct and Social Norms* (Encino, Calif.: Dickerson Publishing Co., 1975), pp. 169–173. See also Soper, book review, 75 *Michigan Law Review* 1539, 1551–1552 (1977).

51. See Morton Horwitz, *The Transformation of American Law* (Cambridge, Mass.: Harvard University Press, 1977).

52. See ibid., p. xvi.

53. Dworkin, *Taking Rights Seriously*, chaps. 2–4 and pp. 291–369.

54. Thomas Aquinas, *Summa Theologica*, pt. II, first part, quest. 90.

55. The claim that law need only aim at rather than actually achieve the common good distinguishes the theory developed here most markedly from Finnis's otherwise similar account. Finnis also develops a definition of law based on that of Aquinas; but Finnis requires that laws actually "be consistent with the basic requirements of practical reasonableness, though [they] need not necessarily or even usually be the [laws a citizen] would himself have made had he had the opportunity." Finnis, *Natural Law and Natural Rights*, p. 289. Much of Finnis's study is devoted to developing these requirements of practical reasonableness in ways that make the work, in Finnis's own estimate, primarily a moral theory rather than a conceptual theory of legal systems. See ibid., pp. 18, 25, 276–281. Moreover, on the central question of the present study, Finnis concludes (without presenting arguments) that a law inconsistent with the requirement of practical reasonableness cannot yield a prima facie obligation to obey. See ibid., p. 359. The present study, in contrast, concludes that a good faith attempt to meet the requirements of practical reasonableness is all that is required for at least a weak sense of obligation.

56. In responding to Raz's similar suggestion that law connotes an official belief in justice, Hart claims that such a theory is still largely a positivist one. See Hart, *Essays on Bentham*, p. 153. For reasons stressed in the text, that conclusion is from one perspective appropriate. The surface modification I have made to Hart's account is slight: I restrict his "attitude of acceptance," which underlies the rule of recognition, to one that embraces and defends the rule as just. But from another perspective this modification represents a serious blow to theories that deny any conceptual link between law and morality. In order to defend the good faith claim to justice, legal officials will find that normative propositions are as much a part of the stock of legal principles as are descriptions of human (legislative) acts, and one will have to reach deep into political and moral theory, as Dworkin claims, in order to vindicate the claim that a decision is legal. See Dworkin, *Taking Rights Seriously*, p. 67. The tension here for the positivist in trying to draw the line between describing and evaluating law is a reflection of the tension created by trying to draw a line between insider and outsider perspectives on normative systems.

57. The contrast between the theory described here and the theories examined in this chapter, as well as an indication of the task ahead, can be seen most clearly in the following summary:

1. I take seriously the suggestion that law must connote the idea of obligation in the sense described by Hart in Chapter 5 of *The Concept of Law*.
2. I locate this idea of obligation in the concept of law not by observing as a matter of empirical fact that various normative attitudes are often or

sometimes or always found in legal systems but by showing how the view that there is an obligation to obey law is valid as a matter of moral theory.

3. I defend this analysis as a definition of law because it better serves the interests of the person who wants to know what his moral obligations are than does a definition that focuses only on the chance of incurring a sanction. (For an answer to the question why the moral person, rather than the bad man should be the test of an adequate theory of law, see the concluding section of Chapter VI of this book.)

III. POLITICAL THEORY

1. The distinction between prima facie and absolute obligation is usually traced to W. D. Ross, *The Right and the Good* (Oxford: Oxford University Press, 1930), chap. 2. For application and refinement of the distinction in the context of political obligation see Smith, "Is There a Prima Facie Obligation to Obey the Law?" Chapter I, note 13 above. As will become clear, I am using 'prima facie' in a much weaker sense than Ross to mean any moral reason in favor of compliance.

Few writers today defend the position that there is an absolute obligation to obey the law, although Socrates is sometimes thought to have held such a view. See William Powers, "Structural Aspects of the Impact of Law on Moral Duty within Utilitarianism and Social Contract Theory," 26 *University of California (Los Angeles) Law Review* 1263, 1263-1264, n.2, where he points to inconsistencies in Socrates' views as expressed in the *Apology* and the *Crito*.

2. See for example Joseph Raz, *The Authority of Law* (Oxford: Clarendon Press, 1979), p. 235, where he argues that obligation to obey means more than merely having a good faith reason to obey, but that even in this "modest" sense there is no such obligation. See also sources cited in Chapter I, note 13.

3. Smith, "Is There a Prima Facie Obligation to Obey the Law?" Chapter I, note 13, p. 965.

4. R. P. Wolff, *In Defense of Anarchism* (New York: Harper and Row, 1970), p. 16.

5. Recognition of this constraint on any successful solution to the problem of political obligation is widespread. See Smith, "Is There a Prima Facie Obligation to Obey the Law?" Chapter I, note 13, pp. 951-952; Raz, *The Authority of Law*, pp. 233-234; A. J. Simmons, *Moral Principles and Political Obligation* (Princeton: Princeton University Press, 1979), pp. 30-35.

6. See A. J. Simmons, *Moral Principles and Political Obligation*, pp. 31-32.

7. See John Rawls, *A Theory of Justice* (Cambridge, Mass.: Harvard University Press, 1971), pp. 34-49.

8. Compare Lucy v. Zehmer, 196 Va. 493 (1954), with Armstrong v. M'Ghee (County Court of Westmoreland County, Pa., 1795, Addison 261). Statements in the text about what is required to establish a legal claim are for the most part bald hornbook propositions of law. Authorities cited are standard

textbook cases or basic treatises familiar to most American law students. Not all statements of law in the text will be documented by citation to authority. My purpose in this section is not to teach law or to document every claim that is made about a specific legal rule, but rather to indicate how paradigmatic sources of legal reasoning about obligation may be used in confirming judgments or intuitions others reach through independent methods.

9. See *Restatement (Second) of Contracts* §§ 19, 69(1) (a) (1979).

10. See ibid., § 69.

11. See 39 U.S.C. § 3009 (1976). This result admittedly represents a statutory change in the common law in response to modern demands for consumer protection. See *Restatement (Second) of Contracts* § 69(1) (a) and comment e (1979).

12. See *Restatement (Second) of Contracts* § 90 and comment a (1979).

13. This example is paraphrased from Peter Singer, *Democracy and Disobedience* (Oxford: Clarendon Press, 1973), p. 52.

14. Raz, *The Authority of Law*, p. 241.

15. See George Palmer, *Law of Restitution* (Boston: Little, Brown, 1978) vol. 2, § 11.2, pp. 492–493.

16. Ibid., § 10.1, p. 359. For an example of a philosopher independently developing the concept of an officious intermeddler see Robert Nozick, *Anarchy, State, and Utopia* (New York: Basic Books, 1974), pp. 93–95.

17. See Palmer, *Law of Restitution*, §10.4.

18. John Rawls, "Legal Obligation and the Duty of Fair Play," in *Law and Philosophy*, ed. Sidney Hook (New York: New York University Press, 1964), pp. 9–10.

19. In this respect recent philosophical attempts to distinguish benefit-based theories from consent theories are confused. Simmons, for example, reads Nozick as suggesting that benefits can confer obligation only where there is tacit consent. See Simmons, *Moral Principles and Political Obligation*, pp. 124–126. Simmons objects to this view and constructs his own example of a case of obligation based on benefits received without consent. The example is this: a neighborhood well is dug to furnish water for the community. Jones votes against the proposed scheme and announces that he does not agree to it. After the well is dug, Jones nevertheless takes water from the well, still denying that he consents to pay. Here, says Simmons, is an example of a benefit-based obligation not derived from tacit consent. Ibid., pp. 126–127. But the example is simply a case of theft, which does not require "fair play" or "unjust enrichment" to explain why it is wrong or to justify legal recovery.

20. See generally Palmer, *Law of Restitution*, §10.8.

21. See John Dawson, "Lawyers and Involuntary Clients: Attorney Fees from Funds," 87 *Harvard Law Review* 1597 (1974), and "Lawyers and Involuntary Clients in Public Interest Litigation," 88 *Harvard Law Review* 849 (1975).

22. See Rawls, *A Theory of Justice*, pp. 113–114.

23. See Ulmer V. Farnsworth, 80 Me. 500, 15 A. 65 (1888); Palmer, *Law of Restitution*, § 10.7.

24. John Dawson, "The Self-Serving Intermeddler," 87 *Harvard Law Review* 1409, 1457 (1974).

25. Smith, "Is There a Prima Facie Obligation to Obey the Law?" Chapter I, note 13, pp. 956–957.

26. Wolff, *In Defense of Anarchism*, p. 27.

27. See Jeffrey Reiman, *In Defense of Political Philosophy* (New York: Harper and Row, 1972), pp. 12–13.

28. That one must ultimately appeal to reason or value in some sense in explaining why promises create obligations is a point often made; see "Of the Original Contract," in *David Hume's Political Essays*, ed. Charles Hendel (New York: Liberal Arts Press, 1953), p. 56; Ronald Dworkin, "The Original Position," 49 *University of Chicago Law Review* 500 (1973); P. S. Atiyah, *The Rise and Fall of Contract* (Oxford: Clarendon Press, 1979), p. 731. And it is a point just as often forgotten. See Anthony Kronman, "A New Champion for the Will Theory," 91 *Yale Law Journal* 404, 411–413 (1981), a book review noting Charles Fried's failure in *Contract as Promise* to consider why promises bind. Indeed much of the controversy over whether contract obligations are benefit based, reliance based, or promise based is a red herring: if reasons must be given for why promises bind, then tort and contract alike rest ultimately on appeals to what reasonable men ought to conclude. The bare fact of will alone is just that: a bare fact. As with all facts, its relevance must be independently established by reasoned argument.

29. Plato, *Crito* 50d–51d.

30. A good overview may be found in Simmons, *Moral Principles and Political Obligation*, chap. VII. For a cogent analysis that resembles the argument of this chapter in finding governmental and parental authority in necessity rather than in benefits conferred, see Elizabeth Anscombe, "On the Source of the Authority of the State," 20 *Ratio* 1, 6 (1978).

31. Compare Simmons, *Moral Principles and Political Obligation*, p. 178, with *Restatement of Restitution* § 116.

32. Hume, "Of the Original Contract," p. 51.

33. Wolff, *In Defense of Anarchism*, p. 16. The relevant passage is quoted and discussed in the text at note 4, above.

34. See Nozick, *Anarchy, State, and Utopia*, p. 68.

35. For this point I am indebted to Donald Regan.

36. I have cast the theory in terms of respect for "those in charge" only because that is the limiting case of law; in most cases, those who accept the system and thus deserve respect will include citizens as well as officials. That one sometimes shows respect by doing the right thing, rather than what is desired, should not obscure the fact that respect for good faith *effort* is shown by complying. This tension between rewarding honest effort and rewarding virtue does not disappear just because in a particular case the pull toward the latter proves the stronger. That is why, after all, the obligation is only prima facie.

37. Smith, "Is There a Prima Facie Obligation to Obey the Law?" Chapter I, note 13, p. 965.

38. Though I have tried to give a utilitarian cast to the theory, mainly in order

to highlight the change that has been made in the usual argument, I confess that the utilitarian model fits uncomfortably. Thus, one might suggest that a theory based on the reactions of others to one's disobedience only counsels keeping disobedience secret, giving rise to obligation only where disobedience is likely to be discovered. One may perhaps counter that the possibility of discovery (unlike the possibility that trivial acts of disobedience will adversely affect the system) can never safely be ruled out (one might confess, if nothing else), and that this standing possibility is all one needs for a prima facie case of obligation (a rule of thumb?). It seems more persuasive to suggest that it is the hypothetical discovery that one must consider, and thus act like any other rational person in society—a Kantian explanation that forces one to evaluate action from the viewpoint of the rational other rather than the contingent, actual other. In the end, I suspect that difficulties with the utilitarian account stem from the incoherence of the idea of prima facie obligation itself within a utilitarian theory.

39. Smith, "Is There a Prima Facie Obligation to Obey the Law?" Chapter I, note 13, p. 970.

40. Finnis correctly observes that Smith's claim is subject to this criticism. See John Finnis, *Natural Law and Natural Rights* (Oxford: Clarendon Press, 1980), p. 345.

41. Lon Fuller, *The Morality of Law* (New Haven: Yale University Press, 1963), p. 106.

42. The distinction between the general justification of the state and the justification of political obligation within any particular state should not be confused with the quite different question of whether a particular state can be legitimate even though there is no obligation to obey its directives. See for example Rolf Sartorius, "Political Authority and Political Obligation," 67 *Virginia Law Review* 3 (1981); Joseph Raz, "Authority and Consent," 67 *Virginia Law Review* 103 (1981). It is no coincidence that this question has come to the fore at the same time that theorists have begun to conclude that there is no obligation to obey. I do not think a meaningful concept of legitimacy can be separated from the notion of at least a prima facie obligation to obey. See J. Reiman, *In Defense of Political Philosophy*, p. 35. Compare J. L. Mackie, "Obligations to Obey the Law," 67 *Virginia Law Review* 143 (1981), with Robert Holmes, "State-Legitimacy and the Obligation to Obey the Law," 67 *Virginia Law Review* 133 (1981).

IV. CONNECTIONS

1. Joseph Raz raises the objection mentioned in the text about immoral systems that we would nevertheless call legal ("a fact about our ordinary notion of law") in arguing against what he calls "the definitional approach" to linking law and morality. See Raz, *Practical Reason and Norms* (London: Hutchinson and Co., 1975), p. 164.

2. Ibid., pp. 165–167.

3. Ibid., p. 168.

4. See M. B. E. Smith, "Is There a Prima Facie Obligation to Obey the Law?" Chapter I, note 13, p. 952, n.5.

5. Raz, *Practical Reason and Norms*, p. 170.

6. See Chapter II, note 6.

7. See the concluding section of Chapter VI on choosing a view.

V. APPLICATIONS

1. Raz argues for the extreme view. See Joseph Raz, *The Authority of Law* (Oxford: Clarendon Press, 1979), pp. 45–52. Hart (who as we saw begins as a modern positivist with the position that law must include the idea of obligation but ends with a model that seems classical in its assertion that law obligates only in the sense that officials accept it) also seems to accept here the classical view that moral standards may contingently be made a part of a society's laws. See H. L. A. Hart *The Concept of Law* (Oxford: Clarendon Press, 1961), pp. 199–200.

2. See H. L. A. Hart, "Positivism and the Separation of Law and Morals," 71 *Harvard Law Review* 593 (1958); Lon Fuller, "Positivism and Fidelity to Law: A Reply to Professor Hart," 71 *Harvard Law Review* 630 (1958); Fuller, "Human Purpose and Natural Law," 3 *Natural Law Forum* 68 (1958); Ernest Nagel, "On the Fusion of Fact and Value: A Reply to Professor Fuller," 3 *Natural Law Forum* 76 (1959).

3. For another illustration of this strategy for accommodating the theory of a nonpositivist such as Dworkin to the positivist's model, see Soper, "Legal Theory and the Obligation of a Judge," Chapter I, note 4 above, pp. 509–516. Dworkin's response to the strategy has been to claim that it results in "redefining" positivism. See Ronald Dworkin, *Taking Rights Seriously* (Cambridge, Mass: Harvard University Press, 1977), p. 345. This response assumes that the true definition of positivism is one that links law and certainty. But the classical definition entails only "the simple contention that it is in no sense a necessary truth that laws reproduce or satisfy certain demands of morality." Hart, *The Concept of Law*, p. 181. The uncertainty of moral facts may be an additional reason for some positivists to insist on separating law and morality, but uncertainty has never been the primary reason behind the classsical positivist's "simple contention." The classical positivist, even if he thought moral facts were as certain and observable as other facts, would still insist on the logical independence of the concepts. See Hart, "Positivism and the Separation of Law and Morals," note 2 above, p. 626. Dworkin's redefinition of positivism is another indication that the problem of explaining the relationship between law and certainty has overtaken the classical problem of explaining the relationship between law and morality.

4. See Joseph Raz, *Practical Reason and Norms* (London: Hutchinson and Co., 1975), pp. 137–146; Raz, *The Authority of Law*, pp. 45–52.

5. See Lon Fuller, *The Morality of Law* (New Haven: Yale University Press, 1963), chap. 2.

6. Compare Hart, book review, Chapter II, note 49, with Fuller, *The Morality of Law*, pp. 133–145.

7. Fuller, *The Morality of Law*, p. 33.

8. See Learned Hand, *The Spirit of Liberty*, ed. I. Dilliard, 3d ed. (New York: Knopf, 1960), pp. 306–307. See also Edward J. Bander, *Justice Holmes ex Cathedra* (Charlottesville, Va.: Michie Co., 1966), pp. 213, 243–244, 245, which collects anecdotes to the same effect from Charles Butler, Karl Llewellyn, and Alfred McCormack.

9. For illuminating discussions of these issues see John Finnis, "Revolutions and Continuity of Law," in *Oxford Essays in Jurisprudence*, 2d. ser., ed. A. W. B. Simpson (Oxford: Clarendon Press, 1973), p. 44, and J. W. Harris, "When and Why does the *Grundnorm* Change?" 29 *Cambridge Law Journal* 103 (1971). See also Chapter II, note 11.

10. One would be hard pressed to find a better recent argument for restrained judicial review than that contained in John Hart Ely, *Democracy and Distrust* (Cambridge, Mass.: Harvard University Press, 1980). One would also be hard pressed to find a better example of paradoxical premises. A judge reading Ely to find out what he ought to do would discover that Ely's answer is entirely dependent on the assumption that democratic values provide the fundamental test for an adequate theory of judicial review (pp. 87–104). To the judge who wants to know why he should accept democratic values, Ely has nothing to say.

Why should democratic values be excepted from Ely's general attack in Chapter 3 on the ability to establish fundamental values? Is it because everybody agrees with this starting point—with the Constitution and democratic theory? But that response is only another argument from consensus, which, he tells us, does not work (pp. 63–69). Is it because one must start somewhere in reasoning to any moral conclusion? But then why condemn other attempts to reason from other starting points (p. 54)? What is so special about this starting point? If the process of justifying the societal application of force has already been tainted by this leap of faith, does it really taint the justification further if we make other leaps? Is it a case of applying Occam's razor to limit to as few as possible the moral assumptions that have to be made? Why isn't the appropriate image instead that of significant figures in a column, or the weak link in a chain: once you have one, does it really further weaken the chain to add more?

Ely's problem, like Justice Holmes's, is that his skepticism about the possibility of proving ethical statements leads him to strike out against all claims of value without abandoning his own deep commitment to the role he plays and the arguments he makes. If one must choose between the evidence of Ely's "lad studying philosophy" (p. 53) who has just discovered the impossibility of proving anything in morals and the adult who can accept values as valid despite their unprovability, it is the image of the latter that should instruct a conscientious judge. If that is so, he is likely to be far more sympathetic than Ely to what other judges are trying to do in discovering fundamental values beyond those of democracy in constitutional theory.

11. See R. M. Unger, *Knowledge and Politics* (New York: The Free Press, 1975), pp. 88–97.

12. See Duncan Kennedy, "Legal Formality," 2 *Journal of Legal Studies* 385–388 (1973).

13. See Karl Llewellyn, *The Common Law Tradition: Deciding Appeals* (Boston: Little, Brown, 1960), p. 25 ("The single right answer tends, along with pressure of work and human avoidance of sweat, to encourage taking the first seemingly workable road which offers, thus giving the familiar an edge up on the more wise").

14. See Rolf Sartorius, *Individual Conduct and Social Norms* (Encino, Calif.: Dickenson Publishing Co., 1975), p. 202.

15. Presumably, insiders whose interests are heeded, and outsiders as well, would still call a system legal as long as it met the conditions of this study for most or a significant group of citizens. But members of an inside group whose interests were ignored in ways that resulted in no obligation for them, as per this study, could be expected to conclude that official directives were no law at all. Thus, this study accounts for the persistent inclination to admit the possibility that official decrees may not be law despite their pedigree—not because they are too evil, as natural law would have it, but because they do not have even the prima facie moral worth described here. At the same time, one would expect others who are not members of such a group to adhere to the common linguistic practice of calling systems legal if there is overall conformity to the features I have identified.

16. See Robert Nozick, *Anarchy, State, and Utopia* (New York: Basic Books, 1974), pp. 290–292.

17. In suggesting that even slaves may have prima facie obligations to obey the law, I am talking only about slaves who are in that position because officials sincerely believe such treatment can be morally justified. Where the disadvantaged group is treated as not worthy of such moral respect, the reciprocal bond necessary for obligation disappears. It may be that by stressing this demand for moral respect for the disadvantaged group many historical examples of slave societies can be shown to reveal an official attitude inconsistent with obligation.

The above distinction assumes that one can sincerely respect as morally equal someone who nevertheless is treated quite differently and less advantageously. The differential treatment is presumably justified by reference to perceived factual differences, such as ability or need, which make disparate treatment consistent with fairness under a particular moral theory. Thus it is the falsity of either the factual or the normative premises that explains why human slavery can no longer be justified. By analogy, the continued acceptance of what is in a sense animal "slavery" presumably rests on factual differences which allow humans to so use animals without entailing that such treatment is unjust: the animal's dignity (assuming it is appropriate to use such a term) is not degraded if the factual differences between humans and animals are as posited and are also the morally relevant ones.

18. See the illuminating discussion in Patrick Gardiner, "Error, Faith, and

Self-Deception," in *The Philosophy of Mind*, ed. Jonathan Glover (Oxford: Oxford University Press, 1976), p. 35.

19. Compare Soper, "Legal Theory and the Obligation of a Judge," Chapter I, note 4, pp. 518-519, with Dworkin, *Taking Rights Seriously*, pp. 350-353.

20. See Nozick, *Anarchy, State, and Utopia*, chap. 2.

21. Dworkin, *Taking Rights Seriously*, pp. 82-84.

22. See Hart, *The Concept of Law*, p. 195.

23. See Soper, "Legal Theory and the Problem of Definition," Chapter II, note 3, pp. 1173-1175.

24. See Hart, *The Concept of Law*, p. 202.

25. I assume, of course, that the persons or citizens in question, unlike rocks or animals, are in fact capable of discourse—an empirical question to be resolved on the basis of factors engagingly discussed by Bruce Ackerman, *Social Justice in the Liberal State* (New Haven: Yale University Press, 1980), pp. 70-80, where he suggests "dialogic performance" as a test of capacity for citizenship. In other respects Ackerman's concept of dialogue in political theory bears little resemblance to the right of discourse sketched here. For one thing, Ackerman derives political theory from dialogue, whereas I have done just the reverse. For another, Ackerman purports to derive a great deal of substantive content from neutral dialogue, whereas I make no such claims for the power of discourse.

26. See Vincent Blasi, "The Checking Value in First Amendment Theory," 3 *American Bar Foundation Research Journal* 523 (1977). The similarities between Blasi's theory of the "checking value" of free speech and my theory of the value of a natural right of discourse should not be allowed to obscure the obvious differences. Among points in common are these: (1) both theories emphasize values distinct from the traditional free speech values of promoting individual autonomy, diversity of ideas, or self-government (see Blasi, pp. 524, 544-567); (2) both theories entail the possibility that the relevant value of discourse can be realized through surrogates or representatives (pp. 562-564); (3) both theories are concerned with a far smaller range of communication, with government officials as the focus, than are other free speech theories (pp. 558-559). But Blasi derives his theory from one particular society's democratic ideals, which necessarily gives it greater range and content than one derived from legal theory as a prerequisite for obligation in any legal society. See generally Frederick Schauer, *Free Speech: A Philosophical Enquiry* (Cambridge: Cambridge University Press, 1982), chap. 2. (I am indebted to Frederick Schauer for the observation in the text concerning the distinction between the right to speak and the right to have the government speak.)

27. Hart, *The Concept of Law*, p. 114.

28. Ibid., pp. 116-117.

29. See Raz, *Practical Reason and Norms*, pp. 159-160.

30. See Athur Leff, book review, 20 *Stanford Law Review* 879, 886-887 (1977); Nozick, *Anarchy, State, and Utopia*, chap. 10.

VI. IMPLICATIONS

1. See Joseph Halberstam, "The Paradox of Tolerance," 14 *Philosophical Forum* 190 (1982).

2. See Joseph Vining, "Justice, Bureaucracy, and Legal Method," 80 *Michigan Law Review* 248 (1981). See also Vining, *Legal Identity* (New Haven: Yale University Press, 1978), Chap. 9.

3. See Richard Hoggart, *The Uses of Literacy* (London: Penguin Books, 1957), p. 159, where he states that sincerity as an end in itself can be a mark of general indifference to and disbelief in value.

4. See Thomas Nagel, *Mortal Questions* (Cambridge: Cambridge University Press, 1979), chap. 14.

5. For a recent account see G. Edward White, "The Rise and Fall of Justice Holmes," 39 *University of Chicago Law Review* 51 (1971; reprinted in White, *Patterns of American legal Thought* [Bobbs-Merrill, 1978], pp. 194–226).

6. See also Chapter V, note 10.

7. Lon Fuller, *The Law in Quest of Itself* (Boston: Beacon Press, 1940), p. 121.

8. Ibid., p. 123.

9. See Chapter II, the subsection on sterility in modern positivism.

10. H. L. A. Hart, *The Concept of Law* (Oxford: Clarendon Press, 1961), p. 205.

11. See H. L. A. Hart, "Positivism and the Separation of Law and Morals," 71 *Harvard Law Review* 593, 624–629 (1958).

INDEX

acceptability of law, 56, 167n18
acceptance of law: Hart's account of, 18–20, 31, 169n4; attitude involved in, 38–46, 174n38, 176n56. *See also* insider; normativity of law
Ackerman, Bruce, 184n25
analytical jurisprudence, 1
anarchism, 81–83, 122, 128, 136
Anscombe, Elizabeth, 179n30
anthropology, 3, 163n5
Aquinas, Thomas, 52, 55, 175n45
Atiyah, P. S., 179n28
Austin, John, 1, 9–10, 17–26, 28, 30–33, 168nn3–4, 171n11, 172nn21, 22; analytical objections to, 18–19, 22–23, 168n4; connotational objections to, 18, 19–20, 31
authority: and autonomy, 75–77, 140; of parents, 77–79; of necessary enterprises, 79–80
autonomy: 16, 75–78, 81–82, 136, 137, 140, 141

basic norm, 5, 27, 154
behaviorism, 48
Bentham, Jeremy, 23, 50, 131
Blasi, Vince, 184n26
borderline case: function of, in definition, 21–22, 24; coercive system as, 94–95, 98, 157; in judicial decisions, 106, 110; of good faith, 124; martial law as, 144
bureaucracy, 153

certainty, role of in legal theory, 99–100, 101–109, 111–112, 181n3
citizens, 4, 63, 179n36. *See also* subjects
coercion, 4, 7, 18–20, 23
coercive systems: defined, 17, 55, 169n8; and normative systems, 17–18, 25–26; and legal systems, 26, 29–30, 91–95, 157–161, 167n15, 172n21; and moral systems, 55, 169n8; value of, 88, 122, 127–128, 136, 137
collective goals, 130
commands, 18–20, 91, 102
common law, 53, 64, 177n8, 178n11
consent: an explanation of law's normativity, 41–42; as ground of political obligation, 65–67, 116, 178n19
constitution, 115, 182n10
convention, 44–45, 143
courts, 109–117, 129
custom, legal status of, 91, 164n5, 168n4

D'Amoto, Anthony, 173n28
Dawson, John, 73
definition: in general, 3, 20–23, 170n9; as goal of legal theory, 19–26, 165n6, 169nn5,8; of legal system, 14, 91, 94–95, 103, 157–161, 169n8
democracy, 66, 116, 182n10, 184n26
deontology, 62, 80, 86, 180n38
description: as goal of legal theory, 7, 25–26, 37, 93, 167n18; and definition, 21, 95, 164n5

· 187 ·

detached point of view, *see* outsider
determinism, 48, 49
dialogue, 134, 142, 184n25. *See also* discourse, right to
Dickens, Charles, 35
discourse, right to, 134–140, 152–153
discretion, judicial, 11, 54, 115, 117
Dostoyevski, Fyodor, 149
duck-rabbit drawing, 14, 94
Dworkin, Ronald, 54–55, 103, 105, 163n4, 168n4, 181n3; and right answers, 110, 111, 117, 126; and principles, 130; and legal and political theory, 11–12, 114, 115, 176n56

Ely, John, 182n10
epistemology: legal theory as branch of, 7, 11, 101; as test for adequate theory of law, 106, 109, 120; and practical inquiries, 19, 120, 166n10
equality, 121–122, 183n17
essentialism, 7, 170n9. *See also* definition
estoppel, 67–69
external point of view, *see* outsider

fair play, 70–73
faith, 44, 159–160
Finnis, John, 164n5, 172n21, 175nn42,45, 176n55, 180n40, 182n9
force, *see* coercion
free speech, 140–142, 184n26. *See also* discourse, right to
Fuller, Lon, 52–54, 103, 105, 106, 155–156, 175n50

Geach, P. T., 175n44
good faith, 79, 80, 83, 117–118, 119–122, 151
gratitude, debt of, 78, 84

habit, 169n4
Hacker, P. M. S., 166n7, 173n30, 175n41
Hand, Learned, 113
Harris, J. W., 182n9
Hart, H.L.A.: on law and obligation, 8–10, 30–31, 166n14, 173nn26–29, 174nn32, 38; on Austin, 18–19, 24, 167n15, 168nn3,4, 170n10, 171n11, 172n21; and Kelsen, 26; and Raz, 34–38, 167n18, 174n32, 176n56; on sta-

tus of moral standards, 50, 181n1; and Fuller, 103; and Dworkin, 110; and rule of recognition, 113, 164n5, 176n56; on natural law, 130, 131; on definition in legal theory, 165n6, 169n8
Hill, Roscoe E., 172n22, 173n29, 175n38
Hobbes, Thomas, 23, 81, 88, 127, 128
Hobbesian justifications, 119, 131, 132, 145, 148, 156
Holmes, Oliver Wendell, 33, 69, 113–114, 119, 154–155, 182n10
Hume, David, 79, 179n28

ideology, 151, 153
insider, 1–2; relevance of legal theory for, 2–4, 19, 154, 157, 166n10; obligation from viewpoint of, 38–45, 174n38, 183n15
internal point of view, 46–47, 48, 174n38

judges: relevance of legal theory for, 4–5, 19; attitude of toward basic legal rules, 31, 41–46, 93, 98, 104; as law finders, 110–112; as law justifiers, 112–117; obligation of, 41–46, 114, 182n10. *See also* courts; discretion, judicial; reasoning, legal
judicial review, 115, 182n10
jury nullification, 115, 182n10
justice: contingent belief in, versus essential belief in, 34–38; belief in, versus actual, 49–51, 55–56, 89–90, 92, 95–100, 119–120; claim of, 108–109, 117–125, 142–143; natural, principles of, 132–134, 135
justification, *see* Hobbesian justifications; justice: claim of

Kadish, Mortimer R. and Sanford H., 173n31
Kant, Immanuel, 17, 94, 121, 132, 180n38
Kelsen, Hans, 19, 26–30, 34, 50, 89, 95, 114, 172n21, 173n17
Kronman, A., 179n28

laws: commonsense definition of, 4; varieties of, 18–20, 22–23, 170n10; range of application of, 23, 168n4, 171n11; evil, 92–93; martial, 144–145

legal obligation, 30–34, 92–94, 173n26, 173n31. *See also* normativity of law; obligation; political obligation
legal reasoning, 52–54, 125, 129–130
legal systems: preanalytic phenomenon and, 21, 23; primitive, 21, 45, 95, 110, 113, 164n5; and robber gangs, 27–28, 89, 127, 137, 167n15; and social clubs, 34–37; and games, 42, 170n10, 174n37; value of, 81, 84; pathology of, 143–144, 146, 151; utopian, 145–146; place for mercy in, 146. *See also* coercive systems: and legal systems
legislatures, 109–117, 129
Locke, John, 132
Lyons, David, 172n22

MacCormick, Neil, 173n29, 174n38, 175n43
Machiavelli, Niccolò, 120, 149
Marxist theories, 123
monopoly over force, 88–89, 127–128
morality: commonsense definition of, 4; legal theory as branch of, 7–12, 106–109; contingent connection to law, 25, 101–102; conceptual connection to law, 92–95, 97–100, 107–109, 165n6, 176nn56,57; stipulative connection to law, 157–161
Morison, W. L., 168n3, 169n5
motivation, 5–6, 122–125

Nagel, Ernest, 103
Nagel, Thomas, 185n4
natural law, 51–55, 131, 183n15; slogan, 57, 59, 61, 83, 115
Nietzsche, Friedrich, 149
nihilism, 119, 147–154, 159
normative systems: defined, 17; as viewed by insider, 38–46; as viewed by outsider, 46–50. *See also* coercive systems; legal systems
normativity of law, 19, 24–38, 93
Nozick, Robert, 88, 122, 178n16
nullity, sanction of, 23, 170–171n10

obligation: connection to concept of law, 9–10, 14, 92–94, 95–100, 176n57; sanction-based theories of, 30–34; promissory compared to legal, 36–37, 92–94;

internal view of, 30–45, 174n38; external features of, 38, 43–44; practice versus purpose theories of, 44–46; and belief, 51, 90, 92–94, 97–100; to obey the law, 61, 74, 84, 150–151, 179n36; to obey parents, 77–79. *See also* legal obligation; political obligation; prima facie obligation to obey law; respect
Occam's razor, 182n10
officials, *see* judges; respect; rulers; sovereign
officious intermeddler, 70, 71
outsider, 2; relevance of legal theory for, 3–4, 163n5, 164n6; obligation from viewpoint of, 46–51; law from viewpoint of, 97, 164n6

paradigms: in law, 64; in political theory, 65–74; complicity-based versus reason-based, 75–77; of respect, 77–80, 121, 123, 135–136
pardon, power of, 146
philosophy, 12, 15, 83, 182n10
Piaget, Jean, 45
Plato, 7, 94. *See also* Socrates
political obligation: recent accounts of, 8, 39; utilitarian argument for, 60–62, 74, 76, 84–86; generality constraint on problem of, 61, 74; specificity constraint on problem of, 62–63; standard arguments for, 65–74; and filial obligation, 77–79, 135–137, 179n30; and respect for necessary authority, 79–80; necessary and sufficient conditions for, 80. *See also* legal obligation; obligation; prima facie obligation to obey law; respect
positivism, legal: classical, 17, 24, 91, 94, 157; modern, 18–19, 24, 26–38; and natural law, 51–52; and official belief in justice, 95, 96, 176n56; and moral standards, 101–102, 107–109; essence of, 102, 181n3; and logical positivism, 106, 109, 159–160; and practical deliberations, 159
Postema, Gerald, 173n25
predictive theories of law or legal duty, 4–5, 31–34, 173nn26–28
prima facie obligation to obey law: defined, 58, 59–60, 177n1; in utilitarian

terms, 85–86, 179n38; in deontological terms, 86, 180n38; weight of, 87, 150–151, 179n36; content of, 84, 179n36, 179n38; and normativity of law, 92–93; and legal positivism, 159
primitive law, *see* legal systems: primitive
process, 53–54, 117, 118–119, 156
promises, 36–37, 41–42, 65–67, 87, 92–94. *See also* consent; obligation
pure theory of law, 27

Rawls, John, 70, 72, 177n7, 178n18
Raz, Joseph, 9–10, 68, 166n13, 167n15; on law and official belief in justice, 34–38, 95, 167n18, 174nn31,32, 176n56; on law and morality, 92–94, 180n1, 181n1; on obligation to obey law, 166n13, 177n2
realism, legal, 54, 110
reason: and values, 44, 53, 55, 75–77, 150, 160, 175n50, 179n28; exclusionary, 174n31
reasoning, legal, 53, 108–109, 117, 125. *See also* discretion; judges
Regan, Donald, 179n35
Reiman, Jeffrey, 179n27, 180n42
relativism, 50, 147, 154–155. *See also* nihilism
religion, 96–98, 160. *See also* faith; theology
respect: and moral obligation, 59, 82, 137, 183n17; mutuality of, 84, 137, 139–140; for law, 92, 118, 121–125, 135–137; for citizens or officials, 179n36
rights: preexisting, 126–130; natural, 130–134, 140; of discourse, 134–143
rulers, 38–41. *See also* judges; sovereign
rules, 18–20, 31, 91, 102, 169n5, 175n56. *See also* acceptance of law

sanctions, 23, 31–33, 68–69, 91, 94, 102, 170n10. *See also* coercion; coercive systems
Sartorius, Rolf, 163n4, 166nn8,9, 175n50, 180n42, 183n14
Schauer, Frederick, 184n26
science, as model for legal theory, 6, 12
self-deception, 123, 135, 141
Selznick, Philip, 164n6

Shklar, Judith, 166nn7,11
Simmons, A. J., 166n13, 177nn5,6, 178n19, 179n30
Singer, Peter, 68, 178n13
skepticism, 155, 182n10. *See also* nihilism; relativism
slaves, 39, 40, 120–129, 183n17
Smith, M. B. E., 60, 85, 86–87, 166n13, 174n31, 180n39
socialism, 83. *See also* collective goals
sociology, 3, 164n6
Socrates, 70, 77, 177n1. *See also* Plato
Soper, Philip, 164n5, 166n18, 171n13, 174n37, 175n50
sources of law, 101–102, 105–106, 108–109, 159
sovereign: defects in Austin's account of, 19–20, 168n3; and gunman, 89, 127; and Hart's officials, 168n4, 171n11, 172n22
standard case, 21, 24–25, 92. *See also* borderline case; definition
state, 88, 180n42; of nature, 127, 131; withering away of, 145; nihilistic, 151; theocratic, 153; bureaucratic, 153
subjects, 38–41. *See also* citizens

taxes: and gunmen's orders, 16–17, 27–28, 61–62, 88–89; and fines, 32–33
terminology, 13, 58–60
theft, 72, 178n19
theology, 94. *See also* faith; religion
Thrasymachus, 7
tolerance, 139, 141, 152
tradition, 143

unjust enrichment, 69–74, 78, 81, 84
utilitarianism, 60–62, 74, 76, 80, 84–86, 111, 132, 179n38
utopianism, 78, 130, 145–146

validity, legal: and legal theory, 4–5, 11–12, 101, 106, 109–110, 112, 120, 143; of iniquitous laws, 29–30, 52, 158–159; as meaning of legal obligation, 33–34, 93
Vining, Joseph, 185n2

Wolff, Robert Paul, 60, 80